DOWN
WITH
TRAITORS

DOWN
WITH
TRAITORS

Justice and Nationalism in Wartime China

YUN XIA

UNIVERSITY OF WASHINGTON PRESS

Seattle and London

DOWN WITH TRAITORS WAS MADE POSSIBLE IN PART BY A GRANT FROM
THE ASSOCIATION FOR ASIAN STUDIES FIRST BOOK SUBVENTION PROGRAM.

University of Washington Press
www.washington.edu/uwpress

Library of Congress Cataloging-in-Publication Data
Names: Xia, Yun, author.
Title: Down with traitors : justice and nationalism in wartime China / Yun Xia.
Description: Seattle : University of Washington Press, 2017. | Includes bibliographical
    references and index. | Description based on print version record and CIP data provided by
    publisher; resource not viewed.
Identifiers: LCCN 2017026643 (print) | LCCN 2017027880 (ebook) | ISBN 9780295742878
    (ebook) | ISBN 9780295742854 (hardcover : alk. paper) | ISBN 9780295742861
    (pbk. : alk. paper)
Subjects: LCSH: Treason—Law and legislation—China—History. | Treason—China—
    History. | Sino-Japanese War, 1937–1945—Collaborationists—China. | Collaborationists—
    Legal status, laws, etc.—China. | China—History—1937–1945. | China—Politics and
    government—1937–1945.
Classification: LCC KNN4417 (ebook) | LCC KNN4417 .X538 2017 (print) |
    DDC 345.51/0231—dc23
LC record available at https://lccn.loc.gov/2017026643

CONTENTS

ACKNOWLEDGMENTS

There is a Chinese saying that captures the subtly conflated feelings that accumulate in one's heart on the return from a journey: "As one gets closer to home, mixed emotions start to brew inside" (Jin xiang qing qie 近鄉情怯). Similarly, while writing this last piece of my book (although it appears first), I feel closer and more indebted than ever to the colleagues, friends, and family members who have accompanied me during this long journey. Listing them all here is impossible. *Hanjian* is still such a pertinent topic in discussions of history and current affairs that every Chinese person I talked to in the past few years has influenced the way I have grappled with this concept. Here I mention only the institutions and individuals who have directly witnessed and helped with the genesis of this book.

First and foremost, I thank those who have guided and brainstormed with me since the inception of this project. I owe a tremendous intellectual debt to Bryna Goodman, who has seen me grow as a scholar of modern China and enlightened me at key moments in this project. Ina Asim, Andrew Goble, and Tze-Lan D. Sang, with their expertise in Chinese and Japanese culture and languages, were instrumental in helping me probe the cultural roots of the historical problems I examine.

This book gradually took shape through discussions with and challenges posed by colleagues in history, Asian studies, political science, law, and related fields. I presented parts of it at different venues, each time harvesting constructive suggestions from the hosts and the audience. I am particularly grateful to colleagues from the University of Washington, Columbia University, the University of British Columbia, Cambridge University, and Zhejiang University for inviting me to share my work. I also thank those who took the time to read parts or all of the manuscript. While I strove to reveal the peculiarities of the anti-*hanjian* campaigns in China, Diana Lary inspired me to see the comparability of such phenomena with punishment of wartime collaboration in other nations. Conversations with Timothy Brook, David Atwill, and Chen Hongmin, among others, prompted me to investigate the complexity and malleability of the word *hanjian* and to better define the scope of my study. Barak Kushner inspired me to position my study in relation to issues unsolved by or arising after World War II in Asia. I also thank Madeleine Yue Dong, David Crowe, Chihyun Chang, You Shujun, Jonathan Henshaw, Christopher Rea, Lan Shi-Chi, Ting Zhang, Chi-hung Luk, and many other colleagues for their encouraging words and constructive criticism.

My deep gratitude also goes to the supervisors and colleagues who have helped me since the start of my academic career. Liang Kan and Theresa Earenfight at Seattle University were the most wonderful senior colleagues and administrators I could have hoped for at my first academic job. Hazel Hahn, a cultural historian and expert in French Indochina, became a most supportive colleague who offered invaluable feedback on my discussion of "Vietnamese *hanjian*."

The most important work of writing this book took place after I started to teach at Valparaiso University. I thank Charles Schaefer, Zhimin Lin, and John Ruff for the generous support they have offered me at so many different levels. Their insight and friendship are what make Valparaiso University feel like home. I have also had the good fortune of belonging to a particularly collegial department. Since I joined the Department of History in 2012, the three department chairs, Alan Bloom, Ron Rittgers, and Kevin Ostoyich, have created a particularly encouraging environment for junior faculty members to produce scholarship. At department research workshops, I have received important feedback from Roy Austensen, Colleen Seguin, Heath Carter, Robert Elder, and Luis Ramos. I also extend my gratitude to Jeni Prough, Yue Zhang, and George Pati of the Chinese and Japanese Studies program.

I could not have finished this project without the love and support of my family and friends. My parents, Xia Zuchang and Zheng Yuling, are both outstanding scholars and doctors in Chinese medicine, in addition to being exceptionally loving and supportive parents. My mother has always been my role model. While serving as a university president, she produced three films and one book, in addition to publications in her academic field. She is a constant source of inspiration, wisdom, and courage. I thank my husband, Nicholas F. Phillips, for the intimate and intellectual companionship he has brought me. He has read all the drafts I have produced for this project and provided comments down to the very last detail. My dear friend Cao Shuai has been my "knower of tone" (*zhiyin* 知音) in Chinese literature, philosophy, and cinema, which provided much-needed distractions during the long process of research and writing.

While preparing the manuscript for publication, I was extremely fortunate to work with executive editor Lorri Hagman at the University of Washington Press. Her professionalism, patience, and familiarity with the field have made the experience of publishing my first book as pleasant as possible. It took several rounds of discussions between Lorri, me, and art director Katrina Noble from the press to finalize the cover image, and I thank the team for their wonderful work. My gratitude is extended to Margaret Sullivan, Whitney Johnson, Beth Fuget, Julie Van Pelt, Erika Büky, and Roberta Engleman who have helped me in various aspects of refining the manuscript and seeing it through to publication. I am honored to have received funding for this book from the Association for Asian Studies First Book Subvention Program. I deeply appreciate the decision made by Jon Wilson and others on the editorial board of AAS.

Last, I am grateful to this project itself, with which I have spent so much time that it has come to feel like an intimate friend. Working on this book has provided me an escape from the mundane world and changed the way I think about and process many issues. I am glad I was writing this book during these particular years of my life. Looking back, it has been a wonderful journey.

ACKNOWLEDGMENTS

DOWN
WITH
TRAITORS

INTRODUCTION

WRITING AT THE DAWN OF THE TWENTIETH CENTURY, THE YOUNG journalist Zhang Shizhao decided to enlighten his countrymen about what it meant to be Chinese: "Warfare and confrontation have emerged on China's borders since the Han dynasty. Barbarians in the north gradually encroached on Chinese land.... [The Chinese dynasties, in order to settle the disputes,] either fought wars with their northern neighbors or resorted to diplomatic marriages. Thereafter, words like 'hanren' and 'hanjian' appeared."[1]

Zhang suggested that people of the majority Han ethnicity (*hanren*), who accounted for more than 90 percent of the population, were the standard-bearers of China's past and future.[2] However, not all *hanren* merited this designation. Those who succumbed to cowardice and colluded with aggressors when China was under foreign threat were "traitors to the Han," or *hanjian*. Zhang claimed that the demarcation between Han and non-Han had been drawn two thousand years earlier. Even so, according to Zhang, there had always been *hanjian*. Such people were enemies within, whose duplicitous presence troubled Han identity. Zhang's deployment of the old term *hanjian* in the context of modern China's forced encounter with Western and Japanese imperialism and the incompetence of Manchu rule revised its meaning. This new context was foundational to the subsequent use of the term.

These fraught categories of identity retain their dynamism today, more than a century since Zhang's discussion of Han traitors. The People's Republic of China (PRC), which has been proclaiming the nation's "peaceful rise," may seem to have emerged from the long shadow of wars and national insecurities. Urban Chinese born in the 1980s, like myself, grew up in relative material comfort, with the opportunity to see and experience the outside world. Many older Chinese fear that this generation is disconnected from the bitter recent history of their motherland, which has become an essential component of Chinese national identity. Several recent events,

3

however, prove that Chinese youth are not short of nationalistic sentiments or expressions. When a Chinese student at Duke University recently mediated between a pro-China group and pro-Tibet demonstrators on campus, showing more sympathy toward the latter, she was immediately labeled a *hanjian* by fellow Chinese students, who soon posted her photos and personal information online, along with her parents' home address in China, thereby indirectly encouraging harassment of her family.[3]

Widely circulated stories of "contemporary *hanjian*" build on and refresh popular memories of historical *hanjian*, rendering a continued condemnation of the *hanjian* type relevant and necessary. Corresponding to what the French historian Pierre Nora calls *lieux de mémoire*, or places of memory, Chinese frequently relive moments of national crisis and humiliation in modern Chinese history.[4] Preeminent among these events is China's War of Resistance against Japan (1937–45 or 1931–45, according to a recent historiographic change mandated by the Chinese Ministry of Education).[5] Seven decades later, this war remains a popular subject of literary, cinematic, and TV productions as well as of historical studies. Every Chinese film about this war, historical or fictional, features at least one *hanjian*. These traitors are portrayed as more vicious than the Japanese and contrast dramatically with the heroic resisters. In 2015 China invited an international audience of dignitaries to the seventieth anniversary celebrations of its hard-won victory in the War of Resistance against Japan and the "World Anti-fascist War," culminating in a grand military parade in Tiananmen Square.[6] China Central Television's film channel broadcast more than three hundred films on the War of Resistance.[7] Every celebratory production reinforced the condemnation of both Japanese imperialism and Chinese traitors.

Such commemorative projects have increased the recognition of China's role in the Second World War in and beyond academia.[8] Scholars in China and elsewhere are building a more comprehensive picture of the war by representing not only pivotal military events but also the human suffering, the experiences of refugees, and other hitherto unrecognized individuals, moments, and events. At the same time, the resistance narrative that has dominated Chinese historiography and collective memory since the war has not been challenged to the same degree as the resistance narratives of other nations that experienced occupation by Axis powers.[9] Western audiences, for the most part, have only just begun to learn about China's "heroic resistance against massive odds."[10]

In this study, I do not intend to deconstruct this resistance narrative. Rather, I hope to complicate the understanding of Chinese resistance by focusing on its antithesis, the *hanjian*. What precisely constituted the *hanjian* crime? Who was punished and how? What does the purge of *hanjian* reveal about the China that emerged from the ashes of its last major wars? These are the questions that animate this book.

In vast areas of China under Japanese occupation, many people tried to remain apolitical or politically neutral in order to go on with their lives. In general, these people were not considered *hanjian*, then or now. Others worked for the enemy as puppet officials, foot soldiers, or spies. Since the war, they have been portrayed simultaneously as a minority and ubiquitous. Between people's vivid imagination and a lack of nuanced historical evaluation, *hanjian* became the reflexive internal "others" in the minds of the self-consciously patriotic Chinese who constituted a majority of the population.

This book examines *hanjian* both figuratively, as an evolving epithet and a label for criminality, and in the flesh, as embodied by individuals who were tried in judicial courts, public opinion, and historical judgment. Except for a number of prominent political figures who were put on trial in 1945, we know little about acts of collaboration by actual *hanjian* at different levels and even less about the acts of retributive violence against them. The purge of *hanjian* enabled the Chinese state and people to imagine a national community victimized by enemies both outside and within, which needed to be purified and renewed by excising its rotten parts. This imagination was rooted in imperial China's first military encounter with the West, the Opium War (1840–42), and captured the minds of Chinese people from every social stratum during the war against Japan. Since then, political morality, rather than civic virtue and political participation, has become identified in public discourse with the quintessence of Chinese identity.

The experience and memory of the War of Resistance have been pivotal in shaping Chinese politics, national identity, and people's relations with the party state ever since. On the one hand, the war left profound physical and psychological wounds on the nation. At least 14 million people died; 80 million became refugees; and much of the product of China's decades of modernization efforts turned to ruin.[11] The advancing Japanese army forced the central government, under the Nationalist Party (Kuomintang [KMT] or Guomindang [GMD]), to flee to Southwest China, then a poorly integrated frontier region. Its authority was challenged in China proper by various collaborationist regimes as well as by the guerrilla forces in Communist base areas. After Japan's defeat in 1945, the Nationalist government returned to China proper, nominally victorious but with its military capacity, financial basis, and bureaucracy damaged beyond repair. A mere four years later, the Nationalists and their once-proud leader, the "Generalissimo" Chiang Kai-shek, lost the Chinese mainland to the Chinese Communist Party (CCP).

Continuous warfare and instability between 1931 and 1945 interrupted China's pace of modernization and left deep scars on the Chinese landscape. Yet the War of Resistance was fought with determination and in the hope of rejuvenating China. The deepening national crisis forced the Nationalists and the Communists, who had been at each other's throats, into an alliance to defend the nation against internal and external enemies. Both parties represented the War of Resistance as a crucible from which the Chinese nation would emerge anew, strong and morally sound. As the prospect of war improved for the Allies after 1943, China achieved new recognition as a sovereign power with an important role to play in the world. When Chiang Kai-shek attended the 1943 Cairo conference and conversed with Franklin D. Roosevelt, Joseph Stalin, and Winston Churchill about the postwar world order, the Chinese rejoiced at the international prestige their country had gained.

Throughout these years of war, division, desperation, and renewed hope, the threat of *hanjian* was identified both among governing authorities and at the grassroots level. This form of treachery was perceived as a problem unique to the Chinese character. Shortly after the war broke out, the Communists and the Nationalist government respectively issued guiding documents announcing two goals: resistance through war, and rebuilding the nation (*kangzhan jianguo*).[12] Both saw the elimination of *hanjian* as essential to win the war and to cleanse the national soul. Chiang Kai-shek's government mobilized all deployable mechanisms and the general population to catch *hanjian*. During wartime, Nationalist intelligence, military, and affiliated patriotic groups summarily executed countless numbers of *hanjian*. They publicized the ghastly death photos of the executed to deter potential traitors. In borderlands under its control, the Communists combined violent struggle against *hanjian* with a socialist revolutionary agenda.

Forming an accurate estimate of the number of *hanjian* identified and punished during wartime is impossible because of the decentralized and often clandestine nature of the operations against them. The incomplete statistics on the trials of *hanjian*, however, suggest the scope of the campaigns after the war. Between 1944 and 1947, the judiciary processed 45,679 *hanjian* cases, prosecuted 30,185 individuals, and convicted 14,932. Of these, 369 were executed, 979 were sentenced to life imprisonment, and the rest received varying prison sentences.[13] In contrast, the Nationalist government arrested only 2,357 Japanese for war crimes, convicted 442 of them, and executed 145.[14] Many notorious war criminals arrested in China, including Okamura Yasuji, commander in chief of the Japanese army in China, were acquitted. The CCP, too, showed magnanimity in its trials of Japanese war criminals in 1956.[15]

The politics of retribution needs to be understood against the complex backdrop of the Chinese Civil War (1946–49) and the Cold War. Chiang Kai-shek treated Okamura Yasuji as an ally and military adviser in the war against communism. The CCP set free most Japanese war criminals in the hope of encouraging Japan's political neutrality in the Cold War and Chinese normalization of relations with Japan in the near future. Nonetheless, these disparities in prosecution and sentencing make one wonder about the goals of the War of Resistance as well as the intensity and efficacy of campaigns against *hanjian*.

The Nationalist government constituted the crime of *hanjian* not as an offense against individual victims but as a violation of the nation. The crime further represented a transgression of the collective well-being and of the political morality of an imagined Chinese community that transcended national borders. The anti-*hanjian* campaigns of the Nationalists took place at a pivotal moment in Chinese legal reform. By defining the crime broadly and by legalizing popular vigilantism in the prosecution of *hanjian*, these campaigns set Chinese jurisprudence on a path away from the intermittently espoused ideal of the rule of law.

The anti-*hanjian* campaigns reinforced the resistance narrative both for the state and for people who otherwise played no real role in resistance. When common citizens responded enthusiastically to their leaders' encouragement to attack *hanjian*, the campaigns adopted a populist aspect. Those who had long endured as passive victims gained a sense of power to punish and an opportunity to redeem their passivity with a display of patriotic fervor. The punishment of *hanjian* provided objects for the contradictions and prejudices inherent in Chinese politics and society. The anti-*hanjian* campaigns set the pattern and dynamics of state-directed mass movements against perceived internal enemies in the decades to come.

This book retains the term *hanjian* as preferable to both its approximate synonyms in Chinese and the common English translations *collaborators* and *traitors*. *Hanjian* is sometimes used interchangeably with *pantu* (traitor) and *maiguozei* (sellout). Yet neither of these alternative terms is as historically and morally loaded as *hanjian*, which points to a person's traitorous and un-Chinese character, rather than just traitorous deeds. The character *han* 漢 in *hanjian* imbues the word with rich ethnic connotations. The central character of the compound, *jian*, originally existed in two forms: 姦, usually used as a noun or adjective, and 奸, a transitive verb. Both may be found in the *Kangxi Dictionary* (*Kangxi zidian*), the most comprehensive Chinese lexicon compiled before modern times. The first form means "illicit sex," "treacherous," and "cunning." The latter means "to trespass" or "to violate."[16] The modern character 奸 inherits the connotations and implications of both: it refers to a range of illicit sexual conduct and criminal activities, including espionage.

In this last regard, *hanjian* is closer to the French term *collaborateur*, as defined by Jean-Paul Sartre, than to alternative terms in Chinese. Reflecting on collaboration with the Nazis in occupied France, Sartre writes that the collaborator has inherent character traits. Thus betrayal has deep psychological or social roots. Those who are of the collaborator type remain latent in ordinary times, yet in wartime they infest the nation like a pestilence.[17] Similarly, the Chinese saw *hanjian* as those who already possessed certain character flaws, and traces of their betrayal of the nation could be discerned in earlier behaviors or incidents. Following this logic, the Nationalists and Communists did not stop at punishing those who were believed to have committed the *hanjian* crime. They also instructed people how to identify "potential *hanjian*" (*zhunhanjian*, or "those who are getting ready to become *hanjian*").[18] The Chinese state, like Sartre, viewed those who were marginalized from mainstream society and lacked stable social, familial, or communal ties as the most prone to betrayal.

Acts of collaboration during World War II incurred shame in every occupied state.[19] In postwar France, for instance, collaborators were charged with the crime of "national indignity."[20] In any nation under prolonged foreign occupation, mild forms of collaboration are bound to be widespread. More active forms of collaboration, however, were often based on varying degrees of ideological commitment. In Hitler's Europe, Austrian and French collaborators were mostly sympathetic to National Socialist values or to anti-Semitism, as in the case of French police who were complicit in the persecution of Jews.[21] Following liberation from occupation, retributive violence against collaborators was common. Symbolic punishment of perceived collaborators, such as shaving the heads of French women who were believed to have been intimate with the German occupiers, often preceded legal trials.[22] In most cases, these forms of popular vengeance were sanctioned by the resistance governments.

Using the term *collaborator* in the Chinese context certainly has its merits. It provides a convenient basis for comparing patterns and circumstances of wartime collaboration in China with those in Europe. Inspired by studies of collaboration in Europe, several scholars in North America have examined the moral quandaries and constraints of Chinese local elites who worked as mediators between the Japanese and their own communities.[23] The motivations of these individuals, like those of their counterparts in occupied France or Korea, cannot be reduced to a simple thirst for power or an urge for self-preservation. In Korea, collaboration has been seen as "a structural feature of modernity," because working with Japan and learning from its success appeared to be the most viable way for Koreans to modernize their home country.[24] In China, some of those who were alienated or marginalized by the many shortcomings of the Nationalist Party saw new opportunities under Japanese rule.

Considering this context allows more room to probe structural, cultural, or circumstantial reasons for perceived unpatriotic behaviors. The black-and-white judgments that these Western-based historians consciously avoid, however, are exactly the judgments that contemporary and subsequent Chinese intentionally made when they considered that the survival of their nation was at stake. To simply revise and dismiss such judgments precludes understanding of their specific significance in Chinese history. In other words, if comparability is achieved entirely through the adoption of a term such as *collaborator*, which emerges from Western experience, the particularity of Chinese trajectories of meaning is lost.

There are additional reasons why I use the Chinese term *hanjian* rather than its possible English translations. The first is linguistic. Language is foundational to categorization and judgment. What English speakers refer to as drugs or narcotics, for example, Chinese call "poison" (*du*). They see all types of poisons, from cocaine to arsenic, from marijuana to nightshade, as similar in character: virulent and morally corrupting. The difference between this and the English idea of drugs is categorical, as the latter also has benign connotations. This analogy may be applied to the term *hanjian*, which expresses the worst betrayal of the nation and the traitorous nature of the accused without referring to specific acts. No English word conveys the severity of *hanjian* and its rich implications. *Traitor* can be literally translated as *pantu*, a person who betrays the group to which he or she used to belong. While treason is a crime, the word *traitor* is more generic and does not fully connote the culturally flawed and conniving behavior of the *hanjian* who betrays both the Chinese nation and the morality of its people. *Collaborator,* the more neutral term that most Western scholars opt to use, originated from the French context. *Collaboration,* etymologically derived from simply "working together," was the term used by Marshall Philippe Pétain himself in a radio announcement in October 1940 to rationalize and even glorify Vichy France's subjugation to the German occupiers.[25] *Collaborator,* therefore, is a term that the collaborators and their opponents alike accepted as fitting. Those who played similar roles in China, however, had no such self-determined label. By the time *collaborator* acquired its pejorative meaning in France, the word *hanjian* had been in use for years to refer to those who worked with the Japanese. Thus it is not only inaccurate but also anachronistic to refer to *hanjian* simply as Chinese collaborators.

The use of the English term *collaborator* makes more sense in discussing the Korean experience. *Collaboration* offers a fairly literal translation for the Japanese term *kyōryoku,* used in the official propaganda of colonial Korea to describe the relationship between the Japanese and their indigenous helpers. Koreans after World War II called the collaborators *ch'inilp'a:* Japanophiles, or "those who were close to Japan." This term certainly has negative connotations, but it was more matter-of-fact and less inherently judgmental than *hanjian,* especially during the Cold War, when many members of the political and military elites in South Korea were former collaborators. The Chinese word for "collaboration" or "cooperation" is *hezuo,* which appeared after the early years of the War of Resistance. *Hezuo,* however, curiously managed to retain its neutral connotation to a degree that *collaboration* has not enjoyed.[26] It never became a euphemism for treason in the Chinese popular vocabulary, which was instead largely shaped by the resistance discourse during wartime and after.

Collaborator, in addition, has important limitations for analyzing the specificity of Chinese wartime experience. Although China lost its capital and a great deal of territory to Japan, an internationally recognized Chinese state existed throughout the war and endured to at least preside over the task of resistance. The national collaborationist regime that emerged never achieved a solid control of the nation's territory or eliminated the Nationalist government in China. In 1940, Wang Jingwei (1883–1944), a Nationalist veteran and longtime political rival of Chiang, defected from the party and established the Reorganized National Government in the former Nationalist capital of Nanjing. For the displaced Nationalist government in Chongqing, Wang's regime was a much stronger contender for legitimacy than the various local puppet regimes that the Japanese had set up in North and East China beginning in late 1937. Numerous Nationalist veterans, bureaucrats, industrialists and men of letters in the occupied regions followed Wang Jingwei. Later they became key targets of the purge of *hanjian*.

The presence of multiple national governments with competing claims to authority over the nation was not unique to China. In several European nations over which Germany claimed supreme authority, a pro-German or collaborationist government coexisted with one that held high the banner of resistance and often had to take refuge on foreign soil. The Czech government based in Prague, for example, was under German supervision, while Czech refugees in London formed a resistance government in exile. We now consider the Polish, Norwegian, Dutch, Belgian, French, and Greek resistance governments legitimate because the Allies won. But it was not until 1942 in London that they were "accorded all the honors" by the major Allied powers. For years in these occupied areas, to resist "meant to leave the legal path and to act as a criminal." Locally, resistance was unpopular among the resisters' compatriots.[27]

In France, for example, after a brief but disastrous conflict in 1939–40, Pétain sued for an armistice with Germany in his capacity as the head of state. The French parliament granted him enormous power as the highest commander, on which basis he set up the collaborationist government in Vichy. In other words, France emerged from defeat with its legitimate head of state and government working voluntarily with the occupying power. Popular sentiment was on the side of Pétain, not General Charles de Gaulle, whose initial London broadcasts attracted little attention. The French public in general was hostile toward the Western Allies, the Soviets, and the Jews. Only after 1943, when it had become clear that Germany would lose, did the resistance movements gain standing.[28] Patriotism was redefined, new patriotic sentiments were born, and the collaborationist government was delegitimized.

In China, in contrast, the Nationalist government persisted and presented itself as a resistance state, though its resistance was contested and wavering.[29] Wang Jingwei's propagandists condemned Chiang Kai-shek as a running dog of the British and American imperialists, who were no better than the Japanese.[30] This accusation was not without some truth, and it was echoed among some who also disapproved of Wang's regime. Chiang practiced a policy of nonresistance toward Japan for years and did not completely reject the idea of peace talks with Japan until August 1937.[31] In the past decade, historians have also brought to light the existence of individuals, secret deals, shared interests, and a flow of goods between the governments of Wang Jingwei and Chiang Kai-shek.[32]

Nonetheless, to the general public, especially in "free China," Chiang Kai-shek remained the national leader, the living embodiment of China's hope for national independence. The legitimacy of the Nationalist government preceded its wartime victory: it had become the internationally recognized government of China in 1928, and its international as well as domestic standing was further attested during World War II by Allied nations. Chiang's official stance of resistance won him unprecedented authority and respect that lasted until a short while after the war.

The power relations between Chinese "collaborators" and resisters therefore differed from those of occupied Europe. Unlike Korea or Southeast Asian countries, China was not under colonial rule when the war started. Chiang's government continued to function, albeit with reduced capacity. The Nationalist legislature established the *hanjian* crime as early as August 1937. The crime was by definition worse than treason and any existing criminal offenses against national security. In France, no law was drafted for the purpose of purging collaborators until April 1944.[33] The Chinese *hanjian*, in contrast, were declared criminals from the start of the war, and resisters were the heroes. The establishment of the Wang Jingwei regime occurred too late, and other puppet governments were too weak, to reverse this view.

The term *hanjian* therefore serves as a reminder of what the war was largely about, as does the official Chinese name for the war (Kangri Zhanzheng, or the War of Resistance against Japan), which differs from more-neutral Western designations such as the "Second Sino-Japanese War." During the long War of Resistance, *hanjian* were the more visible enemy in vast occupied areas. They were, moreover, easier to kill than the Japanese, yet their deaths boosted morale almost to the same degree. Violence and accusations against *hanjian* constituted the resistance experience for civilians who were not equipped to oppose the invaders and those who hoped to divert attention from their own guilt. *Hanjian* were indeed widespread in wartime China. Many individuals inflicted serious harm on the resistance forces and on the local people. Yet some *hanjian* were unjustly accused, and others had done things that did not warrant the excessive punishment they received. Here, regardless of individuals' specific acts and their varying level of actual guilt, I retain the label *hanjian* for everyone to whom it was originally applied, to show the indiscriminate use of this label.

This study is less concerned with evaluating collaborationism or individual collaborators than with examining the legality and legacies of anti-*hanjian* campaigns. Scholars have undertaken case studies of trials of prominent *hanjian*, which the Nationalist government held to reinforce its political and judicial legitimacy.[34] In contrast, scholarship on the wartime executions and condemnation of *hanjian* is sparse at best. Historians who question the passing of moral judgments on collaborators have urged us to consider what might have happened if the war had gone the other way.[35] Whichever way it went, however, a large number of people died or suffered as *hanjian*. The laws, institutions, and sentiments that accounted for their punishment survived Nationalist rule in mainland China. Following the political watershed in 1949, governments on both sides of the Taiwan Strait continued to persecute individuals for *hanjian* or related crimes. This study examines the consequences of the anti-*hanjian* campaigns and what they suggest about Chinese nationalism, law, and society.

CHAPTER 1

FROM EPITHET TO CRIME

NEITHER THE TRADITION NOR THE IMMEDIATE WARTIME NEED to legalize the punishment of traitors was unique to China. The inclusion of treason in common law can be traced back to the Treason Act of 1351 in England, which defined it as acts against the reputation or the safety of the throne.[1] The US Constitution states: "Treason against the United States, shall consist only in levying War against them, or in adhering to their Enemies, giving them Aid and Comfort."[2] Most treason convictions in recent history date to the two world wars. With the unprecedented scope of the Second World War and the extended periods of occupation, spies emerged from all sides, and numerous individuals gave in to the demands of the occupiers. Extralegal punishment of traitors and collaborators was a widespread wartime phenomenon. Most nations that had endured occupation by the Axis powers passed laws in 1944 and 1945 to guide the trials of collaborators, and decisions by postwar courts bolstered the legitimacy of the resistance governments.[3]

In China, this legislative process started years earlier. Having entered a full-fledged war with Japan in 1937, China faced the problem of treason from the early 1930s onward and became the first state to sanction extralegal punishment of perceived traitors. Moreover, the Chinese state adopted the word *hanjian* from the popular vocabulary and established it as a new crime, in addition to the existing crimes of treason, "internal rebellion" (*neiluan*), and "external aggression" (*waihuan*). The Regulations on Punishing *Hanjian* of 1937 marked the consummation of the tightening of laws for state control and national security. From a legislative perspective, the stipulation of laws in response to the needs of total war brought an end to the overall progressive legal reform in China and set the nation on one of the most chaotic periods in its legal history.

As *hanjian* evolved from an epithet into a crime, Nationalist laws against *hanjian* tightened in response to the changing war situation and political winds. The war created fatal divisions among judicial institutions and personnel along political and ideological lines. A significant portion of China's best-trained legal professionals and clerks were later purged for choosing the wrong side. The authority of the law and the legal system, which had never been fully established before the war, was undermined by the interference of different branches of the government, the military, intelligence, and civilians. The regulations against *hanjian* did not go unchallenged. The combined forces of the state machine, war propaganda, and grassroots patriotism, however, drowned the voices of legal professionals in an emotional outcry.

HANJIAN PRIOR TO THE WAR OF RESISTANCE

Hanjian is an evolving concept rich in ethnic and political implications, which have all added to its weight as a criminal label. An etymological analysis of the word *hanjian* requires review of important moments in the construction of ethnicity, race and nation in modern China. Contemporary Chinese people use this word as if its meaning is self-evident, yet even the most authoritative modern Chinese dictionary fails to grasp all the changing connotations of the word. According to the dictionary *Cihai, hanjian* originally meant "traitor to the Han people," and it can be "widely applied to the wretches who pander to foreign aggressors and betray the interests of their home nation."[4] What this definition fails to convey is that *hanjian* is a historical construct. The term, if properly unpacked, shows the dynamics of ethnic relations as well as the Chinese-foreign relations that had been constantly conceptualized since the late imperial period.

From its first and only appearance in a document from the Yuan dynasty (1279–1368) to its frequent use in the official records of the Qing dynasty (1644–1911), the term *hanjian* was used in a variety of contexts, mostly reflecting the perspective of the ruling elite. *Hanjian* always appeared in conjunction with *yi*, "foreign peoples" or "barbarians."[5] *Yi* first referred to ethnic minorities inhabiting the borderlands, which were of great strategic significance to the central rule yet difficult to control. The concept then extended to include peoples who lived on the edge or beyond the cultural influence of Chinese civilization. Following this logic, the Qing rulers also applied it to those Westerners demanding trade with China, initially treating them as another "tributary state" of China, such as Annam.[6]

Since the Yuan dynasty, we know of only one instance of the word *hanjian* appearing in a context that does not involve outsiders. Hu Zhen, a Yuan scholar, mentioned *hanjian* in his interpretation of the *Book of Change*

(Yijing), using the term to refer to "officials treacherous to the Han court."[7] The Chinese took such pride in their first powerful and lasting empire, the Han dynasty (202 BCE–220 CE), that they used the term *Han* to differentiate themselves from the barbarians who lived beyond China proper. Much later, during the War of Resistance, anecdotes and idioms associated with the Han dynasty were often deployed in anti-*hanjian* rhetoric. When Li Ze, an influential businessman, was put on trial in 1946, his wife claimed that "Li's heart was always true to the Han rule" (*xincun hanshi*), evoking a comparison of Li to the Han general Guan Yu, who personified loyalty and righteousness.[8] In this and other incidents, the concept of Han seemingly transcended a single dynasty or ethnic category and came to symbolize the nation of China as a historically and culturally continuous community. This usage particularly resonated with people at a time when much of China was occupied by the Japanese and run by puppet regimes.

Emperors and officials of the Ming (1368–1644) and Qing dynasties used the term *hanjian* to refer to "guileful Han people" who stirred up unrest among aboriginals and caused trouble for the "central dynasty."[9] Rulers of late imperial China tried to subdue their ethnic borderlands with an elaborate system of ruling tactics, agencies, and segregation policies.[10] The Manchus who established the Qing rule, themselves an ethnic minority, were particularly cautious about ethnic mingling in their expansive and ethnically diverse empire because a vast majority of the population were Han, who held a condescending attitude toward other peoples.[11] The Manchus thus inherited the rationale and discourse of ethnic hierarchy constructed by Chinese statesmen in the past, yet they placed themselves above the Han. When Han and non-Han subjects colluded to rebel against Manchu rule, the Manchus implemented an ethnic quarantine between the two groups. Qing records mention numerous incidents of this nature, condemning the roles of *hanjian* in provoking internal troubles.[12]

In late imperial China, therefore, *hanjian* connoted the ruling elites' frustration with people who overstepped their designated ethnic boundaries. Starting in the mid-Qing, however, the court sometimes used *hanjian* to refer to those who helped foreigners in military and commercial endeavors at the expense of the empire. During the Sino-Burmese War (1765–69), for instance, Qing troops caught four *hanjian* who had spied for the enemy. Increasingly, the term *hanjian* was applied to Han people who violated the Qing bans on trade and interactions with foreigners. Chinese who crossed the border to trade or travel in Vietnam or marry the local people were also considered *hanjian*.[13]

The number of *hanjian* mentioned in Qing official documents increased exponentially during the first Opium War (1839–42). A new and superior group of "barbarians" threatened Chinese civilization, which the emperor and his subjects still considered supreme under heaven. In his daring solution to the problem of opium smuggling, Commissioner Lin Zexu denounced and arrested *hanjian* before taking action against British opium smugglers. Such measures were considered justified and necessary by most Chinese at that time, and Lin had been celebrated as a national hero. The Qing restricted trade with the British in Canton and confined their activities to designated areas of the city. Locals who acted as their translators, language tutors, guides, and middlemen in business dealings were all considered *hanjian*. When Qi Ying, a Manchu official, saw foreigners who held a pencil and wrote Chinese characters, he immediately thought that "this must be a *hanjian*'s work."[14] Here *Hanjian* was similarly used to label those who breached the division between Han and *yi*, *nei* (the indigenous) and *wai* (the exogenous).

When the Qing faced increasing crises precipitated by internal unrest and foreign imperialism, *hanjian* developed new connotations, including that of betrayal. Some Chinese facilitated foreign military operations and pillages in China. To Han and Manchu officials alike, these individuals betrayed the economic interest and security of the multiethnic community under Manchu rule. Lin Zexu, among others, made a priority of catching and eliminating *hanjian*, enemies from within, in response to incidents of foreign aggression.[15] This was exactly the same mentality as that behind the anti-*hanjian* campaigns during the War of Resistance.

At a moment of unprecedented crisis, the connotation of *hanjian* as traitors to the empire was even endorsed by the Manchu emperor. In 1900, the Guangxu emperor declared war against eight nations—Britain, Japan, Germany, Italy, Russia, France, the United States, and Austria-Hungary—which had decided to join forces and punish the Qing court in the aftermath of the Boxer Rebellion. Guangxu mobilized his subjects with the following words: "Those who fight the enemies bravely or donate to the cause will be handsomely promoted or rewarded; those who show cowardice or even reduce themselves to *hanjian* will face immediate execution."[16] The emperor thus drew a clear line between loyal subjects and *hanjian*. In this context, the term referred broadly to any subject of the Qing who surrendered to or worked for foreigners, regardless of ethnicity. One did not have to be Han to be *hanjian*.[17] This edict excluded *hanjian* from "all the people under heaven" in much the same way that later anti-*hanjian* laws excluded *hanjian* from the Chinese national community.

The meaning and usage of *hanjian* changed fundamentally during the fall of the Qing and the conception of a Han-based Chinese nation-state. Chinese literati were possessed by a Han ethnocentric feeling: the more radical called for a revolution to end the Manchu rule, which they blamed for China's loss of sovereign rights and dignity. In his widely circulated *Revolutionary Army* (Gemingjun), the young and hot-blooded martyr Zou Rong (1885–1905) proclaimed, "China is the China of the Chinese. Countrymen, you must all recognize the China of the Chinese of the Han race."[18] The longstanding feuds between the Chinese and the Manchus were now articulated in a new vocabulary of race, nation, and social Darwinism.[19]

Zhang Shizhao's reinterpretation of *hanjian* in 1903 fit well into a new national history that centered on the development of the Han and projected ethnic awareness back into the past. Zhang praised the original *hanjian*, those denounced by the Qing rulers as Han rebels, as "heroes of the Han race fighting for the independence of the Chinese nation."[20] The real *hanjian*, argued Zhang, were those who betrayed the interest of the Han, including Han officials serving the Qing rulers and ordinary people who helped foreigners profit from trade with China.[21] To reinforce this new definition of *hanjian*, Zhang anachronistically identified a number of *hanjian* in history and created a genealogy of Chinese race traitors:

> The real *hanjian* are those who betray their own race by colluding with foreigners. . . . Guan Gan, who served under the Han general Li Ling, surrendered to the Hun tribes and helped them defeat the Han army; Zhang Bin helped the Jie invade the Han-based Jin dynasty; Shi Jingtang sought protection from the Khitans and called the Khitan emperor "father"; . . . Zhang Hongfan led the Mongol troops to defeat the southern Song army and ended the Song rule; Wu Sangui, Geng Jimao, and Shang Kexi helped the Manchus eliminate the Ming forces;[22] . . . these are *hanjian* who deserve eternal condemnation.

This list includes notorious figures in Chinese history, but in their own time they were not called *hanjian* or other epithets that implied ethnic betrayal. A Han ethnicity gradually evolved on the basis of shared language, customs, and traditions, and a Han ethnic awareness was catalyzed at transformative moments such as the Manchu conquest of China. The bitter resistance to the Manchus and the Qing's differential treatment of

Manchus and the Han led to ethnic antagonism and the growth of a Han identity. By juxtaposing *hanjian* from before the Qing era with those from his own time, Zhang Shizhao narrated a continuous history of Han Chinese being victimized by foreign invaders with the assistance of Han traitors.

This historiographical change placed ethnic or racial, rather than cultural, distinctiveness at the core of Chinese national identity. As one scholar observes, as carriers of the dominant culture in East Asia, the Chinese, unlike their neighboring peoples, "did not have to worry about their identity until the twentieth century."[23] The world had changed dramatically, however. Repeated defeats in wars with other nations and loss of sovereign rights led many to redefine *China* and *Chinese* in racial terms. Not only did this national community have no place for *hanjian*, but its very construction was based on defining internal others as *hanjian*.

In the two decades after the Republic of China was founded, the term *hanjian* fell out of fashion, as it conflicted with the rhetoric of the post-1911 Chinese nation-state. Revolutionary leaders such as Sun Yat-sen redefined the Chinese race as encompassing multiple ethnic groups and thus being entitled to all the territory of the former Qing Empire.[24] The Nationalist government, established in Nanjing in 1928 under the leadership of Chiang Kai-shek, inherited this Han-centered, ethnically inclusive discourse. Chiang's government operated with greater confidence and wider support than any of its Republican predecessors. It promised to lead China toward independence, unification, and modernity—an ambitious mission that involved recovering China's lost rights and territories—and seeking a "grand unity" of all its peoples.[25] In reality, the Nanjing government controlled only the core regions of China, including the most populated and developed areas in the lower Yangzi delta, which it was soon to lose to the Japanese.

The word *hanjian* was resurrected in the early 1930s as a keyword in the discourse of national salvation that arose in response to the increasing Japanese threat. From this point, the term lost its complicated historical connotations in popular memory and has since been primarily associated with the Japanese invasion. Japan, now the major Asian colonial power, had annexed the Ryukyu Islands, Taiwan, and Korea by defeating Qing China and czarist Russia. Japan's growing appetite for land and resources, as well as domestic crises caused by the Great Depression, led officers of the Kwantung Army to plot the Mukden Incident in 1931 and seek full control of Manchuria. Enraged by Japan's intrusion into Chinese territory, college students and intellectuals fueled public opinion with a patriotic fervor with which they hoped to urge the government and the people to staunchly resist Japan.[26]

Tracking down the first appearance of *hanjian* in this anti-Japanese context is challenging. As early as 1932, in the aftermath of the Shanghai Incident, an "Iron and Blood *Hanjian*-Eliminating Team" appeared. The six-week exchange of fire between the Japanese naval infantry units and local Chinese troops stirred up patriotic sentiment in Shanghai. This grassroots, anti-*hanjian* organization sent threatening letters primarily to *jianshang*, "treacherous merchants," such as those who were still dealing in Japanese coal.[27] Several years earlier, Shanghai's patriotic entrepreneurs, industrial workers, and students had joined forces to promote "national goods" (*guohuo*) and boycott foreign products.[28] Buying and selling Japanese goods, therefore, had been seen as supporting the enemy's business interests at the expense of Chinese industries. With the crisis of war now escalating, "treacherous merchants" who placed personal gains above the interests of the community were further condemned as *hanjian*.

Since then this term had frequently appeared in newspapers, flyers, posters, and public speeches that championed the national salvation movement. The wide acceptance of the word revealed a conflation of the Chinese nation with Han ethnicity, despite the official discourse on ethnic inclusiveness. Only a few questioned the appropriateness of this label. In 1935, the *New Life* weekly (Xinsheng) analyzed *hanjian* in its "New Terminology" (Xinshuyu) column as a new political catchphrase. Disturbed by its increasing popularity in conversation and in print, *Xinsheng*'s editors proposed instead to use *huajian*, "traitors to the greater Chinese nation." While agreeing with the view that "the Han people are the original and the earliest Chinese," the editors reminded the readers that "the other four peoples [Mongols, Manchus, Tibetans, and Chinese Muslims, known as the Hui] became Chinese while China expanded its territory," so the *hanjian* label was inappropriate for denoting traitors to the entire Chinese nation.[29]

Using *huajian* might have been more in line with the official rhetoric on the nation's ethnic composition, but the editors' reasoning, still based on a Han-centric mentality, misinterpreted a complex historical process. The editors realized that China was a shifting concept, the territorial and ethnic scope of which had developed over time. Such a development, contrary to what the editors implied, was not primarily pushed for or achieved by Han-based dynasties. Even the Ming, the last Han-based empire, did not extend its power much beyond China proper to control Tibet, Xinjiang,

Mongolia, or much of Manchuria. Moreover, a Han-centered Chinese political history had twice been interrupted by two alien empires, the Mongol Yuan dynasty and the Manchu Qing dynasty. "The other four peoples" became Chinese only in the sense that the Republic of China recognized them as members of the national community. None of the peoples, or their homelands, were under the solid control of the Nanjing government. In any case, this lexical alternative did not cause even a ripple.

As the shadow of war descended, the term *hanjian* not only spread fast in the public arena but also gained official endorsement. In 1936, the Nationalist government sponsored the publication of *Biographies of Hanjian in the Fall of the Ming* (Mingmo hanjian liezhuan), with a preface written by none other than Chiang Kai-shek himself.[30] Originally named *Biographies of Twice-Serving Ministers* (Erchenzhuan), this text had been part of the official history compiled during the reign of the Qianlong emperor (1735–95). Included in this section were Han officials who had defected from the Ming court and assisted the Manchus in their conquest. Despite their "small contributions" to the Qing, the Qianlong emperor condemned them for "failing to maintain loyalty to their emperor when he needed them the most."[31] Along with the *Biographies of Ming Loyalists* (Zhongchenlu), this project showcased the Qing rulers' endorsement of the Confucian principle of loyalty as the most important quality of officials.

The 1936 reprinting of the biographies clearly drew a parallel between the fall of the Ming and the present moment. As Chiang stated in the preface: "This is a shameful history of people with no integrity. Those who are thinking of following their examples should feel a cold chill on their back when reading this book. Gu Tinglin once said that the demise of Ming originated from its spineless scholar-officials. . . . I initiated the New Life Movement to guide my countrymen with Confucian virtues of propriety, righteousness, integrity and dignity. . . . those twice-serving ministers of Qing were traitors to our Han race/ethnicity. Therefore I changed the title of the book to *Biographies of Hanjian in the Fall of the Ming*."[32]

Chiang's ostracization of *hanjian* reaffirmed the Confucianist component of the Nationalist Party's ideological foundation. Like the Qianlong emperor, Chiang Kai-shek resorted to the traditional Chinese historiographic practice of evaluating political figures with a polarized "praise or blame" (*baobian*) approach and made himself the ultimate judge of history and individual morality. By reminding the Chinese of *hanjian* in the past, the government warned its people against becoming *hanjian* in the imminent war. Even the enemy would despise such a shameful act, as the Qianlong emperor had made clear in his comment on the Ming traitors.

This preface also manifested Chiang's patriotic stance at a time when he was being widely criticized for prioritizing the elimination of Chinese Communists over resistance against Japan. The widespread discontent with Chiang gave his opponents a chance to challenge his authority. During the Guangdong-Guangxi Incident of 1936, militarists from these two provinces strove for political autonomy in the name of patriotism.[33] They named their army the Anti-Japanese National Salvation Army (Kangri Jiuguojun) and published *A Faithful Record of* Hanjian *Sellouts* as a moral justification for their cause. *Hanjian* identified by the Guangdong-Guangxi clique included contemporaries who had been serving the Japan-sponsored Manchukuo (1932–45) as well as familiar names from the past. This publication also labeled as *hanjian* those "corrupt and abusive officials who sell out our nation in ways less conspicuous yet equally detrimental," echoing criticisms of the Nationalist administration.[34] Chiang Kai-shek's adoption of the word in propaganda and in law, therefore, was a defensive move and a key step in establishing his leadership in the national war against Japan once it proved inevitable.

"HARSH LAWS FOR A STATE OF EMERGENCY"

The outbreak of war on July 7, 1937, led China into a state of emergency (*feichang shiqi*) that would last for eight years. One month later, on August 23, 1937, the Nationalist government issued the Regulations on Punishing *Hanjian* (*Chengzhi hanjian tiaoli*). Old crimes were thus proscribed under a powerful new name in the context of China's unprecedented national crisis. Chinese rulers in the past had been most concerned with the two evils of *neiluan* (internal turmoil) and *waihuai* (external aggression), especially if they occurred in tandem. The Great Qing Code, the most comprehensive legal code of imperial China, listed three acts in these two categories among the ten "great wrongs."[35] "Plotting to overthrow the dynasty," "plotting to overthrow the emperor," and "betraying one's own country by secretly serving another" all warranted the most severe form of the death penalty and harsh punishment of family members of the convicted, based on the principle of "corruption of blood."[36]

The Nationalist government's 1928 criminal code retained both *neiluan* and *waihuan*, redefining them as crimes against the nation-state rather than the monarch.[37] *Waihuan* thus referred to "acts that amount to a breach of allegiance and aiding enemy nations," including ceding the nation's territory, affiliating with enemy troops, willful failure to fulfill contracts for military supplies, and disclosure of confidential information on national defense.[38] The code mandated a prison term of one to seven years for the crime, but the death penalty was applicable depending on the gravity of the offense.[39] Many of the acts punishable as *waihuan* overlapped with those later constituted as the *hanjian* crime.

Chiang Kai-shek's Nationalist government had been a more effective police state than its predecessors. It relied on lawmaking as one means of facilitating state control and suppressing political dissent. In January 1931 the Nationalist government passed the Emergency Law on Crimes Endangering the Republic (*Weihai minguo jinji zhizuifa*, hereafter Emergency Law), which granted military courts jurisdiction over cases that mattered to "national security and social order" in areas under martial law, allowing them extrajudicial powers of arrest and detention.[40] By this point, the government had already showed a tendency to suspend civilian criminal justice when it considered it necessary.[41]

In the expectation of an imminent war with Japan, the revised Criminal Code of 1935 and the revised Emergency Law of 1937 elaborated on the definition of external aggression, prescribing more severe punishment for all offenses of this category. Articles 103–6 of the 1935 Criminal Code mandated the death penalty or life imprisonment for those who "collaborate with a foreign country" in bringing war to the Republic of China or encroaching on Chinese territory. Those who fought against the Republic of China or sabotaged its military operations on behalf of the enemy nation also faced capital punishment.[42] Other new capital crimes included colluding with enemies to disturb the public order, leaking confidential information on national security, and participating in enemy propaganda activities.[43] The establishment of the all-encompassing crime of *hanjian* was a consummation of the legal trends in the 1930s developed against the backdrop of imminent war.

The initial Regulations and their 1938 revision served as the legal basis for the anti-*hanjian* campaigns throughout the War of Resistance. Historians have noted that under one-party rule, China had no constitutional procedure for forming a government, much less claiming the authority of the rule of law.[44] The Nationalist Party was indeed placed above the law by the Constitution of the Republic of China.[45] Even during normal times, the Central Executive Committee of the party had the power to decide the principles of legislation. When it was operating from an insecure position during wartime, the party was inclined to make laws with little regard for due process or the perspective of jurists. Admittedly, the suspension of normal judicial proceedings and the erosion of individual rights in the name of national security occurred in democratic countries as well. In Canada, for instance, the War Measures Act, in force during both world wars, granted enormous powers to the federal cabinet and allowed the violation of the basic rights of Japanese Canadians during World War II.[46]

The particular significance of the enactment of *hanjian* laws lay in their timing and their popular basis. Whereas France and other nations tried collaborators under laws enacted toward the end of World War II, in 1944 and 1945, China's Nationalist government legalized the punishment of *hanjian* at the very start of its war against Japan. This legislative move had important implications for China's nascent modern legal system. In the context of war, the anti-*hanjian* laws resonated with the larger public and thus could claim popular legitimacy despite their shaky legal grounds. Political scientists generally consider legitimacy as coming by degrees and being accorded to political institutions that are considered better than the available alternatives, in spite of their shortcomings and failures.[47] The exigency of the war left the Chinese no choice but to support the central government that promised to lead the nation to victory at any cost.

The Regulations were not only important legal documents but also an integral part of war propaganda, frequently cited in newspapers and pamphlets that explained how to identify and punish *hanjian*. Issued as Japan was gaining a sweeping victory, the Regulations defined the *hanjian* crime as including any possible form of collaboration or sabotage that the lawmakers could envision. (See appendix A for a full translation of the 1938 Regulations.) Any of the following acts, when combined with conspiring with the enemy nation (*tongmou diguo*), could be considered *hanjian* crimes:

Plotting against the home country

Plotting to disturb public order

Forming an army or recruiting labor for military use

Supplying, dealing in, or transporting military supplies or stock

Supplying, dealing in, or transporting grain or other items that could
    serve as provisions

Providing financial support to the enemy

Leaking, stealing, or secretly collecting political or economic information
    (about the resistance forces)

Serving as guide for the enemy or assisting the enemy army in other ways

Impeding the work of government employees

Instigating financial chaos

Sabotaging communications, military infrastructure, or military
blockades of the resistance force

Poisoning drinking water or food for consumption by the Chinese
military or people

Instigating defection or collaboration among servicemen, government
employees, or ordinary citizens

Being enticed into collaboration by a perpetrator of any of the above
crimes

Individuals convicted of *hanjian* crimes faced the death penalty or life imprisonment and loss of all civil rights. In addition, all the *hanjian*'s property, except for a small amount necessary for the support of the family, could be confiscated by the state.[48]

The perceived threat of *hanjian* activities to China's war effort was based on alarming events that unfolded during the first years of the war against Japan. Between 1937 and 1938, vast regions in east and central China became constant battlefields. With the horrifying defeat of the Nationalist army, key cities, including Beijing, Shanghai, Nanjing, Xuzhou, and their surrounding towns and villages, fell into Japanese hands. By the end of 1938, the Japanese advancement started to slow down, and the war entered a stalemate. Resistance propaganda at this stage reported widespread *hanjian* activities that attacked the Nationalist troops from behind.

Newspapers published in these years incited a deep fear and resentment toward *hanjian* spies. Journalists reported on numerous spy activities, some of which were real and others products of rumors or paranoia. Indeed, high-profile Chinese individuals spied for the Japanese Imperial Army and caused substantial damage and widespread panic.

Huang Jun was the first prominent government official to be executed as a *hanjian*.[49] With an elite family background and a degree from Waseda University in Japan, Huang Jun's career peaked in 1935, when he was appointed senior secretary of the Confidential Affairs Office in the Executive Yuan of the Nationalist government. This background made Huang Jun a perfect target for Japanese recruitment. He had access to confidential documents, strategic plans, and military information. His work for the Japanese could have changed the outcome of the war. He recruited his son, Huang Sheng, a staff member of the Ministry of Foreign Affairs, and other government personnel into his spy network. Huang's spy group caused the abortion of several secret military actions planned by the Nationalist army, in addition to making multiple attempts on Chiang Kai-shek's life, which Chiang narrowly escaped. Huang Jun, his son, and a few other members of the network were executed on August 26, 1937, with much publicity.

The early years of the War of Resistance also saw the emergence of "minor *hanjian*," ordinary people who ran errands for the Japanese or facilitated sabotage activities. For instance, those executed as associates of Huang Jun included a head waiter in a restaurant and a fortune teller, who capitalized on their public contacts to collect information or spread rumors, on Huang's orders. Most *hanjian* were reported to be "ignorant poor people," who were paid twenty to thirty yuan at most per month for their *hanjian* activity, a pathetically small amount considering the risks involved (in comparison, the Japanese paid mid-ranking officials 1,500 yuan per month on average).[50] Their decisions to take such jobs demonstrates the war-induced poverty and dislocation that drove people to any means possible to make ends meet.

According to resistance journalism, *hanjian* was like a virus that plagued the nation. *Hanjian* spied for the Japanese, poisoned food and water, assessed China's defense mechanisms, signaled Japanese bomber planes, and more.[51] The Japanese army and their Chinese deputies also organized locally based minor *hanjian* and developed strategies for intragroup communication. As counterintelligence measures, these minor *hanjian* carried identifying marks such as red threads sewn inside their clothes and tattoos in particular patterns. Though one cannot quantify exactly how much damage minor *hanjian* did to the resistance force, their existence was understandably alarming to the Nationalist government, especially when its army kept losing on the battlefront. The two early versions of the Regulations, therefore, targeted all kinds of sabotage in addition to the overarching crime of "plotting against the home country."

With the same fourteen criminal acts listed, the 1938 revision of the Regulations was significantly more punitive than the 1937 version. Whereas the earlier draft stipulated a five-year minimum prison term for those guilty of lesser degrees of the *hanjian* crime, the revised version decreed that anyone found guilty (probably on the basis of a brief interrogation, at most) would be executed or jailed for life. In reality, most of those convicted were summarily executed, avoiding the logistical challenges posed by a sentence of life imprisonment. The offense of preparing or conspiring to commit a *hanjian* crime now carried a seven-year minimum prison term (rather than a sentence of one to seven years). The 1938 revisions also mandated a heavier punishment for people who knowingly harbored *hanjian*.[52]

In addition, the 1938 law granted enormous power to the military and the wartime authorities, bypassing regular civil- and criminal-justice procedures. Article 14 dictated that those who were charged with one of the fourteen *hanjian* offenses should be tried in military tribunals or by the local army branch instead of "being tried in a public court," as previously mandated. The 1938 Regulations additionally curtailed the authority of the Executive Yuan (Xingzheng Yuan) in processing *hanjian* property, giving the power instead to the Supreme Council of National Defense, the highest wartime commanding authority, which oversaw all functions of government.[53] These legislative and procedural changes in part reflected the military and logistical plight of a government in exile.

The Nationalist government also took preemptive measures against social groups who were likely to become *hanjian*. Issued in 1939, the Resolutions on Preventing *Hanjian* Activities and Espionage (*Fangzhi hanjian jiandie huodong banfa dagang*, translated in full in appendix B) aimed to use existing local surveillance networks and turn civilians into proxies for law-enforcement and counterespionage agents.[54] The Resolutions urged local police, volunteer groups, village heads, and common citizens to watch for groups, activities, and individuals that appeared suspicious and to patrol "high-risk locations." Once spotted, such groups and individuals would be followed, questioned, and possibly reported to the local authorities.

In essence, the Resolutions revealed categories of people whom the government had always considered threats to public security because of their particular employment profiles, appearance, behavior, familial structure, and social interactions. By such standards, a substantial proportion of the population could be considered potential *hanjian*. They included, for instance, "those who are generally ill-behaved," "those who are unemployed yet often appear busy," "those who frequently interact with foreigners," and "all other individuals who do not appear normal."[55] The vague criteria and the state's reliance on grassroots informers could easily lead to witch hunts.

The social and behavioral profiles of potential *hanjian* outlined in the Resolutions also reflected widely held stereotypes and prejudices. Among the places denoted as at risk of penetration by *hanjian* spies were main transportation routes, docks, temples, stations, theaters, hotels, and "suspicious news agencies." Many of these were places where unsettled members of the population gathered: travelers, itinerant monks, boatmen, performers, and so forth. This floating population consisted of unstable elements that could not be locked into the "mutual surveillance units" (*baojia*), and they were distrusted by the state and society even in good times.

Counterespionage is usually not a duty that can be properly performed by the regular police, let alone by civilians. Yet at a time when the resistance state could barely hold its defensive position, common citizens were expected to undertake counterintelligence responsibilities. Chiang Kai-shek stated that relying on the people and local militia was key to defending the nation and subduing an enemy better equipped for modern warfare.[56] Case studies show that in many localities, the mutual surveillance systems that the Nationalist government had constructed for eliminating the "Communist bandits" were now fortified for catching *hanjian* and spies.[57] In free China as well as in occupied zones, the campaigns against *hanjian* acquired a populist nature and accounted for numerous arrests and executions. The fact that the Resolutions were issued by the Ministry of Internal Affairs demonstrates that the Nationalist government saw the process of *chujian*, or eradicating *hanjian*, as the same as identifying and cleansing suspicious parts of the population. The involvement of common citizens in this national war was not only logistically necessary because of the state's limited resources; it was also regarded as fundamental to stabilizing the populace and purging it of corrupting elements.

The Resolutions were part of a sizable body of wartime laws and ordinances on crimes against the state and public security. The Nationalist government had been accelerating its legislative pace and simplifying lawmaking procedures since the 1930s. Below is a small selection of laws and regulations passed in the name of managing this "state of emergency":

> Regulations on Punishing *Hanjian*, August 1937
>
> Emergency Law on Crimes Endangering the Republic, September 1937
>
> Revised Regulations on Punishing *Hanjian*, August 1938
>
> Resolution on Preventing *Hanjian* Activities and Espionage, 1939
>
> Resolutions on Maintaining Public Order at a Time of Emergency (*Feichang shiqi weichi zhi'an jinji banfa*), July 1940
>
> Prohibitions on Opium and Other Narcotics (*Jinyan jindu zhizui zanxing tiaoli*), February 1941
>
> Wartime Military Laws of the Republic of China (*Zhonghua minguo zhanshi junlü*), April 1942
>
> Regulations on Punishing Robbery and Banditry (*Chengzhi daofei tiaoli*), April 1944.[58]

These wartime laws provided for "special criminal procedures," which allowed the arrest and trial of suspects according to military criminal procedures. The Nationalist government justified the severe laws and abridgment of due process with the traditional Chinese legal principle of "harsh law for a time of turbulence."[59]

The swift promulgation of laws during wartime was made possible by the creation of powerful government agencies in the exigency of a total war. To streamline legislation and decisionmaking, the Chongqing government established the Supreme Council of National Defense (Guofang Zuigao Weiyuanhui, hereafter the Supreme Council) in January 1939 as the highest wartime commanding authority. This body was responsible for making all strategic decisions necessary for the state and its army to win the War of Resistance. Chiang Kai-shek placed all ministries and five branches of the government (known as the Five Yuan) under the command of this council.[60] He chaired the Supreme Council himself, and its executive committee included heads of the administrative branch, the judicial branch, the legislature, the party and the army, in addition to the chairman's handpicked advisers.

The Supreme Council possessed the ultimate legislative power. Once laws were made, the Legislative Yuan had to pass them without revision. If the laws were enacted in response to an emergency, they could be immediately announced and implemented. This concentration of power eroded the political system and alienated even the senior members of the Nationalist Party. "I never see any calm or detailed discussion," Zhou Fohai, one of Chiang's close followers, who had taken important positions in Chiang's administration, commented on the meetings of the Supreme Council. "They just pass the regulations silently. No wonder decisions can't be carried out well."[61] Zhou's disillusionment with the system was partly why he lost faith in the resistance and decided to facilitate Wang Jingwei's "peace talks" with Japan.

The Supreme Council produced additional laws and supplements that increased the scope of applicability of the *hanjian* crime. A 1939 supplement, for instance, specifically identified as *hanjian* those who joined the "puppet militia" (*weijun*), because they "adhered to the enemy nation and rebelled against the state."[62] The Resolutions on Maintaining Public Order at a Time of Emergency of 1940 allowed immediate arrest and "termination" of *hanjian* by the military, the police, or intelligence officials.[63] The same rule was applied to those who were found guilty of conspiring to commit a *hanjian* crime.

Other government agencies and branches produced their own amendments to the Regulations, resulting varying definitions and punishments of the *hanjian* crime. The Supervision Commission, for instance, decided to punish party members who turned into *hanjian* for betrayal of the party as well as the nation.[64] All party members found guilty of *hanjian* activity, regardless of the extent or form of their involvement, were considered "major *hanjian*" (*zhongyao hanjian*). Many provincial governments drafted their own regulations, prescribing additional punishments and incriminating "local *hanjian*" who would have escaped conviction under the central government Regulations.[65]

Furthermore, the Nationalist anti-*hanjian* laws and measures shaped the ways in which the Chinese Communists identified enemies within.[66] The Communists developed their base areas in the vast rural areas of north, central, and eastern China, where the Nationalist administration had been driven away and the Japanese were too stretched to exercise control. The anti-*hanjian* laws in many base areas, including the Shaanxi-Gansu-Ningxia Border Area, were modeled directly on the 1938 Nationalist Regulations.[67] In some areas, the CCP leadership implemented the Nationalist guidelines on preventing *hanjian* and spy activities.[68] The people's war against traitors gave rise to the organization of "safeguarding and *hanjian*-eliminating committees" and "*hanjian*-eliminating squads" in all base areas. In the Shaanxi-Gansu-Ningxia area alone, more than seven hundred county-level committees and nine thousand squads were established, with more than one hundred thousand members active on the anti-*hanjian* front.[69] The CCP also sanctioned unusual measures against *hanjian*, stating, "Once a *hanjian* is identified, anyone can immediately arrest and hand him or her in to the local military or government."[70] The CCP's anti-*hanjian* campaigns were key to the expansion of the party's reach, to its organization of various local resistance movements, and to its growth as a political force. The legacies of the CCP anti-*hanjian* campaigns are discussed in more depth in the epilogue.

LEGAL GUIDELINES FOR POSTWAR *HANJIAN* TRIALS

In August 1945, the Chiang Kai-shek administration returned to its former capital in Nanjing, where it could now sit comfortably as the central government. By then, *hanjian* had ceased to pose real threats to national security, but the campaign against them did not end; rather, it entered a new stage. On September 29, 1945, the government issued a new set of guidelines, Regulations on Handling *Hanjian* Cases (*Chuli hanjian anjian tiaoli*, translated in full in appendix C). They provided a legislative framework for postwar trials of *hanjian*, which helped the Nationalist government to reinforce its image as the resistance state and to consolidate its regime. In addition, the 1945 Regulations set up criteria making it easier for the common people to identify *hanjian* that the judiciary or the intelligence failed to catch.[71] The new measures led to nationwide arrests and investigations of *hanjian*, particularly in cities, towns, and villages that had endured years of occupation.

The postwar Regulations differed from earlier laws by defining the crime based on an individual's title, position, and political affiliation. All officials who had served at or above the third level of civil administration (*jianrenzhi*) or higher in the collaborationist regime could be convicted of the *hanjian* crime; so could those of lower ranks if they were proved to have "infringed upon the life or property of the people through association with the enemy."[72] Special agents of the puppet regime, members of the puppet national assembly, and puppet Nationalist party members were also identified as *hanjian*. In other words, in the postwar phase of the anti-*hanjian* movement, Chiang's administration was mainly after those who had founded, supported, or followed the regime that had opposed his government.

Under the new laws, an individual did not have to have personally "conspired with the enemy nation" to be convicted of the *hanjian* crime, as had been the case in wartime. Affiliation with the puppet regime was sufficient grounds for guilt. Considering the scope and duration of wartime occupation, the *hanjian* label could be easily applied to anyone who had participated in any economic, financial, educational, cultural, publishing, or entertainment enterprises affiliated with or approved by the puppet regime: all that was necessary was for someone to bring a charge against that person. *Hanjian* cases examined in subsequent chapters reveal that those who remained employed in occupied areas, if accused of the crime, had a difficult time proving their innocence to the prosecution or in public opinion.

The more expansive postwar definition of *hanjian* grew, to a large extent, out of the agony over the defection of Wang Jingwei and his foundation of the Reorganized National Government in 1940. Unlike earlier puppet regimes, Wang Jingwei's was declared a national regime, and it operated from Chiang Kai-shek's old capital and power base.[73] Moreover, Wang claimed to represent the orthodoxy (*zhengtong*) of the Nationalist Party, a plausible claim given his important role in the early history of the party and his close relationship to Sun Yat-sen, the founding father of the Republic of China and the Nationalist Party.[74] After Sun Yat-sen's death, Wang Jingwei became the head of the party and the new administration in July 1925, carrying on Sun's strategy of working with the Soviet Union and the CCP to unify China. The turn of events between 1926 and 1928 enabled Chiang Kai-shek, then commander of the Nationalist army, to rise to power and overshadow Wang in the leadership of the party and government.[75]

Wang's repeated defeats in his political rivalry with Chiang might have been a factor in his decision to collaborate with Japan, though Wang's considerations also resulted from his assessment of China's prospects in the war. In his evaluation of Korean collaborators, John Treat correctly points out that whereas we have the benefit of knowing the outcome of the war, people living then could only choose a course of action that seemed viable for the time being.[76] Before the United States entered the war in 1941, China did not seem to stand a chance of defeating Japan. Chiang Kai-shek was aware of Wang Jingwei and Zhou Fohai's negotiations with Japan, and he did not resolutely veto the idea.[77] Similar judgments about China's war prospects, and perhaps Wang's personal charisma, explain why a large number of senior politicians and officials joined Wang. Many influential businessmen, members of the cultural elites, and celebrities were then coerced or enticed into Wang's camp, some more actively than others.

From 1940 on, therefore, the anti-*hanjian* campaigns focused primarily on striking down Wang and his close followers. Many common people continued to collaborate with the Japanese or puppet rule, for which they continued to pay. Yet the Chongqing government's priority was demoralizing and eliminating the Wang Jingwei regime. The Supreme Council issued lists of most-wanted *hanjian*, all of whom were attached to Wang's government or to organizations in its service.[78] The postwar Regulations thus underpinned a transition that had been taking place since 1940.

Yet to punish people for their wartime positions and political affiliations under the 1945 Regulations could have been construed as a violation of the legality principle that forbids retroactive criminalization. This issue was a source of controversy in the postwar international tribunals that tried war criminals, which many criticized as "the victor's justice." At the Nuremberg trials, individuals were subject to arrest and prosecution solely on the basis of their membership in a proscribed organization such as the Schutzstaffel (SS).[79] In the Chinese *hanjian* trials, the legality problem was more complex. In the words of the historian Timothy Brook, "Serving as the director of a bank or the head of an insurance board, or even as the foreign minister, is not in itself a criminal act," even under the wartime National-ist laws.[80] Before the 1945 Regulations redefined the *hanjian* on the basis of affiliation, however, anti-*hanjian* laws based on conduct had been in force for eight years. Vigorous anti-*hanjian* propaganda and threatening letters sent to puppet officials and collaborating lawyers made it difficult to argue that these individuals were unaware of the consequences of their choices. Their conscious decision to collaborate in the face of the wartime anti-*hanjian* laws did not entirely erase the legal problems raised by the 1945 Regulations, but it certainly helps explain why the general public thought they deserved the punishment.

The 1945 Regulations were also significant in that they set out new pro-cedures for dealing with *hanjian* cases. In China, as in France, the resis-tance government tried to restore the full authority of the judiciary and minimize the role of military and intelligence agencies in postwar crimi-nal justice. The 1945 Regulations mandated that all *hanjian* cases, except for those involving puppet military officers, be transferred to civilian crim-inal justice system.[81] As early as 1944, the Nationalist legislature passed a series of laws aimed at restoring order and preparing for a return to nor-mality, including the Regulations on Prosecuting Special Criminal Cases.[82]

Yet it would be naive to assume that the Nationalist government made such moves purely out of respect for the rule of law. The shift was also due to power struggles within the Nationalist government. Chiang Kai-shek handpicked the person in charge of arresting *hanjian* in Shanghai to end the competition for control over this financial and industrial capital of China. Xuan Tiewu, whom Chiang deeply trusted, was appointed the head of the Shanghai municipal police, which assumed the authority to arrest *hanjian* soon after the war ended. Dai Li, the spymaster who rushed his special agents into Shanghai for the arrests and takeover, lost favor with Chiang as the generalissimo reset his priorities and manipulated the bal-ance of power in postwar China.

Major *hanjian* such as Wang Jingwei were crucial to facilitating Japanese rule in China and rallying support for the occupying regime, but the daily functioning of the regime relied on numerous faceless employees. A large number of Chinese with decent educations and professional credentials filled the puppet administration and institutions that acquiesced in the Japanese occupation. Their collaboration was often not voluntary but a means of survival. Many, in their officials roles provided essential public services in the occupied regions. Most were not influential or guilty enough to be incriminated under the 1945 Regulations. From the perspective of the central government, however, these people could not be easily forgiven. Despite their obscurity, these employees constituted the flesh and blood of the puppet administration, without which Japan could not possibly have preserved its control over the vast occupied areas.[83]

The Nationalist government placed these individuals in a different category from *hanjian*, labelling them *weiyuan*, "puppet staff."[84] They included the staff of cultural and occupational associations, chambers of commerce, schools, and presses that continued to function under Japanese occupation.[85] The criterion for deciding whether individuals were *weiyuan* or *hanjian* was whether they had used their position to blatantly harm the interest of the nation or the people. The government did not punish *weiyuan* as criminals, but it still made them pay a price for their disloyalty. Once identified, *weiyuan* were immediately removed from public positions, and since the state kept their names and short biographies on file, their chances of obtaining public positions again were significantly reduced.[86] In addition, the Ministry of Justice nullified lawyers' licenses obtained under the puppet rule. Lawyers who had been certified before the war but renewed their licenses under the puppet regime could apply for the new licenses for a fee of two thousand yuan, providing that they had not been classified as *hanjian*.[87] These individuals, therefore, suffered the collateral damage of the government's complete delegitimization of the puppet regime.

Although retributive in nature, these policies also grew out of the government's concern with the livelihood of citizens whom it deemed more patriotic. During the War of Resistance, numerous clerks, intellectuals, students, and other people from all walks of life followed the Chiang Kai-shek administration to Chongqing and other "free regions." A greater number, however, could not afford to relocate. Following Japan's surrender, those who had followed Chiang returned home only to find that their old jobs and places in the communities had gone to people who had stayed. People from the latter group were no less qualified than the former, but they had one fatal disadvantage: their political integrity was open to question.

In important ways, therefore, the campaigns against *hanjian* was about re-creating living space and employment for people who had chosen Chiang's side in wartime. A decree issued by the Ministry of Justice in September 1946 is one of the rare documents that reveals this hidden agenda. It urged local governments to "encourage unemployed patriots to expose *hanjian*." If the informant and the accused held comparable credentials, this decree mandated, the informant should take over the position of the accused.[88]

The penalties and restrictions on those who had passively collaborated with or accommodated the enemy rule, therefore, created divisions among the people and impeded postwar reconstruction. Such policies were thus challenged by professional groups and in some cases by local governments. In 1946, in order to retain certain members on the municipal council, the Shanghai Social Affairs Bureau decided that occupational associations were not to be considered as affiliated with the puppet regime. Occupational associations had flourished in Shanghai since early 1920s and had made great contributions to Shanghai's social and economic vitality as well as the overall development of the city. The issue was debated at the ministry level of the government. The Ministry of Internal Affairs ruled against the municipal government's decision, insisting on disqualifying members of wartime occupational organizations for public positions. The Ministry of Social Affairs, however, supported its branch office in Shanghai. The more forgiving side won the debate, and the decision resulted in a clearer and less incriminating definition of "puppet organizations" as those established under the direct order of, and with members appointed by, the puppet government. Members of occupation-based, self-formed associations with elected chairs, therefore, should be exempted.[89]

At a time when openly challenging the anti-*hanjian* cause was politically risky, social and occupational organizations sought to protect their groups' interests, sometimes at the expense of certain members. As one of the earliest and best-organized professional organizations in China, the Shanghai Bar Association (SBA) guarded the reputation and interests of the legal profession by disbarring well-known "collaborating lawyers." The Shanghai Chamber of Commerce crafted a petition to the central government cosigned by fifty-five occupational associations. These associations affirmed their loyalty to the nation and emphasized their contributions to the economy and local society. Asserting that they had dealt with the puppet government "courteously yet perfunctorily" (*xuyu fuyan*), they pleaded for the government's understanding of their plight and warned against the overly broad definition of *hanjian*, lest everyone who had remained in the occupied regions be liable to prosecution.[90]

Such a petition was not unreasonable, particularly in light of the government's lenient treatment of the Japanese. Not only did it acquit some of the most notorious Japanese war criminals, but the Nationalist government also allowed most Japanese employees to keep their jobs in China, requiring only their close supervision.[91] With the wounds inflicted by the Japanese still fresh, many Chinese were disillusioned by the government's apparently preferential treatment of the Japanese.[92]

NATIONALISM OVER LAW: LEGAL PROFESSIONALS UNDER THE ANTI-*HANJIAN* REGIME

The making and promotion of the Regulations was a result of government decisions that resonated with grassroots patriotism and popular anxiety over *hanjian*. Legal experts played a minimal role in the process, and the upholding of nationalism muted doubts and concerns that they might have raised. During wartime, judicial clerks and lawyers in occupied areas were no different from other citizens who struggled with the choice between starvation and collaboration. Since they were equally vulnerable to the *hanjian* charges, those who worked in or closely with the justice system were reluctant to comment candidly on the anti-*hanjian* campaigns. Yet an understanding of their wartime quandary and subsequent position on this issue is important, given that they prosecuted, defended, and processed numerous *hanjian* cases. Some became defendants themselves.

Chiang Kai-shek fully understood the importance of maintaining the facade of lawful rule, even though he had suspended normal legislative and judicial procedures during wartime. The Nationalist government recognized that maintaining a functional judicial system was essential to determining "whether or not we retain popular support" (*renxinxiangbei*). Therefore, in February 1938, when the Japanese army swept through east and central China, the Ministry of Justice decreed that no matter how bad the situation had become, "courts and judicial personnel must function as normal." To maintain the operation of the legal system and loyalty of judicial staff, the government squeezed its tight budget to subsidize the clerks. In 1937 and 1938, when the Nationalists were losing vast areas to the Japanese, the Ministry of Justice still managed to provide registered personnel with limited support for living expenses.[93] As more regions fell under Japanese occupation, however, local judicial branches and courts alone could not continue to function. Their collapse not only forced judicial clerks to choose sides but also devastated lawyers in private practice.

Lawyers, as "free professionals," had always had a delicate relationship with the state. Bar associations in China were less independent and assertive than their Western counterparts. As the SBA grew in size and influence, the Nationalist government reorganized it in order to keep the legal profession under control.[94] Still, as the best-established bar in China, the

SBA negotiated with the state on behalf of its members and fulfilled its role as a leader of civil society. The SBA had been among the most vocal participants in the national salvation movements since the Manchuria Incident in 1931, criticizing the government for not standing up against Japanese aggression. It also promoted the expertise and social responsibilities of the legal profession by familiarizing its members with international agreements and treaties concerning the political hot spot of Manchuria.

As the national crisis deepened, lawyers struggled to find a balance between professional ethics and nationalism. Though they were in no position to forestall the passing of increasingly politicized laws in the 1930s, lawyers in Shanghai tried to protect defendants by restoring some semblance of due process in the cases prosecuted.[95] Some lawyers played leadership roles in various endeavors for national salvation. The famous female lawyer, jurist, and social activist Shi Liang was a standing member of several committees dedicated to raising funds for the resistance efforts and wartime welfare of women and children. She was also a strong advocate for the role of women in saving the nation and upholding its morality.[96]

As the war escalated, however, many lawyers lost control over their professional lives as well as their moral choices. Lawyers who remained in occupied areas could hardly keep practicing while claiming loyalty to the central government. Prior to 1941, three of the five courts in Shanghai—the District Court of Shanghai, the Second Special District Court, and the Third Branch of the Jiangsu High Court—had already been taken over and reorganized by the Wang Jingwei regime. After Japan declared war against the United States, Wang's judiciary took over the remaining two courts in the International Settlement (the First Special District Court and the Second Branch of the Jiangsu High Court). Shanghai lawyers who refused to appear in puppet courts could hardly make ends meet.

The Japanese were eager to recruit lawyers to act as their local representatives because of their education, their familiarity with current affairs, and their influence in the community. Many of China's first generation of lawyers had been educated in Japan and maintained professional and sometimes emotional ties to Japan. This background contributed to many lawyers' choices to comply with Japanese rule rather than risk their lives for a war that China seemed to have little chance of winning. Dong Kang, an influential jurist and legal reformer, joined a collaborationist government just months after China and Japan declared war. A majority of lawyers belonged to the local elites whom the Japanese enticed or coerced into collaboration. According to Ren Tianqiang, a lawyer from Wu County,

Jiangsu, a majority of lawyers there had participated in some kind of puppet organization, and most of them did so in order to make a living.[97]

Toward these private practitioners the Nationalist government employed
a carrot-and-stick approach that was ineffectual in both respects. Despite
its promise to provide material assistance to lawyers, in 1938, in response
to petitions by numerous lawyers and bar associations for a subsidy for
"righteous" lawyers, the financially distressed government could only suggest that they move to free regions. It could not afford to reimburse the
lawyers' travel expenses unless they were from Shanghai, which, after all,
"attracts both domestic and international attention."[98] For those who
wished to stay in Shanghai without appearing in puppet courts, the government promised a monthly subsidy of two hundred yuan, a paltry
amount considering the cost of living in this metropolis.[99] Meanwhile, the
government singled out lawyers from all occupational groups and warned
them against collaboration. In 1938, the Ministry of Justice ordered that all
lawyers who had associated themselves with the Japanese or puppet rule be
disbarred, reprimanded by the chief prosecuting attorney of the local court,
and renounced by courts at all levels.[100] The government in exile, however,
could hardly fulfill this threat.

Where the state failed to reach, the Shanghai Bar Association filled in to
guard the integrity of the profession. Following the establishment of the
Wang Jingwei regime in March 1940, numerous institutions and organizations resumed their routine functions, signifying their acquiescence in
the new rule. Yet the SBA responded with passive resistance. Yan Lunkui,
Wang Jingwei's handpicked chief justice for his reorganized District Court
of Shanghai, set up a five-person "accommodation committee" to take
over the SBA, consisting of members of the SBA who had switched allegiances. The committee, however, had a difficult time convincing their colleagues to do the same. In newspapers, the Wang Jingwei administration
cheerfully announced the SBA's "consent to the change and possibility of
further cooperation." In reality, the bar association terminated its daily
operations, leaving only one security guard in the office.[101]

As the war went on and more people compromised with the puppet
regime, the SBA exorcized its rotten members to preserve the standing of
the profession. By December 1941, the Japanese controlled all five courts in
Shanghai, and more than 1,300 lawyers were desperate for work. Political
chaos and economic pressure weakened their ties with the bar. The executive committee of the SBA received updates on suspected or confirmed collaboration by its members, mostly from news reports and anonymous

letters.[102] The bar sent out warnings to these lawyers, along with instructions on how to redeem their reputation: by publishing an announcement of their loyalty to the nation in major newspapers for three consecutive days and submitting three letters of support from upright colleagues.[103]

Almost all lawyers refused to comply with such requirements for fear of retribution from the Japanese or the puppet regime. Hu Yuanjun and Hu Yuansheng, for instance, were reprimanded by the bar for practicing in a puppet court. They argued that when even the bar association had to keep a low profile, it had no grounds for demanding that ordinary lawyers openly proclaim their "loyalty to the Han" (hanzhong).[104] Other lawyers, such as Chen Yijiong and Wu Bin, simply ignored the letters.[105] The SBA considered their lack of action solid evidence of collaboration and disbarred them.

In its edicts, the Nationalist government signaled a clear distinction between lawyers who practiced in puppet courts and those who held puppet positions or membership. The government considered the latter group guilty of the hanjian crime and urged their immediate exposure by others. They could thus be disbarred and their licenses revoked, if more harsh punishment did not ensue.[106] In July 24, 1939, the Ministry of Justice issued a most-wanted list of "lawyers who adhered to the enemy" (funi lüshi), requiring their immediate surrender or arrest. This list included high-profile lawyers and officials who had contributed to China's legal reforms. Their credentials and influence were precisely why the Japanese and the Wang Jingwei regime had solicited their services. First on the list was Dong Kang, who had by then been disbarred by the SBA.[107] When the Qing court embarked on legal reforms during the last decade of its rule, the young Dong Kang was a member of the Law Codification Commission. Working alongside Shen Jiaben, Dong Kang drafted codes that set China's legal system on a new path, including the first constitutional work in China, Outline of the Imperial Constitution (Qinding xianfa dagang).[108]

After receiving an advanced law degree in Japan, Dong Kang held several high-ranking public positions, in addition to practicing and teaching law. Dong was successively chief justice of the Supreme Court, president of the Law Codification Bureau, minister of justice, and acting minister of finance of the Beiyang government.[109] During the Nanjing decade, Dong taught at Shanghai Law School and served in its administration. He was also one of the most successful and expensive lawyers in Shanghai.[110]

Dong Kang was among the first Chinese scholars and officials to yield to the Japanese, partly because of his longstanding connections with Japan. In December 1937 he joined the Provisional Government in Beijing, headed by Wang Kemin, as the director of its Judicial Commission and chief justice of the Supreme Court. During his tenure in this puppet government, Dong Kang continued to publish scholarly works and proposed revisions to the Civil Code.[111] On the establishment of Wang Jingwei's government, he was appointed a member of Wang's congress. As one of the Nationalist government's most-wanted *hanjian*, Dong Kang was arrested and prosecuted in 1945. In his seventies by then, Dong died of distress and illness in the middle of his trial.

When evaluating Dong Kang as a public figure, the postwar media and public opinion focused on his wartime conduct and cast scandal on every aspect of his life. The Nationalist government and independent presses published short biographies of Dong, all of which glossed over his contributions to the modernization of China's legal system and other achievements. Even his calligraphy, which had been highly regarded among collectors, was now said to be unsophisticated in style and desirable only because of his fame and status. In the words of one biographer, Dong "dug his own grave by surrendering to his desire for high rank and becoming a *hanjian*."[112]

Profiles of individual "*hanjian* lawyers" show their diverse backgrounds and the varied circumstances of their collaboration. Like Dong Kang, Wang Manyun was a lawyer turned bureaucrat. A graduate of the Shanghai School of Law and Politics, Wang worked for the Shanghai Municipal Party headquarters while practicing as a lawyer. He later joined the Wang Jingwei regime and headed several offices in the Ministry of Agriculture and Mining as well as the Ministry of Justice. Convicted of the *hanjian* crime, Wang was sentenced to fifteen years' imprisonment.[113]

Ye Changyi was not as influential or successful as Wang or Dong, yet unlike the other two, his *hanjian* conduct had individual victims. A former member of the SBA, Ye went back to his home county of Qingpu and became the head of the puppet regime there. He aided the Japanese army in its violent extraction of local resources and in robberies, which resulted in several deaths. To conceal his crime, Ye relocated in 1939 and adopted a pseudonym under which he continued to feed intelligence to the Japanese intelligence. During the postwar anti-*hanjian* campaigns, an anonymous letter sent to local law enforcement officials revealed Ye's wartime conduct and current whereabouts. Ye was soon imprisoned for the *hanjian* crime.[114]

A majority of lawyers and judicial clerks had neither taken prominent positions, like Dong, nor willingly served the Japanese, like Ye. They had nonetheless associated themselves with the puppet bureaucracy and were penalized similarly to *weiyuan*. The Ministry of Justice imposed a two-year suspension on the licenses of lawyers who had practiced in puppet courts.[115] "Puppet judicial clerks" who did well in an examination held by the Ministry of Justice in 1946 were denied eligibility for positions in the restored judicial system. Under the Restrictions on the Candidacies and Qualifications of Former Puppet Staff issued later that year, the Examination Yuan annulled the scores of those who passed the exam yet had failed the loyalty test.

This decision provoked debates and protests among legal experts nationwide. Ling Hui, a human rights activist with a legal background, petitioned to the Ministry of Justice for the right of all qualified legal professionals to be considered for government positions. This application of the Restrictions, as Ling Hui argued, violated the legality principle, since the recently issued restrictions could not retroactively disqualify those who had been considered eligible for the positions. Earlier law, in this case the Regulations, should apply, and they prescribed a much shorter suspension period.

In this petition, Ling Hui argued for the innocent nature of judicial work, an opinion that was shared by many legal professionals yet voiced by few: "The work of judicial personnel was to process civil and criminal cases. It had little to do with political establishments and activities. During wartime, political criminals were under the supervision of military and police branches. Therefore, the judicial personnel served only the interests of their fellow countrymen by resolving disputes, not those of the Japanese or major collaborators. Since there was no Japanese working in the judicial branches of the puppet government, the Chinese staff was not taking orders from the Japanese."[116]

Ling Hui took the opportunity to criticize the ways in which the government handled the *hanjian* issue, though he considered it necessary to restore the political morality of the nation and the integrity of its civil service. Because the government had left its people to the mercy of the enemy when it fled to Chonqing, it had no right to blame those people for trying to survive. Ling Hui's petition gained the attention, if not the sympathy, of the Minister of Justice, who forwarded it to the examination committee. It failed, however, to rescue the qualified yet ill-fated judicial clerks.

Ling Hui was not alone in questioning the laws and policies on the punishment of *hanjian*. Whereas public opinion for the most part demanded harsh treatment of *hanjian*, lawyers and jurists cautioned against the potential negative effects of the anti-*hanjian* movement on China's legal system, which was yet to be rebuilt. Such voices grew stronger at the end of the war, when most citizens anticipated a return to a normal way of life.

On the promulgation of the 1945 Regulations, prominent judges, attorneys and jurists voiced their concerns about the anti-*hanjian* laws and their effects on criminal justice. A number of legal experts, including Ju Zheng, head of the Legislative Yuan, pleaded with the government to show clemency, especially toward low-ranking staff members of the puppet regime.[117] Now that the war was over, they argued, these people could no longer do real harm to the nation.

Some acted with discretion by providing annotation and clarifications for the Regulations, subtly warning against the abuse of such laws. Zhang Yuanjie, a jurist and attorney who had practiced in Shanghai as well as in smaller cities and towns, understood the uneven development of legal institutions and the lack of basic knowledge of law among common Chinese people. He annotated the 1945 Regulations and included the two earlier versions in his edited volume for reference. This publication was intended partly to facilitate the processing of *hanjian* cases, a daunting task for a judiciary that had lost many of its best people. It also aimed to provide jargon-free guidance to common people who were eager to expose *hanjian*.[118]

The renowned educator and law professor Yu Qichang emphasized a principle that was set in the Regulations yet often overlooked or misread by the general public. Based on a careful reading of the text, Yu argued that the Regulations should be applied only to those who conspired in the formation of the puppet regime and committed one of the fourteen listed crimes, not those who joined the puppet regime after its establishment. The latter offenses should be tried as "internal rebellion" under the criminal code, not the *hanjian* crime, which merited a harsher punishment.[119] Yu thus interpreted the Regulations in the most lenient way possible to reduce the number of potential targets.

A primary problem with the Regulations, as more than one jurist pointed out, was that they encouraged malicious or false accusations (*wugao*). Yu Qichang noted that in many *hanjian* cases, the informants were motivated by jealousy, conflicts of interest, or personal feuds. He urged the police and the procurators to use discretion and conduct careful investigations before making an arrest.[120] Li Zuyin, a law professor and expert on civil law, analyzed malicious accusation as a historical and contemporary phenomenon, examining its causes and proposing possible solutions. Among the various statutes he referred to, Li highlighted Article V of the 1938 Regulations, which prescribed the same punishment to accusers for crimes of which they had wrongly accused others.[121] Yet Li observed that in reality no measure had ever been taken to punish those who filed false accusations, while countless innocent people had suffered long prison terms or even capital punishment.

Articles and comments like these mostly came out in legal journals with a limited audience, but they had a wider influence. Family members and sympathizers of victims of the anti-*hanjian* campaigns borrowed the vocabulary and legal reasoning of the experts. In August 1947, family members of former puppet staff petitioned to the National Judicial and Administrative Conference (Quanguo Sifa Xingzheng Huiyi) for help, citing a legal treatise published in *Law and Regulations Weekly* (Faling zhoukan).[122] Alternating between emotional pleas and calm analysis, the petition pointed out that most so-called *weiyuan* had worked for the puppet regime only in order to support their families. It also raised questions about the compatibility of the Regulations with the Constitution, as the term *hanjian* "contradicts the principle of ethnic equality established in the Constitution."[123]

No one dared to oppose the anti-*hanjian* cause openly, yet often a lawyers' actions and comments betrayed what they really felt about the campaigns. Several reputable and well-connected lawyers defended high-profile *hanjian*. Li Ze, a retail magnate tried as an "economic *hanjian*," for instance, hired three lawyers from the top of the profession: Zhang Shizhao (who, as a young journalist, had reinvented the word *hanjian* in 1903), Chen Tingrui, and Guo Rui. Chen Tingrui also defended Yuan Lüdeng, another major economic *hanjian* tried in 1946. When asked why he was willing to do so, Chen replied that he had been a longtime legal consultant for Li Ze's company, and his friendship with Yuan went back to the times when both had struggled to gain success and status in colonial Shanghai.[124] The relatively light punishment Yuan ended up receiving was largely thanks to Chen's familiarity with the inner workings of the legal system and the Nationalist bureaucracy.

Now an authority on the law and respected among different political parties, Zhang Shizhao showed sympathy to at least two notorious *hanjian*. One was Li Ze, and the other was Yin Rugeng, a minister of the puppet Eastern Hebei government (Jidong Zhengfu, 1935–38), whose death sentence Zhang Shizhao openly criticized as too harsh.[125] Zhang observed that the government largely followed an unspoken rule when deciding whom to punish for the *hanjian* crime: if the collaboration had been initiated before the 1937 Regulations, it did not merit capital punishment or life imprisonment. If consistently applied, this rule geared the purge primarily toward followers of the Wang Jingwei regime, and it also avoided violating the legality principle. In the case of Yin Rugeng, however, this unspoken rule was not applied. Yin had represented the Nationalist government in the signing of a peace treaty with Japan in 1933 and conspired to establish an "autonomous" government in Hebei in 1935. His crimes partly resulted from Chiang's own policy of nonresistance before 1937, as Zhang Shizhao subtly implied. Yin was executed.

While some lawyers questioned the legal rationale of the anti-*hanjian* campaigns, others, out of either patriotism or a desire to reduce competition, took the initiative in exposing colleagues who had "affiliated with the enemy," urging the Ministry of Justice to revoke their licenses.[126] Those who were determined to oust their *hanjian* colleagues established a Shanghai Lawyers' *Hanjian*-Elimination Team (Shanghai Lüshi Sujiantuan) to carry out the intragroup purge.[127] On July 27, 1946, the team exposed the "unforgivable" crimes of seven lawyers to the Shanghai Local Court. Investigation revealed that the accusations were mostly ungrounded.[128] Legal professionals, like the rest of the population, were divided by the anti-*hanjian* campaigns.

CONCLUSION

By writing the *hanjian* crime into law, the Nationalist government seized the leadership of war propaganda from other political and social forces. The statutes, judicial explanations, and indictments governing *hanjian* in turn became an integral part of the resistance discourse. The combined application of legal and propaganda tools had fundamental effects on the individuals who were accused of the *hanjian* crime, whether or not they were convicted. The shame of being labeled a *hanjian* extended to their families. As an anonymous contributor wrote to the journal *China Critic* in September 1945: "Even those who should be given light sentences can hardly expect to go through their remaining years with their heads up. . . . Their ancestors will shamefacedly turn in their graves; their children will, in a society given to cruelty and callousness, carry the stigma of their forebears. They have ridden high for eight years; they must sink low in eternity."[129] As the abundance of television and cinematic dramas about notorious *hanjian* figures attests, this curse has come true.

The making of anti-*hanjian* laws and their propagandization had profound implications for China's history of legal reforms and the role of law in China thereafter. From the late Qing to the Nanjing decade, successive governments had regarded legal reform as one of the most important missions of the state. Although the push for modernizing China's legal system was largely driven by the practical goal of recovering China's judicial sovereignty, decades of legal reforms produced positive results. The human rights movement in the 1930s was a case in point. Concerned with the Nationalists' illegal arrest, torture, and execution of political dissidents, a group of lawyers, left-wing Nationalists, and liberal intellectuals joined forces to appeal misjudged cases and to demand compensation for the wronged.[130] Behind the immediate goal of implementing due process for political criminals (*zhengzhifan*), this movement aimed to impose some checks on the power of the Nationalist party.

At a time of national emergency, however, the focus of social movements shifted toward national salvation, and different patterns of interactions emerged among the state, society, and the legal profession. Those who were well versed in law found it politically imprudent and morally difficult to question the laws against *hanjian*. Although legal reasoning and public opinion had enabled them to advocate for the rights for political dissidents in general in the early 1930s, such instruments were no longer available or useful in the cases of *hanjian*. Moreover, presiding over the resistance cause from a distance, the Nationalist government enlisted the common people as prosecutors of *hanjian*. The Nationalists' definition of the *hanjian* crime corresponded with and guided public opinion on what constituted betrayal of the nation. As a result, the Regulations were relevant and appealing to a much larger sector of the society than were other laws, and they were widely celebrated because of the way they upheld Chinese political morality. The legal and political trends that allowed nationalist sentiments to overrule reason laid the groundwork for the purges to come.

CHAPTER 2

ARBITERS OF JUSTICE IN A LAWLESS STATE

CHINA BETWEEN 1937 AND 1945 WAS IN A STATE OF TOTAL WAR. As records, oral history, and scholarship have shown, the Japanese army committed atrocities against surrendered Chinese troops and civilians in areas that had fallen into its hands. The exigencies of war and the formidability of the enemy called for the mobilization of the whole nation in the resistance cause, erasing divisions between combatants and civilians. The elimination of *hanjian* was an integral part of this total war. During the eight years of war and dislocation, the Nationalist government enacted a body of politically and morally charged laws against *hanjian* and mobilized the people to identify and strike down those judged likely to betray the nation. After the war, popular justice and clandestine operations against *hanjian* during wartime gave way to semiregular judicial procedures.

The Nationalist laws were meticulous in listing the various offenses punishable as the *hanjian* crime but inattentive at best in specifying the procedures for prosecution. In practice, they sanctioned the use of violence against individuals suspected of being *hanjian*. Chiang Kai-shek's special agents and military disposed of *hanjian* in occupied areas by means of assassination and summary execution. Where the arm of the law failed to reach, people took matters into their own hands. Many *hanjian* and suspected *hanjian* fell victim to self-constituted or state-sanctioned *hanjian*-elimination groups. The state and local communities formed an alliance in the name of justice, although the goals and the targets of the two often failed to align.

The Nationalist government envisioned different modes of punishing *hanjian* in war and in peace. With the prospect of the end of the long war, the government intended to put an end to the lawless state. The attempt to transfer authority for punishing *hanjian* back to the judiciary, however, met with various obstacles. The sheer number of *hanjian* cases, pressure from public opinion, behind-the-scenes operations, and difficulties with witnesses and evidence overwhelmed the understaffed judiciary. The *hanjian* cases examined here highlight the political complications and practical obstacles involved in the administration of justice. More importantly, these cases demonstrate how the anti-*hanjian* campaigns hindered attempts to rebuild China's legal system after the war.

THE ANTI-*HANJIAN* ALLIANCE AND THE REGIME OF TERROR

Chiang Kai-shek's government issued harsh laws in a declared state of emergency, but even the abridged judicial procedures were not followed during wartime. The 1938 Regulations required a formal trial of *hanjian* suspects by a military tribunal and approval of the verdict by the Supreme Council of National Defense. In theory, the Regulations also allowed those convicted to appeal to a higher authority. Yet the Nationalist military, police, and intelligence often bypassed these steps and carried out swift extrajudicial killings of *hanjian*.

During the War of Resistance, there was no clear separation between the home front and the battlefront, and *hanjian* activities were perceived to be widespread, as were reports on their arrests and execution. Below is a selection of reports from the many submitted in 1937 and 1938:

> Kaifeng, Henan: Liu Yingqiao and two others were caught and executed by the 78th Division of the Nationalist Army for "colluding with local bandits and conducting *hanjian* acts."
>
> Chaozhou, Guangdong: Jiang Guiting and four others were caught and executed by the local army for "spying on the defense infrastructure."
>
> Baoding, Hebei: Gu Bin and five others were caught and executed by an unspecified party for wearing a certain pattern of tattoos and carrying other identifiers in their pants that led to the suspicion that they were *hanjian* spies.
>
> Bengbu, Anhui: Wang Ganchen and six others were caught and executed by the county government after confessing to *hanjian* crimes.
>
> Changshu, Jiangsu: Da Yi, Neng Ren, and Miao Ding (all dharma names adopted after their conversion to Buddhism), either disguised as Buddhist monks or real monks working for the Japanese, were caught and executed for spying on the local Nationalist army.

Songjiang District, Shanghai: more than twenty individuals, including five children, were caught by the local Railway Bureau and executed by the local army for collecting information on the Chinese railway.[1]

As these reports attest, *hanjian* who engaged in minor sabotage or espionage were usually interrogated only briefly, if at all, before their swift execution. The local government and army often resorted to torture to extract confessions and information on other *hanjian* in the area. Sometimes crude or extraordinary methods of execution were used, such as burial alive.[2]

Individuals did not have to be Han, or even Chinese, to be at risk of identification and punishment as *hanjian*. The Nationalist government claimed in late 1937 that since the outbreak of the war, it had executed more than two hundred *hanjian* along the Beijing–Shanghai and Hangzhou–Ningbo railways, including quite a number of White Russians. In the wake of the Russian Revolution, a large number of émigrés left Soviet Russia, and many came to the Chinese cities of Harbin and Shanghai to join the established Russian communities there. In China as in Japan, they were known as White Russians. In one incident in 1937, five White Russians were arrested carrying maps, telescopes, guns, and ammunition. When interrogated by members of the army stationed along the rail lines, the White Russians confessed that they were spying for the Japanese for a monthly payment of two hundred yuan each. They were shot to death.[3] In comparison, White Russians arrested for the *hanjian* crime after the war received much lighter punishments. A White Russian woman spy, for instance, was sentenced to two and a half years' imprisonment.[4]

News stories of elimination of *hanjian* were often accompanied by chilling photos of their execution or exposed bodies (as in the photo below). With succinct and powerful captions, these photos served to deter those who were considering working for the enemy. Resistance propaganda aroused such patriotism and resentment toward *hanjian* that these sentiments overruled reason and sympathy for former compatriots. Before and during the War of Resistance, propaganda in China owed its effectiveness to efforts by the most liberal and articulate groups of the population: progressive intellectuals and hot-blooded youth. The Nationalists and Communists both had propaganda agencies that operated behind the scenes. Their impact, however, did not overshadow that of independently produced newspapers, pamphlets, plays, and slogans. Although they often

Two Chinese men convicted of the *hanjian* crime kneeling before being executed by Chinese soldiers, 1938. Courtesy of the Everett Collection.

employed sophisticated rhetorical techniques, these were effective mainly because of their crudely authentic voices.

Exposure and Elimination of Hanjian (Hanjian xianxingji), a collection of wartime reports and editorials, was a typical piece of war mobilization literature that placed the elimination of *hanjian* at the center of the resistance cause. The compiler, Bing Ying, explained the high stakes of the anti-*hanjian* movement:

> At this moment, our work on the warfront is to fight the Japanese and eliminate *hanjian* at the same time. We often catch seven or eight *hanjian* at a time—so many to get rid of! Of course, these rotten bastards who sell out their own country should not dream of being allowed to live once they are caught. We end such low lives with cold gunshots.
>
> Fellow countrymen behind the enemy lines! You have to accelerate your pace of eliminating *hanjian!* Every single one of you should realize that *hanjian* are the greatest enemy of our nation. If we don't eradicate them, our national revolution will never succeed![5]

Opinion pieces and reports of this type abounded during the early years of the war, boosting a sense of solidarity among the people based on the excoriation of the traitorous minority.

At a time when the Japanese army was gaining the upper hand on the battlefield, the execution of *hanjian* boosted morale. In many resistance newspapers, news stories of the destruction of puppet organizations outnumbered those about victories at the battlefront. To show that betrayal would bring only condemnation from one's own people and no trust from the enemy, resistance newspapers frequently reported on the Japanese army's abuse of its puppet officials. *Resistance Daily* (Kangzhan ribao), for example, reported how the Japanese, out of suspicion, arrested and beat up puppet county officials in Pinglu and Yuci of Shanxi, in addition to executing a dozen puppet policemen.[6]

Confidential government documents confirmed the scope and intensity of wartime operations against *hanjian*. Chiang's most infamous intelligence

TABLE 2.1. *Hanjian* executed by Juntong, 1938–1945

Function in puppet government, military, or institutions	Number executed
Officials	37
Military officers	14
Prominent members of Wang Jingwei's reorganized GMD	4
Economic *hanjian*	16
Cultural *hanjian*	8[a]
Lawyers	4
Intelligence agents	18
Leading members of social organizations	9
Policemen working in foreign settlements	6
Taiwanese spies	1
Mongolian spies	1
Other spies	53
Translators for the Japanese army	3
Police officers	404
Low-ranking officers and soldiers	339
Uncategorized *hanjian*	13

[a]In addition, two were killed in 1935 on Dai Li's orders before Juntong was formally launched.

agency, Juntong (short for Junshi Weiyuanhui Tiaocha Tongjiju, or Bureau of Investigation and Statistics under the Military Affairs Commission), was responsible for killing at least 930 alleged *hanjian* between April 1938 and 1945. Its postwar report on secret operations during the seven years provided statistics on individuals who were executed as *hanjian* (table 2.1).

A geographical distribution of Juntong's "cleansing" operations is as follows:

Anhui	262
Beijing	1
Fujian	14
Guangdong	134
Guangxi	8
Guangzhou	18
Hankou	11
Hebei	4
Henan	304
Hubei	308
Hunan	51
Jiangsu	98
Jiangxi	424
Shandong	37
Shanghai	159
Shanxi	69
Suiyuan	7
Tianjin	9
Zhejiang	100
Macau	9
Hong Kong	1
Manchukuo	1
along the Zhegan railway (Hangzhou–Zhuzhou)	5
along the Longhai railway (Lianyungang–Tianshui)	3
along the Yuehan railway (Guangzhou–Wuchang)	20
along the Jinpu railway (Tianjin–Nanjing)	18
along the Beijing–Hangzhou highway	18
along other rail lines or highways	116[7]

As this list shows, Juntong targeted Chiang Kai-shek's former power bases (such as Shanghai), key cities under Japanese occupation (such as

Guangzhou), and cities along transportation routes. This pattern corresponded with the duration of the Japanese occupation in each locality, as well as with the intensity of Japanese espionage.

As table 2.1 shows, a substantial number of Juntong's victims were higher in status and perceived as more dangerous than *hanjian* spies executed by the local army or community members. Other than identifying and destroying spy networks organized by the Japanese and by the Wang Jingwei government, Juntong mainly targeted individuals blacklisted by Chiang Kai-shek's government. From 1937 onward, Chiang's government, now based in Chongqing, distributed lists of most-wanted *hanjian* to expose the enemy and to reinforce its own legitimacy. Such lists included leaders and top officials from all collaborationist governments: in particular, Wang Jingwei and his closest followers, as well as their spokesmen in various social circles.[8] These lists served to inform resistance forces of the identities of those who had turned against the nation; they were also the basis on which Juntong planned and carried out assassinations. Many individuals found on these lists, including Fu Xiao'an, the mayor of the puppet Shanghai municipal government, were killed in meticulously planned operations.[9]

The numbers in table 2.1 do not include the operations undertaken against *hanjian* before Juntong was formally established in 1938. However, Dai Li, the notorious spymaster who directed Juntong throughout the war, had trained and ordered special agents to dispose of troublemakers for Chiang years earlier.[10] Among his famous victims in the early 1930s were Zhang Jingyao, a warlord conspiring with the Japanese; Deng Yanda, the leader of the left wing of the Nationalist Party; and Yang Xingfo and Shi Liangcai, human rights advocates and critics of Chiang's administration.

Chiang certainly was not the first to employ the ancient tradition of political assassination in modern times. "Revolutionary assassinations" frequently occurred in the last days of the Qing, when "men of determination" took the lives of Manchu governors for racial retaliation and to weaken the Qing rule.[11] When its first United Front with the Nationalists collapsed in 1927, the Communist Party organized a "dog-killers' squad" (*dagoutuan*) to purge traitors from the party.[12] The revolutionary context receded in political assassinations ordered by Chiang, whose targets were mostly political dissidents. Still, the Chinese public tended to believe that assassins in certain historic contexts were martyrs who took extreme measures for the greater good or a higher principle.

The War of Resistance provided new pretexts for political assassination, which helped neutralize the images of Nationalist special agents as killing machines for political oppression only. By 1937, Dai Li's special agents in Shanghai had developed a standard modus operandi for kidnapping, which required four assailants and one automobile, in addition to research on the target's daily routine.[13] Against the backdrop of China's military losses, Dai Li's extensive network of well-trained spies and clandestine operations seemed a vital component of the resistance war. Juntong's operations were efficient, systematic, and widespread, creating constant fear among influential collaborators in occupied regions.

Lai Guomin, a Juntong special agent, expressed his pride in the agency's work during the seven and a half years of the occupation of Xiamen.[14] According to Lai, a close follower and trusted subordinate of Dai Li, Juntong began its underground work right after the Japanese takeover of Xiamen in 1938. Juntong agents destroyed enemy warehouses and military infrastructure, assassinated *hanjian* and Japanese officers, and prepared the way for the Nationalist troops to retake Xiamen. Local *hanjian* who died at their hands included Hong Lixun, head of the local chamber of commerce, and Huang Lianfang, councilor of the municipal assembly.[15]

Among all the occupied cities and regions, Shanghai witnessed the most intensive secret operations by Chiang's special agents. As the showroom of modern China in the early twentieth century, Shanghai boasted the highest concentration of industries and financial institutions. Many of the city's economic and social elite, as well as leaders of the underworld, had been Chiang Kai-shek's allies, funneling money and support to Chiang's administration in legitimate or shady ways.[16] For the same reasons, Shanghai was important to the Japanese and the Wang Jingwei regime. Yet Shanghai's multiple jurisdictions made it difficult for any single political force to maintain law and order in the city. Before 1937, the city was divided among the Chinese jurisdiction, the French Concession, and the International Settlement, which was under British and American control. In November 1937, after a bloody three-month battle, the Chinese parts of Shanghai were taken by the Japanese. Until the Pacific War broke out in December 1941, the Japanese did not risk entering the International Settlement or the French Concession.

During this period, the Japanese occupation formed an island in the middle of Shanghai, and the puppet police force engaged in a tug-of-war with secret agents sent by the Chongqing government. The Western

Shanghai area (*huxi*) was particularly chaotic. A triangular region west of the International Settlement and northwest of the French Concession, Western Shanghai was under no effective control by any authority and thus became a fertile ground for both common crime and terrorist missions. In the spring of 1941, a wave of "patriotic terrorism" resulted in 14 dead, 60 wounded, and 128 kidnapped during the week of March 22–29 alone. The historian Frederic Wakeman has vividly described some of these events and how they affected the general political milieu in Shanghai.[17]

The patriotic coalition against *hanjian* consisted of Chiang's special agents, the military, Shanghai's racketeers, and temporary recruits with diverse backgrounds. Dai Li had been a sworn brother of Du Yuesheng, the "Godfather" of Shanghai, since the late 1920s, and he absorbed many members of Du's Green Gang into his army of spies and assassins.[18] During the Battle of Shanghai in 1937, Chiang created several "emergency service groups" and "defense and protection squads" to fight the Japanese in urban guerrilla warfare. The 87th Division of Chiang's conventional army was involved in commanding such groups, whose rank and file consisted largely of gangsters and unemployed workers.[19]

After the loss of Shanghai, this alliance grew in importance for the Nationalist government, now waging an intelligence war from afar. In May 1938, Dai Li reorganized scattered Nationalist soldiers, the remaining guerrilla forces from Shanghai, and resisters among the local population into a "Loyal and Righteous National Salvation Army" (Zhongyi Jiuguo-jun).[20] The army's main duty was to support conventional troops in major battles. It also carried out other tasks deemed necessary for the overall resistance cause, including assassinations of *hanjian*. Yet Chiang's agents and many of their local helpers supported this cause for different reasons. Following the assassination of the detective Yin Zhanqing of the puppet Shanghai Special Police Force on May 27, 1941, the investigation by the Japanese military police revealed the identities of eight *hanjian* assassins. The main culprit was a Juntong agent disguised as a casino boss, who recruited several racketeers for this mission with a bounty of eight hundred yuan each, in addition to monthly remuneration to be collected at the casino.[21]

The success of the operations ordered by Chongqing prompted the Japanese and the Wang Jingwei regime to fortify their security and counterintelligence. According to reports by the Western Shanghai Area Special Police Force (WASP), the Japanese Military Police and Wang's law enforcement agents treated any potential Nationalist agents with deep suspicion.[22] The WASP, for instance, went through rounds of detailed interrogation and meticulous background checks on one of its own staff members, Tan Zhifang. Tan came under suspicion because he was seen to have recorded the names of the entire WASP staff and had used a pseudonym during his trip from Yunnan to Shanghai.[23] The investigation never uncovered any solid evidence to connect Tan to Chongqing, but the final WASP report on this incident reflects enduring doubts about his true identity. Unfortunately, no other archival material reveals who Tan really was or what happened to him thereafter.

Over time, the WASP and the Japanese military police grew more effective in spotting Chiang's agents. Detective Guo Shaoyi of the WASP reported in March 1941 the arrival of a one-hundred-strong "Iron and Blood Youth *Hanjian*-Elimination Team" sent by Chongqing. This squad merged with three other similar groups already in Shanghai, including the Revolutionary Youth Group (Geming Qingniantuan) and Dai Li's Action Team (Dai Li Xingdongdui), all of which were under the command of Juntong. A week later, the WASP learned that Chongqing had transferred two hundred more agents from Jinhua and Jiaxing to Shanghai, a move that pointed to extensive underground operations in the lower Yangtze delta. These three hundred agents, equipped with explosives and stationed in different parts of Shanghai, were on a mission to destroy automobiles and assassinate important followers of Wang Jingwei.[24]

The discovery of Juntong's plans did not prevent these agents from carrying some of them out. Juntong later claimed direct responsibility for twenty-seven assassinations in Shanghai from September 1939 to June 1941. Sixteen of the victims were from different branches of the Wang Jingwei administration, two were renowned cultural figures identified as *hanjian*, and the other four were underworld bosses.[25] In late 1941, however, Juntong experienced its greatest setback, as the Japanese military police began to take the security of Shanghai into their own hands.[26] Juntong's entire Shanghai station was wiped out by arrests and defections. The director of the Shanghai station, Chen Gongshu, was arrested and his photo published in major newspapers.[27] Similar disasters befell Juntong's Xiamen station in June 1940: four leading members were executed, six agents tortured to death, and twenty-one imprisoned.[28]

Juntong's work in Shanghai continued, however, with young blood replenishing the organization. In June 1942, the Japanese military police discovered that Juntong agents were working with local "resistance elements" to place time bombs outside the offices of key collaborators. In July 1943, Chongqing sent another three hundred young agents to Shanghai. Disguised as students, they enrolled in universities and high schools to gather intelligence and to recruit among the student body.[29]

The war against *hanjian* also provided a testing ground for Chiang Kaishek's handpicked reserve force for the Nationalist party: the Three People's Principles Youth League (Sanminzhuyi Qingniantuan, Sanqingtuan for short). Chiang founded Sanqingtuan in 1938 to absorb young, patriotic members from different political parties and train them to carry out secret missions.[30] According to the WASP's investigation reports, it was clearly aware of Sanqingtuan's wartime role and activities. Among other actions, Sanqingtuan sent out threatening letters to key figures in the Wang regime. Yuan Houzhi, the head of Shanghai's Municipal Bureau of Finance, received such a letter from the "suicide squad of Sanqingtuan" on August 12, 1941. The letter warned Yuan that "if he imagined that he could secretly continue with his *hanjian* deeds," Sanqingtuan would prove him wrong by drastic means.[31] Similarly, in October 1940, the Shanghai Bar Association received a letter from Sanqingtuan with a list of thirty-four lawyers who supposedly had participated in puppet organizations or courts.[32] Sanqingtuan demanded that the SBA disbar these lawyers in order to restore the reputation of the entire profession and remain a "legal organization" (*fatuan*) without guilt. The news spread fast, and most lawyers fearfully denied accusations of being a Han traitor (*hanzei*).[33]

The measures taken against *hanjian* resembled those used by the Nationalist government to suppress its political dissidents, but much of the impetus for anti-*hanjian* activities came from grassroots initiatives. Patriotic members of local communities often acted years before Chiang's special agents and military to forestall *hanjian* activity. Before 1937, Chiang focused on suppressing and spying on Communists and political dissidents in general rather than *hanjian* in particular. Between 1932 and 1937, Shanghai's newspapers took the lead in advocating the prevention and elimination of *hanjian*.[34] Contributors warned the common people about the enemy's dangerous agenda of "using Chinese to rule the Chinese" (*yihuazhihua*). Progressive intellectuals and enthusiastic readers exchanged ideas on how to reduce the number of *hanjian* by eliminating some and educating others.

Sending potential *hanjian* threatening letters, as a means to deter their activity and to provide a chance for redemption, was a measure first devised by ardent community members. Shortly after the Shanghai Incident in 1932, the Shanghai Coal Association received a threatening letter from a *hanjian*-elimination team, accusing one of the association's members, Gu Zhongshou, of having recently purchased more than a thousand tons of Japanese coal.[35] If the coal association did not take actions against members who conducted such "unpatriotic deals," the team threatened to take matters into its own hands.[36]

To appreciate the gravity of this matter, one needs to consider the important role of coal in the Chinese economy and social life, as well as the campaigns promoting Chinese goods in the 1920s. Coal had been a major source of energy in China for centuries, and coal mining had sustained the local economy in places like Shanxi before foreign investors became involved. The increasing demand for coal from the 1910s onward brought new opportunities for China's nascent industries.[37] To protect national industries, Chinese entrepreneurs, industrial workers, and patriotic students joined forces to promote domestically produced goods (*guohuo*) among consumers and encourage the boycott of foreign products. In 1932, the memories of the *guohuo* movements were still fresh, and the city had just suffered Japanese bombing and a full-scale battle. Purchasing enemy goods, therefore, stood out as a form of *hanjian* conduct that was intolerable to the local people, especially those whose interests were harmed by the deal. The letter also implied rage against those who continued to make profits at a time when others from the community were suffering great losses. Many cases brought to the judiciary after the war revealed the same mentality. People assumed that those whose wealth increased during the war must have done something treacherous.

A traditional distrust of merchants was also at work. The locally based *hanjian*-elimination team was completely oblivious to the coal association's patriotic actions following the Shanghai Incident, which included generous donations and assistance to injured troops and refugees.[38] The team continued to spy on the coal merchants and before long provided the association further instructions for self-rectification:

> Our research shows that various stores dare to sell Japanese coal, and your current executive committee dares to allow such behavior. Despite our repeated warnings, you have paid no attention to this matter. Now we present to you a hand grenade, this time a relatively small one. Please take the following actions to avoid more serious consequences:
> 1. Within a week, stop all transactions involving Japanese coal.
> 2. Publish an announcement in major newspapers stating that you will never buy or sell enemy products.

Publishing announcements was a common way of expressing political integrity. It also had the effect of forcing individuals who had held ambivalent positions to sever current or potential ties with the enemy.

Through verbal threats and physical violence, the state and its patriotic citizens aimed to demonstrate that collaboration came at a price: that being a *hanjian* would have worse consequences than resisting Japanese coercion. This plan succeeded, at least in some cases. The historian Parks Coble records how, after the assassination of the businessman Lu Bohong in December 1937, Rong Zongjing, Shanghai's textile tycoon, panicked and fled the city. Other members of the Rong family, the largest family group in the textile industry, subsequently avoided collaboration as much as possible.[39] Faced with threats from above and below, occupational organizations in Shanghai shed members whose patriotism was questioned. The Shanghai bar disbarred lawyers who took puppet positions or practiced in puppet courts. Similarly, the coal association asked its members to sign an oath of allegiance, ironically titled "A Pledge of Voluntary Promotion of National Products."[40] At this point, the coal association decided to join forces with the *hanjian*-elimination team. It established a twenty-person "suicide squad" in September 1932, which swore to apply "iron and blood" pressure to fellow merchants who were still engaged in trade with Japan.[41]

The extent to which measures of intimidation actually curbed wartime collaboration is difficult to measure. The stories of the Rong family and the coal association, nonetheless, demonstrate that state-sponsored and grassroots anti-*hanjian* activities forced many to reconsider their choices. Members of the resistance did make assassination attempts against Japanese during wartime, but with far less frequency and success. The few Japanese civilians in China and the well-equipped Japanese military personnel were almost impossible targets. More importantly, the state and the people considered the Japanese an enemy that should be conquered on the battlefield. *Hanjian*, on the other hand, were seen as harmful yet cowardly figures who could be disposed of by noncombatant resisters.

POSTWAR TRIALS OF *HANJIAN* AND THE PLIGHT OF THE JUDICIARY

China's victory in August 1945 marked the beginning of a new chapter in Chinese history and a new stage of the campaigns against *hanjian*. The international standing of the Republic of China greatly improved when it joined the ranks of the Allied powers. In 1943, to motivate the Chinese to fight on, the United States and Great Britain gave up various treaty privileges they had obtained in China, including extraterritoriality. China's victory against Japan, therefore, also meant liberation from Western imperialism and the recovery of long-lost sovereign rights.[42] To demonstrate China's intention and ability to administer war-related justice to the same standards as its democratic allies, the Nationalist government's ambassadors abroad collected information about European and American laws against treason.[43] The legal discourse and acts of retribution against collaborators in Europe, therefore, informed similar processes in China. Following the example of Charles de Gaulle in France, Chiang Kai-shek planned to restore the civilian criminal-justice system for the trials of *hanjian*.

To align the anti-*hanjian* cause with these global trends, the Nationalist government put China's most notorious *hanjian* on trial, following the example of the French justice system in the trial of Pétain, although with abridged procedures.[44] These public trials had more political than legal significance for the Nationalist government. Those who followed Wang Jingwei in his defection and took high positions in his government were sentenced either to death or to life imprisonment. These figures included Wang Jingwei's wife, Chen Bijun, and his loyal associates, such as Chen Gongbo, Chu Minyi, and Lin Baisheng. Wang Jingwei himself had died from illness in November 1944. Other major players in the Wang Jingwei regime were sentenced to at least fifteen years' imprisonment.[45]

Though the outcomes of the trials were entirely foreseeable to everyone at the time, the Nationalist judiciary tried to demonstrate that proper judicial procedures were followed and the convictions were based on sufficient evidence. For the trial of Chen Gongbo, the puppet mayor of Shanghai from 1940 to 1944 and a core member of Wang's clique, the court scrutinized over fifty volumes of documents for evidence of collaborationist activities by Chen's administration. Subsequently, the court charged Chen with organizing the collaborationist government, negotiating peace with Japan, forging secret contracts with the enemy, ceding Chinese sovereignty, resisting the central government, disturbing the financial order, and imposing on the Chinese people in occupied regions an education of enslavement to the Japanese.[46]

Covered intensively in the media and witnessed by crowds in the courtrooms, the trials of *hanjian* served to reiterate the leadership and moral authority of the Nationalist government. The prosecution produced elaborate indictments of the leading *hanjian* and read them aloud at the end of each trial. The indictments consisted of three parts: a list of the criminal acts of the defendant, the court's verdict, and the legal reasoning behind the verdict. The indictments, therefore, can be read as the official annotation of the Regulations. Moreover, they were public clarifications of the Nationalist government's positions on war, political legitimacy, and nationalism.

The courtroom debates and their foreseeable results reinforced outright resistance as the only acceptable expression of nationalism.[47] For Chiang Kai-shek, emphasizing resistance was important precisely because his policies toward Japan were ambivalent until 1937. The direct equation of resistance with nationalism also saved Chiang's government from having to consider its responsibility in leaving vast regions and their inhabitants vulnerable to Japanese exploitation. For this reason, the prosecution rejected Chen Gongbo's argument of "collaborationist nationalism," which collaborators in other countries, including Pétain in France and Yi Kwang-su in Korea, had advanced in their own defense.[48]

The court denied any independent decisionmaking power on the part of the Wang Jingwei regime and any possibility that it had made the occupation less exploitative or painful for the people. Chen Gongbo argued that people like him had helped preserve the nation's strength, allowing Chongqing the time to muster resources and mobilize for war.[49] Another major *hanjian* convict, Chu Minyi, described Wang's strategy as "peaceful resistance to the Japanese." The court dismissed all such arguments. "The puppet government," stated the prosecution, "was merely a tool for the Japanese army to achieve the goal of using Chinese to control Chinese."[50] It also painstakingly criticized the main policies of the Wang Jingwei administration, including extracting grain from Chinese peasants for enemy use, trading in opium, implementing the education of enslavement, issuing its own currency, and pushing for the notorious Clearing the Villages movement (Qingxiang Yundong).[51]

The court also denied that the Wang regime or its members had played any positive role while governing the occupied regions. Chu Minyi claimed that he had devoted himself to the reconstruction of Nanjing and the recovery of foreign settlements and thus was "not without contributions."[52] Chen Gongbo argued that Wang's government maintained the security of Nanjing after the Japanese surrender and prepared for its takeover by Chiang's army. In response, the prosecution pointed out that the puppet regime was then in disarray and was incapable of reconstructing Nanjing. Even if the two *hanjian* had maintained local order, they did so only to give themselves bargaining chips for the future. In addition, the prosecution maintained that by negotiating for the recovery of foreign settlements, Chu Minyi had arrogated to himself the power of the central government over diplomatic decisions.

Some of the offenses with which these *hanjian* were charged show that Chiang Kai-shek considered defying his government as one and the same as turning against the nation. Chen was found guilty of "plotting to oust the central government and acting as its chief enemy."[53] Wang Jingwei had nullified all policies and regulations issued by Chiang Kai-shek and urged all government staff in Chongqing to return and follow him instead.[54] In a way, Chen Gongbo, Chu Minyi, and the others were punished for loyalty to the wrong person.

Chen Gongbo's self-defense and the court's rebuttal revealed different concepts of loyalty, which all had a place in Chinese culture but were often in tension. In explaining his motivations for joining the puppet regime, Chen, among others, focused on his personal loyalty to Wang Jingwei. Chen confessed that he had always believed that "the party cannot be divided, and the nation should be unified" (*dang buke fen, guo bi tongyi*). Though he never agreed with Wang's plan of working with Japan, he failed to dissuade Wang and then had to follow him out of personal loyalty. Chen Gongbo's son Chen Gan recollected decades later that his father decided to "jump into the fire pit along with Wang" because Wang had no one else he could trust.[55]

In the trial, the court took the view that personal loyalty was a valued quality in traditional patron-client relations and among friends, but not in the context of a nation at war. The prosecutor argued that Chen showed the utmost loyalty to Wang (*jinzhong*) but no allegiance toward the nation. In other words, loyalty to the nation should always take priority over personal attachments, just as political integrity (*dajie*) should precede personal duty (*xiaoyi*). (Ironically, Chiang himself was known for cultivating close, pater-nal relations with his followers. Dai Li, for instance, was first Chiang's per-sonal bodyguard and later his "hound and horse," cruelly and illegally eliminating enemies for his master.) The prosecution also rejected Chen's claim that he merely tagged along, a claim discredited by his announce-ment after Wang's death that he was determined to carry on Wang's "unfulfilled will" (*yizhi*) by filling in as the acting president of the National government.

Beyond seeking to completely delegitimize its enemy, the Nationalist government also held these trials to distract people from various problems that had surfaced or resurfaced after the war. In his study of the trial of Chen Bijun, the historian Charles Musgrove describes how the audience applauded when Chen accused Chiang Kai-shek's government for its irresponsibility and ineptness during the early years of the war. The audience also followed Madame Wang out of the courthouse and asked for her autograph.[56] The audience's sympathy with Chen was fueled by their disappointment at the returned government's failure to swiftly stabilize the society and revitalize the economy.

So much was at stake in these trials that the judiciary could not reach any judgment other than the one expected. Still, while representing the party line, legal professionals occasionally revealed their personal views on the complex issues of collaboration. The newspaper *Zhoubao* reported that during Chen Gongbo's trial, the judge, Sun Honglin, commented, in apparent sympathy with Chen, that "noble men always take the blame in history" (*chunqiu zebei xianzhe*). Chen was reported to be "so flattered by this comment that he repeated it several times during the trial."[57] *Zhoubao*, however, condemned the judge's remark and accused him of failing in his role as a legal authority and public official.

In cases that did not involve well-known individuals and attracted less media attention, the judiciary had greater leeway to conduct investigations and make judgments. The processing of these cases, however, often foundered on other problems. One complication was the participation of individuals and forces outside the justice system in the exposure and trials of *hanjian*. The authorized or self-proclaimed arbiters of justice that had emerged during wartime, especially Chiang's intelligence and military forces, were not ready to give up their power in the postwar legal campaigns against *hanjian*.

Juntong, for one, aimed to extend its control over the realm of law and order rather than retract its claws. Following the Japanese surrender, Juntong was the authority designated with the power to arrest the vast majority of leading *hanjian* figures.[58] Dai Li acted on this opportunity to seek control over the police forces in major cities.[59] In January 1946 he proposed to Chiang the establishment of a special tribunal for trying and reviewing *hanjian* cases, observing that various local courts had difficulties in "maintaining a uniform standard" when processing such cases.[60] To win Chiang over, Dai Li solicited a supporting letter from his well-connected and articulate friend Zhang Shizhao. Although Zhang provided the letter mainly as a favor to Dai Li, his observations reflected a legal professional's genuine concerns with the problems of malicious accusations and overburdened local courts. Determined to reestablish the authority of the judiciary in meting out criminal justice, however, Chiang vetoed Dai's proposal. If anything, this incident made Chiang wary of Dai Li's growing ambition.

Branches of the Nationalist army that temporarily maintained security over recovered regions considered themselves the obvious authorities to handle *hanjian* cases. They were also interested in the handsome material gains from seizing enemy and *hanjian* property. In control of the Guangdong and Guangxi areas, the commander of the Second Front Army, General Zhang Fakui, even ventured into lawmaking. He proposed two sets of provisions, respectively governing the confiscation of *hanjian* property and citizens' duty to report on *hanjian*, to replace the official Regulations.[61] According to General Zhang, these resolutions were drafted by the military court of the Second Front Army and were approved by a committee consisting of representatives from the party, the government, and the military. The committee's approval, in General Zhang's opinion, was sufficient to legitimize the new provisions.

The ensuing correspondence between the Ministry of Justice and the Second Front Army had a smell of gunpowder. The Ministry of Justice pointed out multiple contradictions between the new provisions and the 1945 Regulations, not to mention the fact that the army had no role in writing legislation at all. Such provisions, according to the ministry, would prolong the sense of terror, hostility, and insecurity produced by the war. They would subvert justice by encouraging anonymous accusations and promising minor *hanjian* lighter punishment if they became informants. Furthermore, the provisions would mean that the Guangdong and Guangxi areas would be placed under military rule rather than under civil administration. The Executive Yuan and the National Military Council both supported the Ministry of Justice on this matter.[62]

The challenges posed by the participation of common people in *hanjian* trials were more complex, as it pushed the investigations in unexpected directions. The involvement of informants, defendants, voyeurs, cheerleaders, and critics influenced and complicated the anti-*hanjian* movement, creating tremendous pressure on the judicial system. Most ordinary citizens lacked a basic understanding of the purpose and limits of law, and many brought accusations against *hanjian* for reasons other than the restoration of justice.

The judicial system had yet to recover from the disruptions of the war. In March 1947, the Ministry of National Defense requested every province to provide statistics on *hanjian* cases for the sake of compiling a history of the War of Resistance. Reports from Shandong reflected the chaotic state of the court system there. The seventh branch of the provincial court had yet to be reestablished, and the fourth and fifth branch courts had already been taken over by the Communists.[63] Because of continued political instability, statistics on *hanjian* from Shandong were incomplete at best, and the Shandong courts were severely compromised in fulfilling their duties. Unfortunately, the state of the court system in Shandong was representative of courts all over the nation.

The judiciary was also short of personnel. The personnel newly dispatched by the Ministry of Justice were insufficient to staff local courts. Although in theory, those with work experience or credentials gained under the Japanese occupation were not permitted to process *hanjian* cases, the shortage of lawyers and judicial staff made this scenario unavoidable. Many local governments allowed individuals to change their names to escape the registry of the disloyal so they could be hired. Students who had attended law schools under the occupation were employed as lawyers or judicial clerks. One can only wonder how the murky backgrounds of some judicial personnel affected the dynamics of individual *hanjian* cases.

For a judiciary already faced with financial, staffing, and ethical challenges, the sheer number of *hanjian* cases alone was overwhelming. The *hanjian* cases added to civil and criminal caseloads that were proliferating at a time of transition and recovery. Since the government set a deadline of December 31, 1946, for exposing *hanjian*, accusations received by local courts peaked between April and August that year.[64]

Courts in areas with large populations or that had spent a long period under occupation had a heavier *hanjian* caseload than others. Henan, as one of the most populous provinces in China, had had one-third of its territory taken over by the Japanese by 1938. The rest of the province was a constant battlefield for the Japanese and Nationalist troops. In addition, Henan suffered a series of man-made and natural disasters, including a flood that Chiang deliberately caused in 1938 with the goal of stopping Japanese advancement, which instead devastated the local agriculture and produced countless refugees. The famine of 1942–43, furthermore, caused millions to die or flee to neighboring provinces.[65] Observing the hellish scenes during the famine, the American journalist Theodore White commented that the people's loyalty to the state "had been hollowed to nothingness."[66] Whether or not he was right, Henan was among the three provinces with the highest number of *hanjian* cases after the war.[67] For

TABLE 2.2. *Hanjian* cases received by the Henan High Court and its branch courts, 1946

Month	Cases accepted	Cases concluded	Cases under review	Number of defendants convicted	Number of defendants not convicted
May	1804	709	1095	413	322
June	1767	568	1199	259	299
July	1335	647	1088	359	359
August	1573	617	956	383	347

Source: "Yulu geyuan banli hanjian anjian qingxing biao" (Progress report on *hanjian* cases brought to courts in Shandong and Henan), March 1947, Academia Historica, Taipei, 151–1707.

several months in 1946, the Henan High Court and its six branch courts were overwhelmed by accusations of *hanjian* (see table 2.2).

Given the daunting nature of the task, local courts in general demonstrated extraordinary patience and meticulousness in their investigations. Reports from several provinces show that on average, it took the judiciary forty-five days to conclude a case, with multiple cases being processed at the same time.[68] Some cases were closed in as little as twelve days, while others took months or even years.

A progress report involving the judiciary and government at different levels illuminates the painstaking and detailed investigation involved in a *hanjian* case. In March 1946, the Henan High Court accepted a case brought by Cheng Liansan, who accused Li Bocen and several others of assisting the enemy and exploiting the local people. When the High Court ordered the local court to conduct an investigation, clerks from the fifth branch court went to several villages in Deng Xian and interviewed villagers, the head of the "mutual surveillance unit" (*baozhang*), members of the local militia, and local government staff. Based on these investigations, the court decided to prosecute several of the accused but drop the charges against others.[69]

As many officials and professionals had foreseen, the problem of malicious accusation was widespread in *hanjian* cases. The National Advisory Council voiced a concern with *hanjian* lawsuits that were resulted from personal feuds.[70] The attorney Zhang Shizhao observed that many people were using this chance to get back at their personal enemies. Even if the informants could not always succeed in sending their targets to jail, the lawsuit still damaged the reputations of the accused and cost them a great deal of time and money. Well aware of the consequences of wronged cases, the judiciary paid particular attention to the relationships between the informants and the accused, as the following cases demonstrate.

The *hanjian* case of Ding Guitang sheds light on institutional reorganization and personnel reshuffling in the restored Nationalist administration. Ding Guitang and Shen Bochen were both senior employees of the Chinese Maritime Customs Service (CMCS), an institution with a unique history and wartime experience.[71] Since its inception in the mid-nineteenth century, the CMCS had been staffed with high-caliber foreign directors and Chinese as well as foreign employees.[72] After the attack on Pearl Harbor of December 7, 1941, the Japanese took over the CMCS and appointed one of its Japanese employees, Kishimoto Hirokichi, to be the inspector general. Shortly thereafter, Chongqing established its own customs service, which made great efforts in the following year to persuade the Chinese members of the Japanese-controlled CMCS to relocate to Chongqing.[73]

As the most experienced Chinese member of the CMCS and an ethical yet savvy individual, Ding Guitang played a key role in the establishment of the Chongqing CMCS and the postwar purification of the Shanghai CMCS, which was affiliated with the Wang administration. Ding had joined the CMCS in 1916. In addition to amassing an impeccable work record, Ding took major steps to ensure that Chinese employees were treated on an equal basis with their foreign colleagues.[74] Following the Japanese takeover, Ding Guitang made repeated attempts to escape Shanghai and eventually succeeded. He joined the Chongqing CMCS in December 1942 and was appointed to the second highest position in this institution.[75]

After the war, Chiang Kai-shek entrusted Ding Guitang with reorganizing the puppet CMCS and investigating collaborationist conduct among its employees. Ding had begun to make plans for reorganizing and restoring the CMCS as early as 1943. With a full understanding of the Chinese CMCS employees' wartime plight, Ding took a lenient approach. He also recognized and valued the experience and credentials of all CMCS employees, Chinese and foreign.[76] Among the more than five thousand employees who had remained in the puppet CMCS, Ding placed only 142 high-ranking members under investigation. The investigation committee ended up terminating the employment of two Chinese and two foreign employees. One of them, Shen Bochen, faced accusations of colluding with the Japanese in preventing Chinese employees from relocating to Chongqing.

The case of Ding Guitang reveals how personal grudges found outlets in the anti-*hanjian* campaigns. Shen's resentment of Ding went way back. In 1936, Shen had accused Li Tonghua, a custom officer in Jinan, of embezzling embargoed goods. The accusation was disproved, and Shen was demoted, a disgrace for which he held Ding responsible. Now Shen Bochen again blamed Ding for his dismissal, even though it was other CMCS employees who had disclosed the information about Shen's collusion.[77]

The process of screening CMCS employees for *hanjian* was just one case in which Chiang authorized the extralegal investigation of collaboration, which evidently obstructed the restoration of judicial authority. Many "takeover committees" were established after the war to reclaim occupied institutions and purge staff members with questionable allegiances. Decisions reached by these temporary yet powerful committees were often the result of the inner workings of each institution and a concern to preserve the organization. Ding Guitang's decision to dismiss only four employees out of thousands who had continued to work under the occupation was a case in point.

After a yearlong investigation, the court decided to not prosecute Ding for the *hanjian* crime, mainly because Ding went out of his way to join the Chongqing government. Ding's fifty-page letter in his own defense, which elaborated on his activities from the 1920s to the present with attached evidence, was vital to the investigation. Ding's later career illustrates his loyalty to the nation rather than to the government—either that or his skill at adaptation and self-preservation. By the time of the Communist takeover in 1949, Ding had facilitated the nationalization of the CMCS, and he became the first inspector general of the Customs Service of the People's Republic of China.[78]

In many cases, informants used fabricated or irrelevant evidence to frame others as *hanjian*. Though the courts often dismissed such evidence as insufficient, these cases shed light on the motivations of the informants and social perceptions of *hanjian*. In November 1945, Wang Xungao, a forty-six-year-old Shanghai resident, brought an accusation against Wang Xuechen, the editor of two tabloids, for his "notorious deeds and willingness in aiding the enemy" (*niji zhaozhu, ganxin funi*).[79] Wang Xungao provided no solid evidence that Wang Xuechen had engaged in any *hanjian* conduct. Instead he focused on the content of Wang's tabloids, which he considered full of "hooligan literature" (*liumang xiaoshuo*) and "sex scandals" (*taose xinwen*). He trivialized Wang Xuechen's *Shanghai Daily Digest* and pointed to the fact that it had been banned.[80]

When accusations were based on questionable evidence, the judiciary made decisions by considering the wartime and current activities of both parties involved. In the Wang Xuechen case, the court discovered that the *Shanghai Daily Digest* had been suspended and eventually banned in 1943 by Wang Jingwei's Central Propaganda Committee. This fact was taken by the court to demonstrate the innocence of the accused, or at least his lack of ties with the Wang regime. Furthermore, the court found indications of Wang Xuechen's financial distress and speculated that he was unlikely to be a *hanjian*.[81] During the trial, Wang Xungao admitted that he and the accused used to be colleagues but never got along. Having realized that this lawsuit probably would not go as he had hoped, he withdrew the charge against Wang Xuechen.

Weak evidence and misinformation also complicated the cases of Zhou Feicheng and Wu Jie. In late 1948, several individuals accused Zhou Feicheng of being an opium addict and *hanjian*, and Wu Jie of being *hanjian*.[82] According to the informants, Zhou, as the principal of Shanghai Gezhi Middle School, had "hooked up" important figures in educational circles to the Wang Jingwei regime."[83] Wu Jie was said to be a lawyer and the secretary of Yuan Lüdeng, an infamous economic *hanjian*. The subsequent investigation revealed that Zhou Feicheng had been a teacher for many years and had only recently become a school principal. He thus was not influential or well connected enough to do what he had been accused of. Furthermore, the prosecutor found no evidence of Zhou's active collaboration. The court observed that the name Wu Jie written with the characters 吴介 was nowhere to be found either on the list of wanted *hanjian* or among lawyers. There was a Wu Jie 吴玠 who was indeed a lawyer and professor of law, but nothing indicated that he had collaborated, either.

The court decided to not prosecute the cases against Zhou and Wu for lack of witnesses as well. The accusers, who signed their names as Shi Yujing, Ding Wen, and Ke Ren, could not be found at the addresses provided.[84] They also failed to show up in response to a court summons. The court thus suspected that the accusations were based on rumor or hearsay, which explained the misspelled names, the vague description of "criminal facts," and the inclusion of trivia unrelated to the *hanjian* crime.

As in the case of Wang Xuechen, the accusers listed other misconduct by the accused as proof of their immoral or corrupt nature and thus their susceptibility to becoming *hanjian*. The informants hoped that accusations of the publication of pornographic material or an addiction to opium would influence the court's judgment. Fortunately, this was not the case. The accusation of Zhou Feicheng's opium addition was dealt with separately, and Zhou was found not guilty on that count either.

In this case, as in almost all *hanjian* cases, financial status was pivotal to the nature of the accusations and to helping the investigators to evaluate the entire case. The three individuals who accused Zhou Feicheng and Wu Jie stressed that both owned cars. In addition, they claimed that Zhou was "too wealthy for an educator." The investigators discovered that Zhou did own an automobile. Moreover, many in education circles disliked him for his arrogance. Wu Jie, on the other hand, was in serious financial trouble and could not possibly be a member of the automobile-driving class.[85] The accusation and the court judgment both assumed that wealth was an indicator of questionable wartime behavior. Individuals who survived the occupation with a good financial standing easily aroused suspicion concerning the source of their wealth. The court, however, considered evidence of actual harm done by the accused before deciding to prosecute them.

Patterns in the judiciary's dealing with *hanjian* cases recurred across localities. Difficulties in locating witnesses and finding sufficient evidence were the main reasons for the judiciary to turn down cases. Table 2.3 provides a summary of all the cases dismissed by procurators of the third branch of the Hunan High Court from three counties: Huarong, Xiangtan, and Hengshan.[86]

To encourage the common people to come forward without fear of retaliation, the government allowed anonymous accusations. For the same reason, the state ordained that the presence of plaintiffs or informants was not required for the court to pursue a case and conduct an investigation.[87] This decision substantially obstructed the judicial process. In many *hanjian* cases, the informant was the one most familiar with the activities of the accused, especially if he or she was a direct victim. Without the presence of the informant, investigation was difficult to carry out, and the court had to dismiss the case.

Cases dropped by the procurators reflected another important pattern. The judiciary tended to forgive passive participants in puppet institutions when little proof existed that they had done any substantial harm to the nation or given concrete assistance to the enemy. Judicial officials frequently quoted Article III of the Regulations in their legal reasoning and emphasized "real harm done to the people" or "contribution to the enemy" as what truly constituted the *hanjian* crime. This article, which came with no clarification or guidance, was interpreted differently by different courts and in

TABLE 2.3. Summary of *hanjian* cases dismissed by the Third Branch of the Hunan High Court, 1946–48

Accusers	Accused	Charges brought	Reasons for dismissal
Xu Yunqing	Chen Xikang and 15 others	Participation in local puppet administration	No such person as Xu Yunqing was found. The 16 people were not among *hanjian* wanted by the government. Letters of support for the 16 from the local party organ, local police, and local gentry were presented to the court.
Anonymous	Li Zhizhen	Participation in the mutual surveillance group established by local puppet regime in Chengshi County	No evidence suggested that Li used his position to do anything beneficial to the enemy or harmful to the people or the nation. He Zhenhuan, the county chief of Chengshi, testified in his support.
Anonymous	Yi Nanzhen and 30 others	Participation in the local puppet administration and the puppet chamber of commerce, among other organizations	The accuser could not be located, and the letter of accusation used a fake seal (not made by the shop whose name the seal carried). The court also received a letter stating that Yi was a Juntong agent.
Deng Yunxuan	Li Biying, Ai Zulian, Li Biren, Liu Gengxin, Huang Jiancheng, Qin Dachun	The 6 accused had earlier accused Deng Yunxuan of heading the local mutual surveillance group in Chengshi County and of embezzling money collected for the salt tax. Deng Yunxuan in turn accused Li Biying and Ai Zulian of serving as translators for the Japanese, and the others of participating in the local puppet administration.	Li Biying and Ai Zulian were only 16 years old in 1945, with only an elementary school education, and thus were unlikely to have served as translators. Qin Dachun was an illiterate carpenter. Only Li Biren had worked for the local puppet administration and was now at large.
Tan Shoujie	Xin Wenqing and his wife	When Hengshan County was under occupation, Xin partnered with the enemy in running a Great East Asia Cooperation Store and incited the enemy to rob local people. This resulted in the killing of a resident, Feng Jiaolian. Xin's wife coaxed local women into entertaining the enemy.	No supporting evidence was offered for any of the accusations against Xin Wenqing or his wife. The court continued to investigate the robbery and murder as a separate case.

Accusers	Accused	Charges brought	Reasons for dismissal
Ye Rong (former Zhongtong agent)	Su Zefan (female)	When Xiangtan County was under occupation, Su was an informant for the puppet security committee and used this position to extort funds.	No supporting evidence was found for the accusation. Yan Licun, a mutual surveillance head (*baozhang*), testified in Su's support.
Feng Desheng, Huang Guomin	Luo Shaojun	In 1945, Feng worked as an intelligence agent for the local guerrilla force under the command of the Nationalist army officer Lin Zhiyun. Luo took the Japanese to Feng's home, arrested 9 people, and killed Feng's cousin. Huang's father was also an intelligence agent investigating *hanjian* in Xiangtan County. Luo discovered his identity and took the Japanese to kill him.	Neither Feng nor Huang witnessed the killings in person, nor did those who informed them of the incidents. No other supporting evidence was offered for the accusations. Luo Shaojun stated that he was hired by the Japanese to clean their rooms for two months for a payment of 9 kilograms of rice. He was never paid. The court dismissed the case, arguing that Luo was merely a janitor and had no power to take the Japanese to arrest people.
Wen Zejia	Kang Lezhong	Participation in the puppet security committee in Hengshan County and extortion of local resources, including lumber Wen had stored.	Kang admitted that he worked on the puppet committee but denied the other accusations. It was Kang's wife who appropriated the lumber, for reasons deemed "irrelevant to Wen's puppet position."

varying circumstances. "Real harm" to the nation or "contribution to the enemy" were particularly tricky to define in cases involving "cultural" *hanjian* and propagandists. The more lenient interpretations were likely to come from judicial personnel who were genuinely sympathetic to passive collaborators because of their own wartime quandaries.

In addition to problems with the reliability of evidence and witnesses, another source of frustration for the judiciary was that people often brought cases first to other authorities, which could lead to both inconvenience and political interference. In Shanghai, many informants wrote directly to the mayor, Qian Dajun. On receiving the letter accusing Wang Xuechen, Qian ordered the Shanghai Bureau of Social Affairs to investigate the matter. When the case eventually reached the Shanghai High Court, the Bureau of

Social Affairs instructed the court on how to proceed and render judgment.

Other informants exposed *hanjian* with great enthusiasm by writing to newspaper editors. In this scenario, a *hanjian* case was effectively tried in the court of public opinion before it entered the judicial process. The public would then question the efficiency, competence, and ethics of the judiciary throughout the proceedings.

HANJIAN WITH COMPETING LOYALTIES

Cases involving special agents were particularly revealing of the issues discussed above. During wartime, different intelligence offices that reported directly to Chiang Kai-shek dispatched special agents on various missions, with little communication between agencies. Chiang deliberately created multiple layers of power in his administration and played one faction against the other so that no single individual or clique would threaten his central authority. Just as he used Sanqingtuan to counter the power of the Nationalist Party, Chiang established and commanded two intelligence agencies: Juntong, led by Dai Li, and Zhongtong (Bureau of Investigation and Statistics of the Party Central Office), directed by Chen Guofu and Chen Lifu.

Dai and the Chen brothers were in constant rivalry, and so were the men under their command. Each bureau sent numerous agents to sabotage or infiltrate collaborationist regimes without the knowledge of the other. This lack of coordination often created danger for their agents, as the assassination of Mu Shiying shows. On June 28, 1940, Mu Shiying, a renowned writer in Shanghai and then chief editor of a newspaper sponsored by the Wang Jingwei government, was shot in a rickshaw on his way home. Mu's wartime role and his assassination have aroused much speculation and debate. Since the 1970s, scholars have tended to believe that Mu was sent by Zhongtong as an underground agent and inadvertently fell victim to the schemes to assassinate *hanjian*.[88]

The intelligence offices' secret wartime operations caused tremendous confusion for the judiciary while investigating *hanjian* cases, as the identities of many secret agents were almost impossible to determine. Shen Zui, one of Dai Li's most trusted officers at Juntong, later revealed that most of his informants were double agents working in Japanese intelligence. Although Chongqing's use of double and undercover agents became public knowledge soon after the war, not a single person, not even Chiang, had access to full information about these agents and their activities. To complicate matters, some agents secretly defected to the other side. Numerous *hanjian* suspects took advantage of this state of confusion and claimed that they had been ordered to work within the enemy camp. Many managed to obtain exculpatory letters from powerful acquaintances or patrons. Unable to distinguish truth from perjury in these cases, the Ministry of Justice decided that only letters from the commanders of military districts and those from the directors of Juntong and Zhongtong were acceptable as evidence.[89]

Juntong took advantage of the situation to expand its network, buy influence, and interfere with judicial decisions. Not only did it provide letters of support for its own agents in *hanjian* cases, but it also attempted to rescue government officials, economic tycoons, and agents sent by other powerful offices or individuals. For instance, Juntong helped prove the secret identity of Xia Wenyun, an agent sent by General Li Zongren to work in Shanghai and North China.[90] In an official letter to the Ministry of Justice in January 1948, Juntong demanded the right to participate in all cases in which defendants claimed to be undercover agents.[91]

Some cases that involved secret agents were easier to resolve because the evidence was abundant and persuasive. Tang Chengbo and Li Hexiang had joined Juntong before the war and were ordered to infiltrate the puppet regime. Juntong provided a large quantity of documents and correspondence, in addition to a letter of support, to prove the contributions Tang and Li had made to the war effort and their allegiance to the central government. The court found the evidence convincing and dropped the charges.[92]

In other cases, when a single-page letter on Juntong stationery was the sole evidence of the innocence of the defendant, the judiciary became suspicious and frustrated. The investigation of Luo Hongyi's wartime conduct and connections, for example, revealed a complex relationship between Chiang Kai-shek's government, the intelligence community, and Shanghai's underworld, constructed on exchange of favors and shared political and economic interests. To do their job properly and in good conscience, the Capital High Court in Nanjing and the Shanghai police had to solve multiple puzzles related to this network and overcome multiple impediments.

A notorious drug kingpin in Shanghai, Luo Hongyi was accused of collaborating with the Japanese and poisoning the Chinese people with opium. The Capital High court accepted this case and started the investigation immediately. Luo's involvement in opium trafficking was beyond dispute.

The key question in this case was whether Luo was a shareholder of the Central China Grand Charity Hall (Huazhong Hongjishantang) sponsored by the Japanese in September 1939.[93] This was an entity enabling the Japanese and the puppet administration to monopolize the sale of opium in Shanghai and the surrounding provinces. Though the chair of the board of directors was a Japanese national, the person who conducted business and networked for the Grand Charity Hall was Sheng You'an, also known as Sheng III. Born into a prominent family and an infamous prodigal, Sheng III had descended to facilitating the narcotics trade operated by the Japanese.[94]

Both sides in the War of Resistance had stakes in the opium business. The cultivation and sale of opium in China was an important means by which the Japanese extracted local resources. The Japanese monopoly on opium also cut off a main source of income for Chiang Kai-shek and his allies in the underworld. In Shanghai, the center of the opium trade, the traffic of narcotics before 1937 was largely controlled by the Green Gang under its legendary leader, Du Yuesheng. The Nationalist government had maintained a close relationship with the Green Gang since the 1920s and benefited tremendously from the narcotics trade.[95] When the Japanese took over Shanghai in November 1937, Du left for Hong Kong.[96] The Japanese then controlled the opium trade through the Grand Charity Hall and a General Bureau for the Opium Embargo (Jinyan Zongju) that, despite its name, protected the selling of opium by the Japanese and their Chinese collaborators.

The Japanese profited tremendously from the opium trade in China. From 1939 onward, they transported large quantities of opium grown in north and central China to Shanghai, selling it at a price affordable even to the laboring class. An opium regime had taken shape with convenient and cheap supply, a large sales network of opium shops and dens, and Shanghai's puppet police escorting the drugs in transit.[97]

The fact that Luo Hongyi was one of the shareholders of the Grand Charity Hall was easy to confirm. In a report produced in May 1946, the Shanghai Municipal Government listed in detail various Japanese policies and institutions related to the opium trade. This report listed Luo not only as a Chinese shareholder of the Charity Hall but also as the owner of an opium store in Nanjing.[98] A judicial investigation of Luo's case started shortly after the issue of the report. The Capital High Court, however, could not get a hold of an original copy of the list of shareholders, despite repeated requests to the Shanghai Municipal Government.

Who was shielding Luo? The first to be exposed was Wang Xinheng from the Office of Confidential Documents in the Shanghai Municipal Government, who had refused to cooperate with the court. A former Communist party member, Wang had been a follower of Dai Li since the early 1930s. Wang worked as a supervisor for Dai Li in Shanghai, maintaining close communication between the spymaster and Du Yuesheng.[99] In his replies to the questions of the Capital High Court, Wang Xinheng claimed that when the Grand Charity Hall was formed, Luo was in Hong Kong and thus could not have been a shareholder or an executive member of the organization. Wang provided one witness and one piece of evidence for Luo. The witness was Du Yuesheng, who was also in Hong Kong at the time and could confirm Luo's alibi. The evidence was a list of shareholders of the Grand Charity Hall that did not include Luo's name. Zhao Chen, chief justice of the Capital High Court, was full of doubts on receiving this photocopied list and immediately asked for the original copy. He was told that it had been lost.[100]

Subsequent investigation by the court unveiled the hidden connections among several individuals involved in this case. Luo was a protégé of Du Yuesheng, who then pleaded Luo's case to Dai Li. Although Dai Li found Luo's wartime conduct despicable, he had his reasons to pardon Luo. Other than his connection with Du, Luo had made a handsome donation to the resistance forces and had facilitated the work of Juntong agents in wartime. The donation was minimal considering Luo's wealth, which exceeded 3,700 gold bars at market price. A good portion of this fortune was accumulated during the war.[101]

Du Yuesheng and Dai Li soon rounded up a solid team of witnesses for Luo Hongyi, including several Juntong agents in Shanghai, a high-ranking military officer, and Du's butler, Wang Molin. Together they forged a new identity for Luo as an underground Juntong informant. The Capital High Court instructed the Shanghai police to interrogate the witnesses thoroughly. Perhaps because the evidence against Luo was beyond dispute, or perhaps because Dai Li died in a plane crash in March 1946 and Chiang Kai-shek decided to weaken Juntong's power, Luo was convicted of the *hanjian* crime at last. He was released in 1949, however, and left mainland China for Hong Kong.

The *hanjian* case of Shi Xixia reveals another problem, namely the difficulty of differentiating between double agents, underground agents, and agents who had defected. In 1948, Xiang Yingquan, a former contact for Juntong's Korean Salvation Group (Hanguo Jiuguotuan), filed a lawsuit at the Shanghai High Court against Shi Xixia and Wu Mingfang, a "female *hanjian*."[102] According to Xiang, in January 1945 he came to Shanghai from Chongqing to purchase educational supplies. His identity and whereabouts were discovered by Wu Mingfang, then the mistress of a Japanese national. Wu reported this information to Shi Xixia, a former Juntong agent who had defected and was then working for the puppet Shanghai Municipal Police. The two detained Xiang and blackmailed him for a handsome amount of money. Xiang could not come up with the money, so Shi, Wu, and another accomplice kept Xiang's purchased supplies.

When the Shanghai High Court found Shi Xixia guilty of the *hanjian* crime, Shi appealed to the Supreme Court. He pointed out several discrepancies in the plaintiff's statement and what he considered an incomplete investigation by the Shanghai High Court. He claimed that he was an agent for Zhongtong, under whose command he had pretended to surrender in order to infiltrate the puppet police force. Shi presented a letter of support from one of Zhongtong's contacts in Shanghai. Yet witness testimonies and records of earlier trials suggested that Shi had forged evidence. From the time of interrogation to his initial trial, he admitted his identity as a Juntong agent and never indicated otherwise. When asked why he had surrendered, Shi replied that his imprisonment had demoralized him, without reference to any secret mission or order from Zhongtong or Juntong. The evidence Shi presented later did not testify to his assignment as an underground agent; rather, it was part of earlier correspondence regarding a secret mission. Shi's appeal was overruled, and he was sentenced to four years' imprisonment and deprivation of his civil rights.[103]

The case of a White Russian *hanjian* contained multiple elements that complicated the anti-*hanjian* campaigns: the role of intelligence, the involvement of foreign nationals, assassinations, unreliable loyalties, and unstable alliances. Tao Ci, as he was known by his Chinese acquaintances and in the media, was a White Russian who "collaborated with the enemy" and was thus sentenced to a fifteen-year prison term. The direct victim of his *hanjian* crime was Chen Sancai, who was later recognized a heroic martyr by Chiang Kai-shek himself. A graduate of Tsinghua University and an electrical engineer, Chen ran his own company and made a fortune selling refrigerators. From the outbreak of the war, Chen had made generous donations to the resistance cause, and eventually he was recruited by Juntong. In 1940, Chen undertook an assassination attempt on Wang Jingwei after enlisting Tao Ci and a White Russian nurse. As a non-Chinese, Tao Ci required a strong financial incentive in order to risk his life for such a mission. Unsatisfied with what Chen was able to offer, Tao Ci sold out Chen to Wang Jingwei's intelligence service, directly causing Chen's torture and execution.[104]

Tao Ci almost escaped punishment for this betrayal by switching to the right side at the right time. Chen Sancai's nephew, who was arrested with Chen but soon released, was one of the few who knew the cause of Chen's exposure and death. He reported Tao Ci to the Shanghai Municipal Council, which could not do anything at the time because of pressure from the Wang Jingwei administration. Chen's nephew kept a photo of Tao Ci, determined to find him and avenge his uncle's death. In 1944, however, a politically savvy Tao Ci joined the Loyal and Righteous National Salvation Army under Dai Li and was able to pose as a "resistance element." His eventual downfall was a result of instructions from Dai Li and petitions by the Tsinghua University alumni association.

CONCLUSION

The War of Resistance and the anti-*hanjian* campaigns occurred at a pivotal stage of China's legal history. The drafting of new laws and institutional reforms in the early twentieth century was championed by legal professionals and social organizations in the name of social progress. Though the Nationalist government often obstructed judicial independence, it by and large supported legal reforms in the interests of abolishing extraterritoriality. The outbreak of war in 1937 interrupted this process and changed the primary concern and functions of Chinese law under the Nationalist government.

Between 1942, when the Allied nations promised to give up their extraterritorial privileges in China, and 1947, when the Civil War escalated, a window of opportunity appeared for renewed legal reform. The abolition of extraterritoriality was a goal toward which China's reformers had worked long and hard. Ironically, it was achieved at a moment when China's legal system was in utter disarray and far from independent. Chen Tingrui, a renowned lawyer, a national congressman, and a leader of the Shanghai Bar Association, published a long and passionate article in *Dagong bao* in November 1942 regarding the urgency of legal reform.[105] In his opinion, it was the establishment of the rule of law, rather than the abolition of extraterritoriality, that should be the ultimate impetus for legal reform. Therefore, China should continue to work toward this goal even in a time of war and even after it had recovered its judicial sovereignty.

Chen's suggestions won little sympathy from the state, which had more urgent matters to worry about, such as the devastating famine in Henan and the Burma Campaign. Some important members of the party, however, echoed Chen's concerns for legal reform. Ju Zheng (1876–1951), a Nationalist veteran and the head of the Judicial Yuan from 1932 to 1948, published important works in 1944 and 1945 on the pressing need to rebuild the legal system.[106] Ju Zheng called for the integration of indigenous legal wisdom and the core political thoughts of Sun Yat-sen into a modern legal framework. Published in the middle of a high-level power struggle within the Nationalist Party, Ju Zheng's work can be interpreted as a criticism of Chiang Kai-shek's rule.[107] Nonetheless, Ju Zheng was genuinely keen to see a legal system that could bring justice to the people. The goal of Chen Tingrui and Ju Zheng, among others, was not the restoration of the prewar system but the construction of a new, truly independent and functional legal framework. Such a vision fit well with the announced national mission of "resisting Japan and rebuilding the nation."

Their shared vision, however, never came to pass. Along with the increasingly severe political and economic crises faced by the government, the anti-*hanjian* campaigns sabotaged the chance of revitalizing the legal system. The investigation and trials of *hanjian* placed tremendous pressure on the judiciary, which in many places was half functional at best between the War of Resistance and the Civil War. Considering the sheer number of *hanjian* cases and the practical difficulties of investigation, even a fully recovered judiciary could hardly have handled the matter efficiently and fairly. In addition, political interference and other factors constantly obstructed the execution of justice.

While encouraging a return to regular procedures, the Nationalist state continued to rely on what might be called popular justice. The wartime purge of *hanjian* had adopted the features of a mass movement, and this trend continued after the war, when the state invited the common people to participate in the prosecution of *hanjian*. In August 1946, the Ministry of Justice ordered courts at all levels to release lists of wanted *hanjian* to the public, so that common citizens could help make arrests.[108] Tens of thousands of people took part in the campaigns, so vocally and actively that they made this movement appear more popular than it actually was.

The anti-*hanjian* years also gave rise to a more intimate yet dangerous relationship between the people and the law. Operating from a distant and weakened position during wartime, the state granted citizens the power to bring down its perceived enemies. While celebrating victory, Chiang

Kai-shek allowed the people to launch accusations against *hanjian* anonymously, in the name of protecting plaintiffs and informants from potential retaliation. The decade-long witch hunt did help catch many *hanjian* spies, but it also produced ungrounded charges and unjustified accusations. Moreover, for many, the prosecution of *hanjian* became an outlet for their bitter feelings about the war and frustration with a postwar life haunted by inflation, unemployment, instability, and increasing inequality.

CHAPTER 3

THE POLITICAL ECONOMY OF THE ANTI-*HANJIAN* CAMPAIGNS

VARIOUS ORGANS OF THE NATIONALIST GOVERNMENT MADE nationally or locally applicable provisions on seizing, managing, and redistributing property that had been owned or taken by the Japanese and their collaborators. More like administrative decisions than law, these rules and their implementation failed to bring legal or economic justice to postwar China. The making of such rules and the social repercussions they caused revealed the interplay among law, politics, and economy in the punishment of *hanjian*.

The anti-*hanjian* campaigns took place in a society stricken by high inflation, unemployment, class conflicts, and a widening gap between rich and poor. Laws against *hanjian* were not restorative in nature, and the seizure and redistribution of *hanjian* property did little to help the nation or its people recover from the devastation of the war. Rather, they created new channels for government corruption, embezzlement, and nepotism. The public grew increasingly bitter while watching those with political privileges receiving the lion's share of the wealth and possessions of *hanjian*.

In general, the public hoped that the process of punishing *hanjian* would lead to a clean and honest government that would lead China through its reconstruction.[1] Starting in 1946, and acting partly in response to public pressure, the Nationalist government put major economic *hanjian* on trial. These trials, however, exposed various problems within the government and the judiciary, most noticeably corruption, factional struggle, and backroom deals. The common people expected little direct gain from the confiscation of *hanjian* property. What they longed for was justice, including seeing those who had prospered through suspicious means during wartime lose what they were not entitled to at the hands of the law. The bleak postwar economy and challenges from other political forces pitted the majority

80

of the urban population against the alleged economic *hanjian* (*jingji hanjian*), and the government's poor handling of these trials further pro-voked discontent and civil unrest.

THE LAWS ON REDISTRIBUTION OF *HANJIAN* ASSETS

The Nationalist government and the public generally considered confiscat-ing a *hanjian*'s property as both lawful and reasonable. After all, if *hanjian* deserved death, they certainly deserved to lose their material possessions and civil rights. As numerous opinion pieces applauded the opportunity to "settle accounts" (*suanzhang*) with *hanjian* as soon as the war was over, people expected that *hanjian* would repay what they owed their compatri-ots.[2] Readers of major newspapers such as *Shenbao* eagerly speculated about how much each *hanjian* was worth and what the government would do with their assets.

The heated public discussion of the disposition of *hanjian* property pushed the Nationalist government to clarify and revise the relevant laws and statutes. The wartime Regulations said little about financial penalties against *hanjian*, as the Nationalist government was unable to seize property from most *hanjian* when they were enacted. The postwar Regulations were more specific on this matter.[3] Article IV stipulated that any of a *hanjian*'s assets that were originally public property should be retrieved, those that had been taken from private owners should be returned, and the rest should be confiscated. If these assets could not be retrieved, the *hanjian*'s personal property should be valued at market prices and sold to repay what was owed. In all cases, a portion should be left for support of the *hanjian*'s dependents.

This rule sparked debates among legal experts as well as the general pub-lic on at least three issues: should a *hanjian*'s property be confiscated in its entirety, including assets not related to the crime? What was a proper amount to leave for supporting the *hanjian*'s dependents? And what should be done about a *hanjian* who died before facing trial?

The Executive Yuan and the Ministry of Justice responded with targeted revisions and judicial explanations, which provided official answers to these questions and guidelines for various scenarios that emerged during the implementation of the laws. Both contemporary legal experts and later historians concur that financial penalties against *hanjian* were harsher than previous laws governing comparable crimes.[4] As the law professor Yu Qichang pointed out in 1948, those convicted of "internal rebellion" under the 1935 Criminal Code were required to surrender only assets that were obtained by committing this particular offense. *Hanjian*, however, could be stripped of all their assets, including inheritances and assets accumulated before their crimes.[5] Moreover, these assets could be seized before the accused were actually convicted of the crime and received a sentence. The 1947 revision of Article IV of the Regulations made this rule applicable to *hanjian* who had died before the government had a chance to make arrests.[6] Several leading figures in Wang Jingwei's government, including Wang himself and Fu Xiao'an, the former mayor of Shanghai, had died before 1945. Their personal property and possessions were confiscated by the Nationalist government.

The wholesale confiscation of *hanjian* assets virtually denied an individual's accomplishments before the war and extended the punishment to the entire family. Many at the time, including some judicial personnel, considered such a penalty too harsh. The Capital High Court suggested to the Ministry of Justice that this practice was reminiscent of the traditional punishment of *jimo chaojia*, a house search and confiscation of all possessions. The implications of this policy, therefore, were similar to that of *lianzuo*, or guilt by association, a traditional legal concept by which a criminal's family members and close acquaintances were also held accountable for the offense.[7]

Positioning itself as a modern state operating under the rule of law, the Nationalist government mitigated its harshness toward *hanjian* by elaborating on how to care for their dependents. The state defined "legal dependents" as immediate family members whom the accused was legally obliged to support and who had no other source of income. The amount exempted from confiscation should be sufficient to support minors until they reached adulthood, elders over seventy, and adults who were unable to work. The reserved amount should be between 1 and 20 percent of the total value of the *hanjian*'s property and should enable the family members to maintain an average standard of living.[8] As originally stated in the Regulations, if the value of the *hanjian*'s property was not sufficient to support the offender's dependents, the state would not confiscate the assets.

The rationale behind these provisions for the dependents of *hanjian* was the assumption, shared by the state and the people, that nobody condoned *hanjian* crimes, not even the offenders' families and friends. War propaganda and postwar popular literature frequently conveyed the message that *hanjian* conduct was simultaneously widespread and universally condemned. Wartime resistance newspapers frequently published announcements of patriotic youths who repudiated their traitorous fathers.[9] Postwar newspapers and tabloids often reported on individuals who exposed their *hanjian* relatives with a spirit of *dayi mieqin*, "placing righteousness above family loyalty."[10] Providing for *hanjian* dependents represented a way of rewarding such political loyalty, at least on paper.

The Executive Yuan produced a series of regulations and policies from 1946 to 1948 to supervise the management and redistribution of *hanjian* and Japanese assets. When the news of Japan's surrender reached China, the Japanese withdrew, and their client regimes collapsed overnight, leaving behind a large quantity of materials, facilities, and valuables. The Nationalist government divided "enemy and puppet assets" into several categories: cash (*fabi* or *zhongchuquan*), precious metal coins, foreign currency, gold, jewelry, investments of all types, land, office space, warehouses, docks, factories, all other personal belongings, and immovable property. These assets constituted a rich repository of which all political forces and private parties wanted a share.[11]

Among the regulations, the Solutions for Confiscating Enemy Property for Government Use delineated the responsibilities of the various government organs involved in the takeover. Rules for Granting Rewards to Informants clarified how to encourage people to expose hidden *hanjian* without abusing the system. Revisions to these regulations were frequently made to address problems and confusion that arose in this process.

The regulations aimed to streamline the takeover, safekeeping, liquidation, and redistribution of *hanjian* property. The receiving agents (*chengshou jiguan*) were usually the Nationalist army, as it reclaimed lost territories, or judicial branches that seized *hanjian* property while investigating their cases. The military and the judiciary were required to hand over the confiscated property to the local Enemy and Puppet Property Processing Committee (Diwei Chanye Chuli Weiyuanhui). This committee was responsible for assessing, recording, and auditing all confiscated property and reporting such information to the Ministry of Finance. The ministry kept records of the transactions of confiscated property and any income it created. After the ministry assessed the property, the Central Trust took care of its management.[12]

The state allowed several types of private parties to claim shares of confiscated *hanjian* assets. In addition to *hanjian* dependents, who were allowed a portion for living expenses, those who disclosed information on *hanjian* assets could expect rewards. Ordinary citizen informants received 10 percent of the market value of the assets, not including investment profits and interest. Public servants and intelligence agents received 3 percent, as they were expected to fulfill their duty of reporting any *hanjian* crime and property to the state.[13] The government developed a meticulous system for rewarding informants, taking into consideration scenarios in which more than one person reported on the same property or the same informant reported multiple offenses. Designed to induce common citizens to participate in the anti-*hanjian* campaigns, the reward system greatly added to the workload of the government organs responsible.

The 1945 Regulations briefly mentioned that a portion of the *hanjian* property should be returned to the original owner if it had been forcibly taken. In practice, however, compensating private owners was not a priority of the Nationalist state. Counterintuitive as it may sound, this was not a high priority among the public, either. The *hanjian* crime was mainly committed by prominent national figures against the nation-state. The major *hanjian* were too high up to inflict discrete harms on individual citizens. Minor *hanjian* who had exploited people in their community were numerous, but tracking down each and every of their victims and calculating exactly how much was taken from them would be impossible.

In any case, no evidence suggests that the Nationalist government compensated the losses of individual *hanjian* victims in a systematic and consistent manner. For several years after the war, the receiving agents of the government had the first option on buying or renting confiscated property. The original owners of property forcibly taken by *hanjian* were not mentioned in laws other than the Regulations.[14] In 1948, for the first time, a judicial explanation granted original owners the first option on reclaiming property that had been taken by *hanjian*. If the value of the property had increased during the war, the owner needed to pay an adjusted amount for the added value.[15] Shanghai's capitalists, for instance, had to pay 70 percent of the current market price to reclaim factories they had owned before the war. Even this unfavorable deal was secured only after painful collective haggling with the government.[16] For pieces of land, the government reserved the right to "legally" retain them before they were evaluated and repurchased by the original owners. In other words, the government gave itself priority to use the land in question.[17]

The belief that the nation-state itself was a victim of the *hanjian* crime provided justification for the state's claim to the lion's share of the confiscated property. The Central Trust of China ordered most of the assets to be cashed out in *fabi* ("legal tender," currency issued by Chiang Kai-shek's government) and deposited into the Central Bank of China. For immovable property, the Central Trust held auctions and deposited the auction income.[18] Precious jewelry, antiques, paintings, houses, land, furniture, vehicles, boats, and other property were to be entrusted to the Central Trust Bureau for sale, rent, or auction. The money from the sale or rental of these items also went into the Central Bank.[19] Government offices directly involved in processing *hanjian* cases were allowed a share as compensation for their wartime losses. The Central Trust, for instance, received 5 percent of the rental income for its management of seized property. To remedy the understaffing and underfunding of the judiciary, the Executive Yuan appropriated 8 percent of the confiscated property.[20] The confiscation of *hanjian* property, therefore, was a way to nationalize private property and help get a financially paralyzed government back on its feet.

THE REDISTRIBUTION OF *HANJIAN* ASSETS, IN PRACTICE

The actual confiscation and redistribution of *hanjian* property deviated greatly from what the law and policy had prescribed. The government, while claiming a big chunk of the bounty, overestimated the integrity of its officials and staff. Despite the streamlining of procedures, enemy and *hanjian* property was rarely transferred from one agency to another smoothly or in its entirety. On their return to previously occupied regions, all levels of the Nationalist government found themselves short of office space and supplies, so they used what they could find. Since the liberation of occupied regions was a gradual process, some local governments were already using confiscated property when the first set of guidelines on the redistribution of enemy and *hanjian* assets was promulgated in May 1946.

A sample list of confiscated items and their whereabouts from December 1945 demonstrates vividly the "first come, first served" approach widely adopted in handling confiscated *hanjian* property. Produced by the Beizhan branch of the Shanghai Municipal Police, the list showed items confiscated by this office that never made to the next stage of processing. The headquarters of the Shanghai Municipal Police appropriated some items, including cloth (1 bolt), yarns (11 rolls), cashmere garments (74 pieces), a small passenger car, and so on. The branch office itself kept some items, such as four bags of charcoal, two electric burners, six cotton quilts, a blanket, two silver cases, and a serving set. A few items on the list, such as a piano, a pipe organ, two mattresses, a rug, and a mirror, were "borrowed" by staff members of the branch office. Curiously, the head of the office took half a gold bar, weighing about 250 grams, for "safekeeping."[21]

Aware of widespread petty embezzlement by its officials and employees, the government ordered all branches that had borrowed confiscated office buildings to register with the Ministry of Finance and to pay a proper amount of rent. Similar rules applied to other real estate, such as docks and storehouses, that had already been taken by the military or local governments.[22] The government also required offices in charge of handling the confiscated property to hand over any rent or auction income as soon as it was received. In practice, however, these policies had no effect on curbing petty corruption or the illegal seizure of goods.

One reason for the administrative failure in handling *hanjian* property was the lack of an independent and efficient authority free of conflicts of interest. The government attempted to create one in the form of the Enemy and Puppet Property Processing Committee, which was not available in all localities. To control the management of *hanjian* assets in places with no processing committee, the Executive Yuan ordered local courts to freeze enemy and puppet property for safekeeping by local governments.[23] The income that a local government obtained from using or managing such property was to be deposited in the Central Bank of China.[24] Correspondence between the central and local governments revealed that the latter habitually kept portions of the loot.

Even in regions where the processing committees existed, they never secured sole authority over the management of property. In Shanghai, a processing committee was established in October 1945 to oversee the whole business of handling *hanjian* property from Shanghai to Changzhou. The committee was soon overwhelmed by all the complications involved in this profitable cause and by challenges from other government agencies. It was abolished in December 1946, when the Central Trust of China took over. The next year, the Central Trust established a Jiangsu-Zhejiang-Anhui Enemy and Puppet Property Processing Committee (Suzhewan Diwei Chanye Qinglichu) to oversee the Nationalist power base.[25] This committee was in operation until March 31, 1949, illustrating the long-drawn-out process of handling *hanjian* property.

Even when rules were clear and special offices were available to take charge, many high-ranking government officials bypassed procedures to take what they desired. In Shanghai, numerous houses, vehicles, and other types of puppet property were "taken for private use" (*juwei siyou*) rather than being put up for resale, auction, or redistribution. The Shanghai High Court compiled a list of fifty-two houses it had confiscated from convicted *hanjian*, mostly single-family homes with gardens in prime locations of Shanghai.

It was the job of the processing committee and the Central Trust to list and process these properties, but most of them were already inhabited when the list was composed. Seventeen were taken or "maintained" by Nationalist government organs or officials, including Zhongtong (4), Juntong (1), and judicial personnel from major courts in Shanghai and Nanjing (7).[26] A presiding judge from the Shanghai High Court was so comfortably settled into his new home that he refused to move out despite several requests from the processing committee. The Executive Yuan and the Ministry of Justice had to issue a formal order to evict him.[27]

In postwar high society, grand houses formerly owned by *hanjian* became the best gifts to exchange for political favors or to build personal networks. So many offices and individuals took advantage of their temporary control over confiscated houses that no supervising authority maintained a clear record. The processing committee was the entity authorized to manage these houses, and with help from the Shanghai police, it sometimes forced occupants to vacate houses, only to make them available for party and government bigwigs.[28] In December 1947, for instance, the processing committee ordered the house at 1827 Linsen Road to be vacated so that it was ready for Yu Youren, president of the Supervision Yuan. In another incident, the Shanghai Municipal Government allotted a confiscated house at 1803 Linsen Road to its secretary general, Shen Shihua. Located in the high-end residential district within the French Concession, this house had been a secondary residence of Zhu Boquan, a well-known Shanghai financier who was charged with the *hanjian* crime. Shen Shihua then gave it to Chiang Wei-kuo, the second son of Chiang Kai-shek, who was then serving in Shanghai Armored Vehicle Regiment. Liu Gongyun, director of the Processing Committee, approved this transfer. Yet by the time Chiang Wei-kuo took possession of the house, 92 of the 228 pieces of the furniture had been "lost."[29]

Powerful figures fought over extravagant houses, which symbolized the comfort, luxury, and modernity of Shanghai, so much missed by those who had been in exile in Chongqing. When Miu Bin, the deputy principal of the Wang Jingwei government's Judicial Yuan, was executed as a major *hanjian*, his "grand mansion with garden" (*huayuan yangfang*) on Shaoxing Road became a hot item on the market.[30] Interested parties included the American embassy, Chiang Wei-kuo, Zou Haibin from the Supervision Yuan, and Xia Qin, chief justice of the Supreme Court.[31] The final competition was between Zou and Xia. Both exploited all their connections and resources to get the property. The Executive Yuan granted the house to Zou. The

Jiangsu-Zhejiang-Anhui Property Processing Committee, however, made the same promise to Xia. The Shanghai High Court, to which Zou and Xia both appealed, was caught in a politically delicate situation. The court suggested that the two families shared the house, but Zou refused. The matter was eventually resolved when Zou was promised another confiscated house.

Such scandals caught the attention of the Nationalist leadership and senior party members. The government ordered the Shanghai Municipal Police to investigate all *hanjian* property that had been taken illegally. Such investigations did not go far, however, because of other challenges faced by the Nationalist government and the escalating Civil War.[32] Cui Zhenhua, a veteran Nationalist and a member of the Supervision Yuan, joined with eleven other highly respected figures from the party to warn the government about the problematic takeover of enemy and *hanjian* property. During the second meeting of the Nationalist Party's Central Executive Committee, Cui and her colleagues demanded a transparent and lawful manner of handling such property.

The petition they drafted started with a summary of all the problems they had observed in this process:

> In many regions, poor transportation delayed the arrival of parties responsible for taking over enemy and puppet property; and when they finally arrived, they appeared ill-prepared, with inadequate guidelines. As a result, some assets were relocated or hidden by *hanjian*, some were taken or destroyed by the Communists, and others disappeared at the hands of unethical officials and local racketeers. The losses were tremendous. The property that our government did get hold of was not properly managed because of the power struggles at all different levels and between different branches. The government established offices solely for the management of such property. Receiving agents, however, either completely bypassed such offices and handled property on their own, or handed over the shell of the property while keeping the valuables inside. As a result, the processing committees existed in name only. Among the small number of industrial plants that have been properly received, most cannot resume production to support their employees. Numerous houses and automobiles have been kept for private use without benefiting the public at all.

Cui then pointed out what was at stake: "The government takes over enemy and puppet property with the intention of benefiting the whole society.

Even if the government cannot find the original owners of many enterprises soon, it should take good care of these enterprises to put people's minds at ease. . . . Those who lost property first to the enemy and then to the receiving agents are agonized, and those who came a long way to reclaim their lost land have been deeply disappointed."[33] Cui and her colleagues urged the government to respect the property rights of the original owners. The priority in processing enemy and *hanjian* property, they asserted, was to track down and compensate the civilian victims of years of occupation, not to enrich the government and its officials.

To judge from laws and policies regarding the enemy and *hanjian* property, the Nationalist government was responsive to public opinion and professional advice. It intended to operate by established procedures. These procedures, however, were harsh on the *hanjian* defendants and oblivious of their victims. The gigantic state machine and its human representatives showed little concern with public interest or the recovery of the society as a whole. After the war, *hanjian* could no longer do real harm to the country or its people. To stabilize society and the economy, the anti-*hanjian* campaign, if conducted at all, should have been more restorative than retributive. The takeover of *hanjian* property, however, proved quite the opposite.

COMPLICATING WARTIME COLLABORATION: THE CASES OF SHANGHAI CAPITALISTS

The War of Resistance, like every other prolonged war, was fought on the economic front as well as on the battlefield. A firm control of the economy and resources became crucial for all parties, especially after the war entered a stalemate. It was clear by 1942 that neither side was likely to achieve a speedy victory. Japan had overextended its manpower and resources, and Chongqing was short of staple goods and military supplies. Shanghai, the major financial and industrial center in prewar China and still the city with the highest concentration of capital, was of vital strategic importance. Consequently, the political positions and choices of Shanghai's capitalists became critical variables in the outcome of the war.

Shanghai's economy followed a roller-coaster trajectory during the eight years of war and dislocation. During the Battle of Shanghai between August and November 1937, thousands of industrial plants and factories were destroyed or damaged.[34] In 1938, most large factories resumed operation, and by 1940 most of Shanghai's industries resumed production and even exceeded their prewar output. As hostilities escalated in 1941 between Japan and Great Britain, embargoes and military maneuvers caused a dramatic decline in production and trade. The market was restrained by the rising cost of energy and the control economy (*tongzhi jingji*) of the Wang Jingwei government, as were people's everyday lives. A burgeoning black market further impeded legitimate and what was perceived to be patriotic business.

Out of nationalistic sentiments and a consideration of their own business interests, Shanghai's capitalists generally avoided collaboration, at least until 1940. In 1938, the Japanese had little success in luring the Chinese industrialists with the promise of reopening factories after the Battle of Shanghai. Many prominent figures in business and finance, including Shanghai's leading textile tycoon, Rong Zongjing, went to Hong Kong to escape the dilemma.[35] Some relocated their businesses to the foreign settlements despite higher land prices there: these offered a temporary haven until December 1941. As the stalemate continued, however, Japan accelerated its extraction of mineral and industrial resources in the lower Yangzi delta and took greater control of enterprises in Shanghai. When the Pacific War broke out, the Japanese moved into foreign enclaves, leaving no safe space for patriotic businessmen or their businesses.

As the postwar trials reveal, only the entrepreneurs who had followed Chiang Kai-shek to Chongqing were safe from suspicion of collaboration, but most of Shanghai's business owners were either unable or unwilling to move their factories, possessions, and families almost one thousand miles southwest. After 1937, only about 150 out of 5,525 factories in Shanghai relocated to Chongqing.[36] While these factories and their owners were praised for contributing to the War of Resistance, those that had remained in Shanghai became easy targets of *hanjian* charges.

Many individuals in Shanghai undoubtedly acted on opportunities created by the war to accumulate wealth by less than legitimate means. Their prosperity came at the expense of the people, the local economy, and the welfare of the community. One of the most notorious *hanjian* in Shanghai, Sheng You'an, made a massive fortune selling opium to the Chinese and salt to the Japanese. With his direct and indirect victims "amounting to hundreds of thousands," Sheng was sentenced to death by the Capital High Court in March 1947.[37]

Many less powerful individuals, too, capitalized on the war for their own gains. Fu Yung Kong, an employee of an American match company, had worked for Japanese employers prior to the war and spoke fluent Japanese.

During the war, Fu usurped the superintendent's position and assisted the Japanese in taking over the match company. For Fu's betrayal of the company and for running his own business with Japanese help, the company terminated his employment in 1946, a decision supported by the local government.[38]

Most of Shanghai's elite businessmen and industrialists, however, were too savvy to collaborate fully with the Japanese and the puppet regime. Some strategically divided their assets among several cities and invested in different political camps to minimize their risks. For instance, Liu Hongsheng, the head of a leading business family in Shanghai, fled to Hong Kong when the Japanese forced him to chair the puppet Shanghai Chamber of Commerce. Liu left four of his sons in Shanghai to preside over the family businesses and founded a new venture in Hong Kong in 1940. Soon after that, he moved to Chongqing on the invitation of Chiang Kai-shek, thus signifying that he now openly sided with Chiang. Liu then ordered his four sons to smuggle skilled technicians and machinery from Shanghai to support production on the home front.[39]

Those who had hoped to continue their lives in Shanghai and preserve China's industrial bases tried to negotiate with the Japanese on their own terms. These individuals did not consider their actions to be collaboration, yet their efforts achieved little other than arousing suspicion from Chongqing. Shanghai's leading businessmen organized a Shanghai Citizens Association to bargain with the Japanese to restore Chinese control over seized industries. Though the leaders maintained that this organization aimed to rescue Chinese enterprises and restore Shanghai's economy, their willingness simply to talk with the enemy was enough to earn them the label of *hanjian*.[40] After all, the Wang Jingwei regime had made similar attempts by pleading to the Japanese for the return of confiscated Chinese industries. It even dedicated two offices, in Shanghai and Canton, to this purpose.[41]

The Shanghai capitalists' relations with the Japanese and with the two Chinese governments shed much light on the complex and ambiguous nature of wartime collaboration. Most prominent capitalists who had stayed in Shanghai throughout the war and made compromises with the Japanese and Wang Jingwei also cooperated with Chongqing through clandestine trade and other means. During the war, trade between Shanghai and inland China was never completely severed for long. Communication resumed between Shanghai and Hong Kong in 1938, making it possible for Shanghai suppliers to meet Chongqing's demand for essential items and provisions. The Burma Road and a maritime smuggling route in Southeast

Asia provided two additional supply lines for Chongqing.[42] The routes through Hong Kong and the Burma Road were cut off after 1941 and 1942, respectively.[43] As a result, strategic trade with Shanghai became particularly important for the Nationalist government in exile.[44]

What made such trade possible was a network of people who walked adeptly between political camps. It included powerful Nationalists, underworld bosses, and capitalists in Shanghai. The establishment of Wang Jingwei's government in 1940 led to a split of Nationalist Party members between the two governments but not to a clear-cut end of long-established connections and contacts. Espionage activities and frequent defections in both directions reinforced such ties. Furthermore, Du Yuesheng, who continued to control the Green Gang even after his escape to Hong Kong in 1937, had developed contacts on both sides as well as in the business world. Du's wartime representative in Shanghai, Xu Caicheng, maintained relationships with Chongqing, Japanese intelligence, and the Wang Jingwei government.[45]

These individuals who flirted with different parties enabled wartime cross-zone trade, and their ambiguous roles complicated the issue of collaboration. Capitalists in Shanghai and in Chongqing shared trading routes and business interests. In dire need of revenue and essential items such as cotton and grain, the Chongqing government gave up its earlier bans on trade with occupied regions and assigned Juntong to secure the smuggling of such items. Wartime trade thus became a source of exbudgetary revenue for Juntong. Operating from Hong Kong and then Chongqing, Du Yuesheng established several companies to purchase goods in Shanghai and transport them to inland regions. Among them were the China Industry and Commerce Trust Company and the Tongji Company.

Many of those who were later tried as economic *hanjian* were indispensable players in this multilateral long-distance trade. The best-known were Wen Lanting, Yuan Lüdeng, and Lin Kanghou, the "three elders of Shanghai."[46] Du Yuesheng's Tongji company had a Shanghai branch, which was organized as a separate company, the Minhua Company. Minhua was established with Japanese approval and launched by Zhou Fohai, a senior Nationalist and a key figure in the Wang Jingwei government. The three elders were among the fourteen directors, whose names had been sent to Chongqing for approval by Chiang Kai-shek himself.[47] When put on trial and faced with an angry public who had no knowledge of the wartime secret trade, the three elders could only vaguely hint at their plight and their unsung contributions to the War of Resistance.

ECONOMIC *HANJIAN* ON TRIAL

The term "economic *hanjian*" frequently appeared in postwar edicts, government correspondence, newspapers, and literature. Perhaps because the speakers and the audience always assumed its meaning to be clear and consistent, no one made an effort to define it. To deduce from relevant articles in the Regulations, an economic *hanjian* was someone who had traded key military supplies or provisions with the enemy, provided the enemy with funds, disturbed the financial order, or taken a position in an economic, financial, or banking institution under enemy control.[48] Perhaps because the popular understanding of this term was vague, however, the label was applied to a broader group of people. In an article in the Shanghai-based newspaper *Zhoubao*, the left-wing intellectual Zheng Zhenduo denounced as economic *hanjian* "anyone who had trade, commercial, or financial contacts with the Japanese."[49]

In other words, whereas Chiang Kai-shek's Nationalist government was more concerned with punishing leading capitalists who had facilitated the economic rule of the Japanese and the puppet regimes, the general public considered the category of economic *hanjian* as largely synonymous with *jianshang*, "treacherous merchants." The popular aphorism *wushang bujian*, literally "There is no merchant who is not treacherous," reflected a deeply entrenched distrust of those whose activities centered on profit seeking. The Confucianist social order had placed the merchant class at the bottom of the social and moral hierarchy, below scholars, peasants, and artisans. During wartime, the fact that some merchants continued to trade with the Japanese and prospered at a time of national crisis reinforced the resentment and cultural bias against merchants.

The punishment of "treacherous merchants" in general, whether or not they had colluded with the Japanese, was a wartime measure to boost the morale and stabilize the market. Following the passage of the National Mobilization Act in spring 1942, the Nationalist government formalized its monopoly over key resources in the free regions.[50] The total mobilization of the economy for the war effort required an elimination of commodity speculation. In November 1942, the National Mobilization Commission punished two "treacherous merchants" as an example to others. Wu Zhaozhang, a branch manager of the Chuankang Bank, was found guilty of manipulating the agricultural market by hoarding large quantities of rice and vegetable seeds. Chen Zhongyu from the Chuanyan Bank was also alleged to have hoarded rice. In an investigation conducted by a military tribunal and a confidential trial by the commission, Wu was sentenced to death and Chen to life imprisonment.[51] The postwar punishment of economic *hanjian* was based on similar charges, though by then the defendants at least had access to some kind of judicial procedure.

For the Nationalist government, the "purification" of Shanghai's capitalists went hand in hand with restoring its control over China's industrial center and its former power base. After the war, one of Chiang Kai-shek's top priorities was to restore economic order and secure government revenue. The recovery of Shanghai's financial and industrial sectors was crucial to saving the government from bankruptcy and to rebuilding the nation.[52] In addition to confiscating enemy and puppet property, the Nationalist government developed new monetary policies, which unfortunately brought more chaos than order. With the return of the government and the businesses that had followed it to Chongqing, an enormous amount of *fabi* flooded into Shanghai's market, when the puppet *zhongchuquan* was still in circulation. On September 29, 1946, Chen Xing, head of the Central Bank, set an exchange rate of two hundred *zhongchuquan* to one *fabi*, a rate that favored the *fabi* but meant disaster for the people. Yet no one dared to protest, as defending the value of the *zhongchuquan* would be seen as *hanjian* behavior.[53]

Having formed a secret alliance with many of Shanghai's capitalists in wartime, Chiang Kai-shek attempted to strike a balance between carrying on the anti-*hanjian* cause and retaining the support he had gained from this group. The Nationalist government produced a list of economic *hanjian* accused of "attaching themselves to the puppet Wang regime" for arrest and trial.[54] The process and results of their trials reflected the power plays of prominent political and financial figures in or close to the Nationalist Party and government. When they attempted to interfere with the trials of economic *hanjian*, they discovered that their power had limits and that these high-profile trials were subject to forces and factors beyond their control.

The cases of Wen Lanting, Lin Kanghou, and Yuan Lüdeng were most revealing of the ambiguous nature of collaboration and the intricate politics involved in *hanjian* trials. All three were model entrepreneurs who had successfully carved out a space in colonial Shanghai for Chinese national industry. Wen cofounded the Shanghai Stock and Goods Exchange, the first exchange in Shanghai.[55] As the owner of a dozen textile factories in the lower Yangzi delta, Wen Lanting had held positions in multiple organizations promoting commerce and philanthropy. Yuan Lüdeng, a leading figure in Shanghai's financial circles, was also an active member of the Young Christian Association and the Welfare Association for Chinese Women and Children. Similarly, Lin's numerous titles spoke for his successful career, social visibility, and enthusiasm for public causes.

Had the Japanese never occupied Shanghai, all three would have been considered patriotic industrialists. During the Shanghai Incident in 1932, Wen Lanting vigorously solicited donations and provided support for the 19th Route Army. During the three-month Battle of Shanghai in 1937, Wen headed the Red Cross Society of China and organized several crews to rescue injured soldiers.[56] Yuan Lüdeng, the secretary general of the Shanghai Refugee Relief Association, also worked tirelessly to collect donations for war relief.

The Japanese takeover of Shanghai and its long-term occupation changed the life paths of the "three elders" as well as numerous others caught in the same quandary. The Nationalist government charged all three with the crime of "contributing to the Japanese control economy" by taking positions in the puppet "Commodity Control Commission" (Shangtonghui) and supplying the enemy with provisions.[57] The so-called control commissions were institutions formed to redirect Chinese industrial output and raw materials to meet Japanese wartime needs. In March 1943, the Wang Jingwei regime reorganized the control commissions already in existence and established the National Commerce Control Commission.[58] A majority of influential Chinese businessmen who remained in Shanghai voluntarily or involuntarily joined the commission, for which they were later charged with a major *hanjian* crime.

In their self-defense, these Chinese businessmen elaborated on the circumstantial reasons for their participation in the commission. Wen Lanting made the decision at a moment when Shanghai's entire textile industry was at stake. After the Japanese took over the International Settlement in 1941, they confiscated several Chinese textile factories that had been relocated there.[59] In exchange for returning the factories to Chinese control, the Japanese asked for a leading textile industrialist to take charge of the Commodity Control Commission and to facilitate the purchase of raw cotton in China.[60] Wen Lanting, as the head of the Textile Industry Association, who was present in Shanghai at the time, was a natural choice.

Wen likely accepted the position with approval from the Nationalist government. At the time, he was seventy-six years old and had little stake in the negotiations: he did not own any of the factories that the Japanese had confiscated. When pressed by the prosecution, Wen Lanting stated that he was instructed by Zhongtong to "penetrate the puppet commission."[61] Zhongtong did not back up Wen's story during his first trial.[62] Yet Wen's involvement in the Minhua Company showed that he apparently had communicated with Chongqing and was then regarded favorably by Chiang.

Wen insisted that he was not guilty of the crimes he was charged with, but he could defend himself only in vague language. He could not reveal his role in the Minhua Company or the trade between Shanghai and Chongqing, which would confuse and even enrage the public. More important, exposing this unknown aspect of the War of Resistance could land him in greater trouble. In his defense, Wen expressed his frustration with the legal ordeals he had had to endure and the involvement of intelligence agencies in this process: "I exhausted myself in philanthropic works. I cannot admit to the crimes listed in the indictment. I did what I did by following orders from the central government. So I cannot agree with what Juntong has written about me in their accusation letter, especially because I rescued many individuals who were arrested by the Japanese. While working with the enemy, I helped preserve national strength."[63] Wen grew increasingly emotional during the trial. Several times the court had to call for medical help, for Wen's agitation exacerbated his already frail physical condition.

The wartime activities of Wen Lanting resembled those of double agents. If they were revealed, the government's clandestine operations would compromise its image as the resistance state. The Nationalist government therefore could not or would not confirm any contributions Wen had made during the war. Judging by the witnesses arranged for Wen, however, Chiang Kai-shek provided or allowed some protection for this conscientious businessman turned *hanjian*. A clear signal was the presence of Qi Zaisheng, a Zhongtong agent, who testified that Wen had facilitated his release from Wang Jingwei's prison several times. In addition, Qi acknowledged that Wen had provided the central government with information on Japanese army provisions and the economic situation in occupied areas.[64]

Other witnesses shed light on the nuances of Wen's collaborationist activities and testified to the positive consequences of his presence on the Commodity Control Commission. Wu Kunsheng, the manager of the Shenxin Factory, confirmed that Wen strove to minimize the amount of raw cotton extracted by the Japanese from China. Yang Zhiyou from the Minfeng Textile Factory argued that Wen used "delaying tactics" (*huanbingzhiji*), a form of passive resistance, when interacting with the Japanese. In Yang's opinion, Wen had indeed contributed to "preserving national strength."[65] Having continued to lead the Shanghai textile industries during wartime, these witnesses were naturally sympathetic to Wen's predicament.

Wen's defense attorney, Lu Huimin, understood well the complicated politics underlying his client's case and tried to use various factors to Wen's advantage. He also felt an obligation to Wen, who had rescued him several times from Japanese detention.[66] While acknowledging that Wen's participation in the Commodity Commission was dishonorable, Lu tried to win Wen sympathy from the court and the public by lamenting the pressure that had been placed on this old man. Since the public assumed that most *hanjian* had collaborated for material gain, Lu stressed Wen's frugal lifestyle before and after his collaboration, pointing out that Wen had no property in his own name and lived on a simple diet. He then asked rhetorically, "How could such a person become *hanjian* and sell out his nation for personal gain?"[67]

Still, on September 12, 1946, the court found Wen Lanting guilty of three main counts of the *hanjian* crime. Wen had published a speech in the puppet-run *Shenbao* celebrating the "Great East Asian War" and the "return" of the Wang Jingwei regime to Nanjing. He was also found to have provided large quantities of grain and cotton to the Japanese army. Lastly, Wen used his social influence to raise one billion *zhongchuquan* for the Japanese air force. Wen was sentenced to eight years' imprisonment (later reduced to three and a half) and deprived of his civil rights as well as his property. Wen appealed to the Supreme Court for a retrial but passed away in July 1947 with his case undecided.

Yuan Lüdeng made a similar choice during wartime and suffered similar consequences. When the Japanese took over the International Settlement and reorganized the Shanghai Municipal Council in 1941, Yuan remained a board member.[68] Reflecting on this decision, Yuan later stated he had made "a minor sacrifice to preserve what was more important" (*baoquanzhe da xishengzhe xiao*).[69] Yuan later joined the National Chamber of Commerce and the National Commodity Control Commission under the Wang Jingwei government. Whatever his motivations, Yuan was well aware of the political consequences of these moves, and he took preemptive measures to appease Chongqing. After he joined the puppet Municipal Council in 1941, Yuan immediately notified Du Yuesheng so that Du would explain his dilemma and considerations to Chiang Kai-shek.[70]

Yuan's long-term friends and contacts in the Nationalist Party lobbied for a significant reduction of his original sentence—from life imprisonment to several years in prison. Chen Tingrui, a renowned lawyer and a personal friend of Yuan, exhausted his lawyerly skills and connections in arguing this case. Following Chen's advice, Yuan focused on contributions he had made when serving on the Commodity Control Commission while also showing remorse. Yuan recounted, for instance, how he forestalled the Japanese confiscatory purchase of rice in the fall of 1943 and helped alleviate the burden on Shanghai's residents.[71] Chen also arranged for several Juntong agents as well as other powerful figures to plead on Yuan's behalf.[72] As a result, Yuan was imprisoned for one year and was released in March 1948 in a "Great Amnesty" declared by Chiang in celebration of his election as president. Five years later, Yuan was again convicted of the *hanjian* crime, this time by the Communist government, and was sentenced to ten years' imprisonment. Yuan died in prison at the age of seventy-six.[73]

The case of Lin Kanghou, the last of the "three elders," shows the recurring patterns in the circumstances of collaboration and trials of the primary economic *hanjian*. Lin was sentenced to two years' imprisonment. As *Shenbao* pointed out, given their notoriety and the importance of their wartime positions, the "three elders" were treated with leniency. News reports and tabloids revealed the public's mixed feelings about the three, in contrast to the utter condemnation of Sheng You'an. During Wen's trials, *Shenbao* kept updating the readers on new developments in the courtroom and Wen's deteriorating health. According to the newspaper, Wen was still respected by Shanghai's residents, so much so that during his hospitalization, his daily visitors had filled three guest books with signatures and messages.[74]

Even the most critical account of *hanjian*, *Hideous Histories of* Hanjian (*Hanjian choushi*), commented that Wen and Yuan worked with the Japanese half-willingly at most. In this widely circulated pamphlet, the author suggested that Wen and Yuan showed indirect resistance while interacting with the Japanese. Wen was said to have appeared uncompromising, even critical, in his negotiations with the Japanese, but his translator would soften his vocabulary to avoid trouble. Yuan's public speeches frequently signaled his political ambivalence, but the puppet-run newspapers changed his words to make him seem a more docile collaborator.[75] Though the stories in *Hanjian choushi* were often based on rumors and hearsay, they nonetheless showed the willingness of the public to accept excuses for the collaboration of Wen and Yuan. These stories, in addition, demonstrated that in most cases, *hanjian* could not converse directly with the Japanese.

Whether or not this was the intention of the author, readers were left pondering the role of translation and propaganda in scenarios of collaboration.

The above are only a few examples of powerful economic *hanjian* on trial. Table 3.1 provides brief information on a selection of individuals convicted of similar crimes. In general, the media followed postwar trials closely, revealing problems with the legal proceedings and speculating on behind-the-scenes deals that affected the outcomes of *hanjian* cases. The media drew attention to the inconsistent sentences given to individuals who, in the eyes of the public, had done comparable harms to the nation. The banking magnate Zhu Boquan, for instance, served on the board of the Japanese-controlled Chinese Industrial Bank and the puppet Securities and Exchange Commission. Considered a "principal economic *hanjian*" (*jingji jujian*), Zhu was found guilty of "collaborating with the enemy nation and disturbing the financial order" and was sentenced to two years' imprisonment.[76] Qian Dakui, the vice president of the Central Reserve Bank, was charged with the same crime but sentenced to death.[77]

TABLE 3.1. A selection of major economic *hanjian* tried and convicted by the Nationalist government

Name	Position in the puppet regime	Sentence
Tang Shoumin	President, Reconstruction Bank	Life imprisonment and deprivation of civil rights for life; later reduced to eight years' imprisonment in a retrial, thanks to his connection with T. V. Soong, Chiang Kai-shek's brother-in-law. Released in early 1949 under the Great Amnesty.
Ma Jiliang	Head of the Department of General Affairs, Central Reserve Bank	Fifteen years' imprisonment and deprivation of civil rights for ten years.
Xu Tieshan	Manager, South Pacific Cigarette Company	Three years' imprisonment.
Wang Wuquan	Chair of Hangzhou Chamber of Commerce	Life imprisonment and deprivation of civil rights for life.
Jiang Shangda	Deputy chair of the Textile Association of Jiangsu, Zhejiang, and Anhui; member of the Cotton Control Commission and Commodity Control Commission	Imprisonment for one year and three months; deprivation of civil rights for two years. Jiang received a light sentence because he could prove that he participated in the Commodity Control Commission with Zhongtong's sanction and helped preserve 220 textile factories.

A good number of individuals with wealth and connections managed to escape legal punishment for their wartime activities. The businessman Liu Hongsheng had picked the right side during the war and established solid connections with Chongqing. Two of his sons, however, had stayed in Shanghai and made certain compromises. They were faced with the charge of the *hanjian* crime. Liu pleaded for help from the head of the Shanghai police and the mayor of Hangzhou before he discovered that his sons had found themselves the ultimate protector. By hosting Dai Li and holding extravagant receptions in his honor on his arrival in Shanghai, the Liu brothers became Dai's privileged guests rather than his political prisoners.[78]

The newspapers commented that only minor *hanjian* who had no connections with the Nationalist government were caught and punished. According to *Dagong bao*, of the thirty-four convicted by the Supreme Court in February and March 1946, most were "minor *hanjian*" whose crimes had had a limited impact on the nation or the war effort.[79] For instance, Xu Xing, a sentinel working for the puppet government in Shenzhuang, Shanghai, was sentenced to eight years' imprisonment for extorting a total of twenty-five thousand *zhongchuquan* from passersby. Those who were convicted were certainly not all innocent, but they did not necessarily do greater wrong than those who walked free.

Corruption of the justice system through the exchange of favors was coupled with power struggles among different government agencies and individuals. The wartime coalition among Chiang's intelligence agents, the military, Sanqingtuan, and the underworld in Shanghai broke up as soon as the war was over. Individuals and institutions that had gained tremendous executive and punitive power during the war attempted to retain their authority and extend it in recently recovered regions. The competition between Zhongtong and Juntong led to a contest for arresting the greatest number of *hanjian* after the war, especially in Shanghai. Economic *hanjian*, because of their handsome assets and money they could offer for assistance leading to their acquittal, were the ideal prey. Many economic *hanjian* had maintained close connections with the Chen brothers and had based their wartime decisions on instructions from Zhongtong. Juntong, however, was the organization in charge of identifying and incarcerating *hanjian*. In September 1945, right after the war ended, Dai Li arrived in Shanghai and launched a Juntong office there to arrest *hanjian* and confiscate their property.[80] Dai Li's office showed no leniency toward those sheltered by Zhongtong. Many, including the "three elders," were arrested by Juntong and faced judicial investigation and trial. The Zhongtong-Juntong rivalry was also evident in the arrangement of witnesses for important *hanjian* on trial.

THE CASE OF LI ZE

Among all the convictions of economic *hanjian*, Li Ze's case was most illuminating not only of the struggles within the Nationalist government but also of the larger socioeconomic background and factors beyond the Nationalist government's control. Li Ze's case occurred at a moment when Chiang Kai-shek was attempting to restore the normalcy of the administration and the civil justice system. It thus provided a good opportunity for the Shanghai Municipal Police and Shanghai High Court to assume the authority of punishing *hanjian*, thereby undermining Juntong's power in the area. The transfer of authority, however, was fraught with contradictions and backlash effects.

This case also captured the increasing social tension in postwar Shanghai.[81] After the Japanese surrender, life did not improve for many. Economic dislocation threatened social stability and weakened public confidence in Nationalist rule. Newspapers, especially left-leaning ones, questioned the integrity of Chinese capitalists, even those who were not identified by the state as economic *hanjian*. Communist propaganda influenced disenfranchised social groups. The Communist Party channeled the anti-*hanjian* momentum in order to strike down its class enemies. Workers at odds with management found it easy to invoke suspicion of the employers' sources of wealth and to act on the state's call to expose *hanjian*.

Li Ze was a leading figure in Shanghai's retail industry. His uncle, Li Minzhou, had founded one of Shanghai's top four department stores, the Xinxin Company. When Li Minzhou was assassinated by a disgruntled employee in 1935, Li Ze became the general manager of this family business. Because of Li's status in the business world, he was pursued by representatives from Chongqing as well as the Wang Jingwei regime. Like the "three elders," Li Ze participated in more than one organization sponsored by the Japanese while secretly financing various projects and operations organized by Chongqing. Among other contributions, Li donated a total of seventy-seven million *fabi* to the Pudong branch of the Loyal and Patriotic Army.[82] Li's background, wartime conduct, and political calculations were fully exposed in the months after Shu Yueqiao, a former employee, accused him of the *hanjian* crime.

In contrast with the obscure accusers of other cases, Shu Yueqiao, by exposing Li Ze, became a celebrity and was portrayed as a model citizen by the media. Shu was a well-traveled, worldly individual. Originally from Zhejiang, he had received a middle-school education in Beijing, attended a military academy, and served in the army. Under the Japanese occupation, Shu worked as a waiter at the Xindu restaurant, a business affiliated with the Xinxin Company, and "depended on tips to survive."[83] Li Ze, then manager of Xindu, confiscated all the tips in the name of the company, leaving the waiters only their meager salaries to live on. Unlike other employees, who were angry but did not dare to protest, Shu asked for a share of the tips. As a result, Li Ze fired him.

While he may have been motivated in part by a genuine hatred of *hanjian*, Shu found the perfect opportunity to get back at Li Ze when Chiang Kai-shek called for the common people to expose *hanjian* whom the state had overlooked. Shu Yueqiao carried out his plan to bring down Li Ze in several stages. He first wrote letters to various branches of the government and the Third Front of the Nationalist army. In a letter addressed to the Ministry of Justice, Shu listed Li Ze's *hanjian* crimes as follows:

1. Purchasing Japanese products in late 1936, while the Shanghai people were boycotting Japanese goods. Moreover, Li Ze had his cargo escorted by a Japanese warship.
2. Taking positions in puppet institutions, including the National Commodity Control Commission and a committee that managed Allied-owned property taken by the Japanese.
3. Donating one hundred thousand kilograms of iron to the Japanese.
4. Hiring a senior captain named Kishida Yutaka from the Japanese navy as a consultant to the Xinxin Company.
5. Sending representatives and gifts to celebrate the foundation of the puppet state of Manchukuo, as well as birthdays and weddings of leading puppet officials.[84]

What enraged Shu was not only that Li Ze had escaped the law but also that he masqueraded as a contributor to the War of Resistance (*kangzhan yougong fenzi*), thanks to his connections to Juntong.

Having received no reply from the Ministry of Justice, Shu turned to the public and the media for help. On October 5, 1945, Shu denounced Li Ze's *hanjian* activities at the front door of the Xinxin Company in a passionate speech while distributing flyers and posters.[85] He then contacted newspapers that had been active in in exposing *hanjian* and covering their trials. The left-wing newspaper *Zhoubao* was the first to take up this case by publishing "An open letter from Xinxin employees" on October 8, 1945.

Compared to Shu Yueqiao's accusation letter, this open letter was more diplomatically crafted to win sympathy from the government and the public. It started with praise of the government:

> The Great War to liberate our nation from foreign control finally ended with our victory. . . . With overflowing joy and excitement in our hearts, we pay respects to our highest leader Generalissimo Chiang. In the last two months, newspapers and magazines have been filled with stories of punishing *hanjian*. A number of *hanjian* have been put on trial, which cheered the common people who had been oppressed by them. The consensus among the people is to expose and eliminate *hanjian* once and for all. It seems that the state has not been able to achieve this goal. For instance, the manager of the Xinxin Company, Li Ze (a.k.a. Li Ruotao), is indeed a problematic figure.

The open letter detailed Li Ze's traitorous activities, as listed in Shu Yueqiao's initial letter of accusation. It ended with an expression of collective determination: "We now act against our own interest to expose our manager, and are determined to carry out this cause. . . . We have always heard that your newspaper holds a righteous attitude on political and social matters, so we hope you could allow us a space in your newspaper to publish this letter. In this way, the sense of justice upheld by this society will bring about an appropriate judgment on Li Ze."[86]

By January 1946, this letter had appeared in several widely read newspapers and magazines. Among them were the *Times Daily* (Shidai ribao) and *Selected News and Literature* (Wencui), which published the story with minor variations.[87] Before long, several others had joined Shu's cause, and the group soon expanded to include eight hundred Xinxin employees.[88]

To develop one individual's accusations into a social movement required organizational skills and a clear political agenda. These were found in Han Wucheng, one of the ten most articulate supporters of Shu Yueqiao. Han, a salesman in the Xinxin Company, was also a leading member of the Shanghai General Labor Union.[89] The CCP had developed a party branch at the Xinxin Company, and at the time, Han was preparing to launch a labor movement at Xinxin. Shu Yueqiao's accusation of Li Ze provided a perfect

pretext for the labor movement and for a campaign against the whole capitalist class in Shanghai.[90] Han Wucheng managed to collect signatures
from the eight hundred employees of Xinxin in three months, making
them the first group of workers in postwar Shanghai to attempt to overthrow
the capitalist order by taking advantage of the government-sanctioned
anti-*hanjian* campaign.

The subsequent developments in the case were characteristic of class
struggle. On January 7, Xinxin employees held a press conference and made
five demands, which they had printed on flyers and disseminated the previous day.[91] They demanded Li Ze's immediate arrest, trial, and sentencing
under anti-*hanjian* laws; confiscation of Li Ze's property to support the
unemployed; and denunciation of Li Ze by any fellow citizens he had
exploited during the occupation. As the organizer of the press conference,
Han Wucheng clarified that the employees did not hold personal grudges
against Li Ze. Rather, they were acting out of a genuine concern for their
nation.

The press conference achieved the desired result. All journalists present
promised to support the employees' righteous cause. One journalist encouraged the employees by referring to a case in Guangxi in which a corrupt
official was sentenced to life imprisonment only because the government
was under constant media pressure. On the day of the press conference,
Xuan Tiewu, the head of the Shanghai police, ordered the arrest of Li Ze.
Newspapers celebrated Li's arrest as a victory of the common people against
the wealthy parasites of society. *Daying Evening Paper* (Daying yebao)
reported on the arrest with an editorial titled "First Anti-*hanjian* Battle by
Common Citizens Produces Result: Xinxin Company's Manager Li Ze
Arrested."[92] *Iron Gazetteer* (Tiebao) ridiculed Li for losing his composure
in the presence of the police and for demanding to ride in his own car to
the police office.[93]

Li Ze's quick arrest, however, was neither a result of media pressure nor
a signal of the victory of the common people. Rather, it was triggered by
personal and institutional conflicts within the Nationalist administration.
The head of Juntong, Dai Li, had seen in the punishment of *hanjian* a golden
opportunity for taking control of China's police force. Immediately after
the war, the Songjiang-Shanghai Garrison Headquarters (Songhu Jingbei
Silingbu), which took orders from Juntong, was in charge of arresting and
prosecuting *hanjian*. With the garrison headquarters and Juntong's Shanghai branch under his authority, Dai Li attempted to encroach on the territory of the Shanghai police force. In response, Chiang Kai-shek appointed

Xuan Tiewu, his trusted subordinate, who never got along with Dai Li, as the head of the Shanghai Municipal Police.[94]

The Xinxin workers' accusation provided justification for Xuan Tiewu to take down Li Ze, a personal friend of Dai Li and a protégé of Juntong. Dai Li was aware that Li's wartime conduct was sufficient to warrant a *hanjian* charge. At the same time, he was grateful for Li's help with Juntong's work and considered Li indispensable to building his power base in postwar Shanghai. Dai Li decided to help Li Ze escape. In November 1945, in the middle of arresting other economic *hanjian*, Dai Li arranged to help Li Ze and Guo Shun, the manager of the Yong'an Company, to flee to the United States. Guo Shun left, but Li Ze did not. When Xuan Tiewu learned of this arrangement, he decided to show off his recently gained power by arresting Li Ze.[95]

There were good reasons to believe that Chiang Kai-shek supported Xuan Tiewu in using Li Ze's case to undermine Juntong's growing power.[96] Chiang personally replied to Shu Yueqiao's letter of accusation, promising to urge the judiciary to conduct a thorough investigation and restore justice.[97] Soon afterward, Bi Gaokui, the superintendent of the Song-Hu Garrison Command, who reported to Juntong, was dismissed from his post. The official reason for Bi's dismissal was "an error in an old case"; yet it takes little to deduce that what really got Bi into trouble was his lenient treatment of Li Ze.[98]

The trial of Li Ze is the best-recorded *hanjian* case in the postwar period, thanks to intensive media coverage all the way through. Newspapers vividly reported on the efforts of Li Ze and his close acquaintances to extricate him from the lawsuit and scandal. *Warfront Daily* (Qianxian ribao) spotted Li buying up the issues of *Shidai ribao* that contained the accusation letter at thirty times the regular price. The editor thus commented that "a major *hanjian* is also a major *jianshang*" (treacherous merchant) for thinking that he could buy his way out of punishment and public denunciation.[99] Days before his arrest, Li was reported to have held a banquet for twenty "distinguished guests" at the luxurious Xin Yong'an Club at a total cost of ninety thousand *fabi*. Managers of the three other major department stores in Shanghai feted government and military officials on Li's behalf. After Li Ze's arrest, Li Shanchu, a loyal subordinate of Li Ze, allegedly attempted to doctor the Xinxin Company's accounts. Li Ze's family members were reported to have hosted two important officials at the Xindu Restaurant.[100] Newspapers then urged the government to take heed of such maneuvers and hold an open trial for Li Ze as soon as possible.

The media also provided the public with information on other parties that played important roles in this case. It was disclosed that *Tiebao*, after publishing the earliest open letter against Li Ze in October 1945, had received a warning from an anonymous source. The editors simply ignored the warning.[101] Shu Yueqiao was now in the spotlight as "the first in Shanghai to have heroically exposed a major *hanjian*."[102] Shu reinforced this impression by revealing that since he had initiated the accusation, several "strange visitors" had come to his house, alternately threatening him to give up the lawsuit and attempting to buy him over.[103] Shu claimed that although he had been unemployed, he would not take money from Li Ze at the price of justice, and he would pursue this case to the end.

The high-caliber prosecution and defense teams of Li Ze's case also attracted media attention. The famous lawyer and patriot Sha Qianli served as the legal consultant for the accusers. Li Ze and his family first sought help from influential political figures, including Wu Tiecheng, secretary general of the Nationalist Party's Central Committee, and Zhang Naiqi, a core member of the China Democratic League. Wu and Zhang decided not to get involved in a case with such "political complications."[104] On their recommendation, Li Ze hired three famous and well-connected defense lawyers: Zhang Shizhao, Chen Tingrui, and Guo Rui.

A tug of war between the prosecution and the defense meant that the first two trials went nowhere. Among the crimes listed by Shu Yueqiao and Xinxin employees, only one seemed beyond doubt: that Li Ze had served on the National Commerce Control Commission. The defense insisted that this was a strategic move, which those who had lived under the occupation should understand. As for Li Ze's relations to the puppet regimes, his business ties to the Japanese, and his facilitation of Juntong's work, neither party was able to present evidence solid enough to settle the case.[105] Shu Yueqiao's motivation for accusing Li Ze also became the subject of court debates. Li Ze's witnesses maintained that Shu Yueqiao was taking revenge on Li after failing in efforts to blackmail him. Shu admitted that he had brought the lawsuits against Li partly because he considered it unfair that a *hanjian* had become so much better off than he was. The court decided that Shu's motivation was irrelevant to the charges against Li Ze.[106]

To bolster Li's defense, his lawyer, Chen Tingrui, flew to Chongqing and brought back a letter from Juntong that elaborated on Li's various contributions to the War of Resistance. On one occasion during the wear, Juntong agents were disguised as Xinxin employees. When several were arrested by Wang Jingwei's secret police on March 8, 1942, Li Ze bailed them out in the name of the company. Moreover, Li Ze responded to Juntong's call for Shanghai's capitalists to make donations to prepare for the return of the central government. His donation accounted for a third of the total collected.[107]

In addition to this official letter from Juntong, an agent, Huang Ruitang, wrote to offer his personal support of Li Ze. Huang elaborated on the circumstances of Li's participation in the Commodity Control Commission. Huang acknowledged that Li had discussed this matter extensively with him, and he had advised Li to accept the position for his personal safety and to facilitate Juntong's underground work. Chen Hao, the head of Juntong's Shanghai branch, was also supportive of this move. Both reassured Li that he would not be blamed for taking the position, providing that he did no real harm to the resistance efforts.[108]

These letters were accepted by the court, but they failed to convince the prosecution and the general public of Li's innocence. The prosecution also questioned the admissibility of these materials as evidence, as they were received after the deadline and could well have been a product of Chen's manipulation of personal connections. *Zhoubao* commented on Li Ze's skills of "political speculation" (*zhengzhi touji*). It observed that many *hanjian*, economic *hanjian* in particular, flirted with both sides during the war to minimize their political risks and financial losses.[109]

To capture readers' interest and to influence public opinion in this case, newspaper editors and reporters dug up back stories on the various parties involved. Some reports worked to Li Ze's advantage. Reporters from *Xinbao* visited his house and published an emotional, sympathetic interview with his sixteen-year-old daughter, who insisted that her father had been wronged. She believed that Xinxin employees had developed a grudge against Li when he prohibited them from performing a play and refused to increase their salaries. His daughter maintained that on this occasion her father was merely following orders from higher up to control spontaneous employee performances, but the employees had interpreted this as a suppression of their rights. She was also convinced that Li Ze was an undercover agent for Juntong.[110]

With the CCP operating behind the stage, reports against Li Ze proliferated in left-leaning newspapers. Small pamphlets condemning him were disseminated on the eve of Li Ze's third trial. A certain Hot-Blooded Press (Rexue Chubanshe) published *The Hideous History of* Hanjian *Li Ze, Manager of the Xinxin Company*, which was apparently modeled after the popular literary series *Hanjian choushi*.[111] This pamphlet was a collection

of news articles critical of Li Ze since the publication of the first open letter. The first page showed photos of Shu Yueqiao and Xinxin employees
who had denounced Li Ze as *hanjian*, thus giving a human face to anti-
hanjian activism.

Those who called for Li Ze's punishment went one step further and
criticized the anti-*hanjian* campaigns for being too lenient and corrupt in
general. Shu Yueqiao related a report from an unspecified source about how
the Italian people executed Benito Mussolini without a trial, commenting
that "those who committed the most heinous crime should be executed
immediately, for everyone has witnessed their crime."[112] As a contrast, in
China, "a major *hanjian* like Li Ze is put on trial several times (as if the court
was not sure of the crimes he had committed)." The length of the trials,
said Shu, allowed time for Li's defense lawyers to produce false evidence.
Shu's comparison and criticisms of the anti-*hanjian* campaigns in China
showed that the Nationalist government's effort to globalize and justify the
trials of *hanjian* backfired. They also revealed the widely held attitude that
the judicial trials of *hanjian* were perfunctory.

Public attention also focused on the ethics of the government officials
and personnel involved in Li Ze's case. One editorial noted that "Li Ze tried
to buy his innocence by stuffing gold bars into officials' pockets" and alleged
that "since the beginning of this case, there probably have been more than
a hundred officials who would be found guilty of corruption."[113] The editor
even compared this case to the late Qing legal case of Yang Naiwu and Xiao
Baicai, which was notorious for the large number of officials incriminated
for the miscarriage of justice.[114] Some officials involved, such as Bi Gaokui,
were indeed removed from office, no less because they were on the losing
side of the power struggle than because the government was concerned
with their integrity.

The court's final verdict on Li Ze included a three-year prison term and
confiscation of all his property, a decision made to balance the interest and
demands of the different parties involved, including Juntong. Though Juntong was denied the power of policing Shanghai, it remained a powerful
and dangerous organ that the court could not just ignore. On the prosecution's side were not only those who wanted to strip Juntong of its power in
Shanghai but also public opinion. Many considered this punishment too
lenient.[115] Some newspapers juxtaposed Li's sentence with those of two
minor *hanjian* convicted on the same day. One was sentenced to seven
years in prison and the other to ten years.[116]

The court's ruling on Li Ze failed to please either side. Li Ze and his accusers both appealed to the Supreme Court for a retrial, for which they launched a new round of lobbying and publicity. Li Ze's family pleaded for sympathy and help from social groups who shared a similar socioeconomic background and wartime experience. Li's wife wrote to the Guangzhou Sojourners' Association in Shanghai, asking for their intervention in regard to the "unjust treatment" her husband had received. She claimed that her husband had not joined the Commodity Control Commission for personal gain and that "his heart has always been with the Han people and their destiny" (*xincun hanshi*).[117] *Hanshi*, literally "the house of the Han dynasty," came to represent China and its cultural essence under legitimate rule. *Xincun hanshi* is an idiom based on the story of General Guan Yu, who personifies loyalty and righteousness in the traditional Chinese value system.[118] Mrs. Li's implicit comparison of her husband to Guan Yu, who made strategic moves in order to continue serving the Han, was effective. About eighty individuals from Shanghai's business circles petitioned for clemency on behalf of Li Ze, while accusers continued to rally media support for a harsher punishment.[119] Despite the efforts made by each side, the Supreme Court upheld the original verdict.

The media followed up on Li Ze's prison life. Locked up in the Shanghai Tilanqiao prison with many other *hanjian*, including Wang Jingwei's widow Chen Bijun, Li Ze apparently did not suffer as much as many had wished. Newspapers reported how *jianshu* (literally, "family members of *hanjian*," though the word can also be interpreted to mean "those of the *hanjian* type") sent food, comfortable clothing, and other daily necessities to Li Ze and other prisoners twice a week.[120] *Lianhe bao* reported bitterly that since Li Ze's arrest on January 7, 1946, Xinxin Company had considered him on leave and continued to pay his full salary.[121]

The repercussions of this case extended from Li and his family to the Xinxin Company and to Shanghai's business world. After his release from prison, Li lost his old position at Xinxin and his credibility among business contacts, acquaintances, and clients. He went to Hong Kong to start afresh.[122] The value of Xinxin's stock fluctuated dramatically during Li's arrest and trial. Other members of the management were also put in precarious positions once Li Ze's wartime activities were disclosed and publicized.[123] Following the Xinxin employees' example, labor unions from other companies and factories denounced their employers.[124] Workers from the Kangyuan Metal Can Factory accused their manager, Xiang

Kangyuan, of the *hanjian* crime on the grounds of Xiang's participation in the puppet Shanghai Municipal Consulting Committee, among other things.[125] To the surprise and dismay of the Nationalist government, the anti-*hanjian* campaigns had provided an impetus to the labor movement in postwar Shanghai.

CONCLUSION

When Li Ze's wife petitioned for help from acquaintances and contacts of her husband, she expressed the following grievances: "If my husband's company had been in the free regions, he would not have been appointed to such a position. Had he not been the manager of a famous company, he would not have encountered such adversity. . . . My husband did nothing more than playing along with the enemy to preserve the company and provide support to the resistance. Yet now he has been found guilty of collaboration. How could this happen in a nation that claims to uphold the rule of law?"[126]

Li Ze could have demonstrated greater resolve in resisting Japanese demands. Many individuals with similar social status and reputation staunchly refused to work with the Japanese or the Wang Jingwei regime. Given the vicissitudes that Shanghai's capitalists had experienced from the early 1930s to 1949, however, Mrs. Li's words were not without some truth.

During the war and occupation, China's leading capitalists had only two options. They could unwaveringly resist, thereby putting their businesses, family and their lives in danger. Or they could collaborate, at the expense of their reputation, conscience, and sometimes their lives. For those who chose to stay in wartime Shanghai, there was no way out. Many of those who were later labeled economic *hanjian* had been community builders and organizers of war relief before the occupation. Many collaborated with Chongqing's knowledge and used their positions in puppet institutions to facilitate resistance efforts. Their political ambivalence might have been a mask, a means of survival, a strategy to preserve the greater good, a psychological defense from guilt, or a combination of different factors.

The postwar political and social environment of upheaval and blame, however, allowed no room for a calm and nuanced analysis of the roles or motivations of economic *hanjian*. As the postwar trials show, the general public applied a simplistic black-and-white approach to evaluating the integrity of public figures. The Nationalist government, especially its leaders, was aware of the ambivalent positions of many alleged economic *hanjian*, but it could not reveal secret wartime alliances and communications to the public. Nationalist intelligence officers selectively testified on behalf of capitalists who were put on trial. In some cases, their testimony was based on real contributions by these individuals, but in other cases it was the product of bribery or nepotism.

Political interference and power struggles impeded justice in the trials of *hanjian* cases and disheartened the general public. A journalist from *Dagong bao* commented that all those who had served in or worked for the puppet regime, regardless of their claims to be underground contacts for Chongqing, should be investigated and put on trial in order to ensure that "the smoke curtain of 'underground work' would not hinder the work of investigating *hanjian*."[127] In the race to reclaim power and resources in key regions, various government branches and institutions maneuvered the prosecution and punishment of *hanjian* to further their own interests.

To the people's disappointment, despite the vigor of the prosecutions, the anti-*hanjian* campaigns did not give rise to a righteous and honest government. To ease budgetary stresses and compensate for financial losses, the state confiscated property that had been appropriated or built by the Japanese and their Chinese collaborators. Despite media and public scrutiny, many Nationalist officials turned the takeover process into a scandalous misappropriation of resources to which the common people had no access.

At the peak of the postwar anti-*hanjian* campaign, members of the Chinese populace who lacked privilege or power were struggling to survive. The economy continued to deteriorate between 1945 and 1949. Class conflicts intensified in major industrial centers, and the gap between common citizens and the privileged few widened. At this juncture, as the case of Li Ze shows, left-wing leaders and advocates capitalized on the mishandled purge of *hanjian* by the Nationalist state. Accusations against economic *hanjian*, in particular, enabled leaders of labor movement to kill two birds with one stone: the capitalist class and the Nationalist state's political legitimacy.

CHAPTER 4

ENGENDERING CONTEMPT FOR FEMALE *HANJIAN* AND CULTURAL *HANJIAN*

CHIANG KAI-SHEK'S GOVERNMENT DIRECTED THE ANTI-*HANJIAN* campaigns mainly to strip power and legitimacy from those who founded and joined opposing regimes. Leaders and high-ranking officials in Japan-sponsored governments and organizations facilitated the expansion and entrenchment of Japanese imperialism in China. Moreover, they marginalized Chiang's government in exile and competed with it for jurisdiction over China. The Nationalists also targeted economic *hanjian* who contributed to a "control economy" under Japanese command and reduced the resources available to the resistance forces. The activities of these political figures and financiers had a direct impact on the morale and fighting capacity of the nation.

The groups purged and publicly denounced also included "cultural *hanjian*" (*wenhua hanjian*) and "female *hanjian*" (*nühanjian*). The former was a loosely defined category of individuals involved in education, literature, journalism, and the arts. Some of these people were powerful government figures and well-established scholars; others were less conspicuous. "Female *hanjian*" was a label applied to an array of women ranging from Shanghai's most popular writers to social butterflies. A few individuals, such as Su Qing and Zhang Ailing, fit into both categories. Writing from occupied Shanghai, Su and Zhang were successful, economically independent women who claimed large audiences. Because their works deviated from the grand narrative of nationalism and resistance and they were personally associated with male *hanjian*, they were branded both "cultural *hanjian*" and "female *hanjian*."

The experiences of cultural *hanjian* and female *hanjian* reveal the discrepancy between the popular understanding of collaboration and the state definition. Most individuals in these two categories were not the primary targets of the state. Because of their news value, however, they featured prominently in popular anti-*hanjian* discourse. After the war, a distinct genre of literature appeared in newspapers, tabloids, and pamphlets. With titles such as *Criminal Histories of Cultural* Hanjian (Wenhua hanjian zui'eshi) and *Hideous Histories of Female* Hanjian (Nühanjian choushi), these works claimed to reveal the unknown stories of alleged *hanjian*.[1] This genre reflected a postwar conservatism in society and the literary world. These vulgar yet lively pieces also catered to the taste of the reading public, who consumed stories of *hanjian* celebrities with pleasure and disdain.

Gendered aspects of the popular anti-*hanjian* literature explained its popularity and highlighted the use of verbal violence as a tool against *hanjian*. The Regulations identified *hanjian* based on their wartime conduct and stipulated punishments regardless of their age, gender or ethnicity. Anti-*hanjian* pamphlets and tabloids, however, regularly deployed a highly gendered vocabulary to diminish the masculinity of male *hanjian* and the personhood of female *hanjian*. Complementing the legal purge, this literature turned these individuals into social outcasts and influenced the ways in which political crimes were exposed and transposed to other aspects of social life.

CULTURAL *HANJIAN* ON TRIAL

As with economic *hanjian*, there was no uniform, official definition of "cultural *hanjian*." The Nationalist state did not coin this term; rather, it adopted the term from popular discourse. According to the Regulations, the state considered the following individuals as potential cultural *hanjian*:[2]

> Principals of any postsecondary schools or administrators of similar institutions sponsored by the Japanese or the puppet regimes;
> Editors, directors, or managers in any press, newspaper, or magazine that produced propaganda for the Japanese army or puppet regimes;
> Members of any movie studio, radio station, or other media or cultural organization in the occupied areas that produced propaganda for the puppet regimes.

Individuals in these categories, on being accused of any conduct that benefited the enemy or harmed the people, were to be prosecuted as cultural *hanjian*. As recorded by Juntong, eight individuals who were recognized as cultural *hanjian* were assassinated between 1935 and 1945. One of them was Mu Shiying, an avant-garde writer who was later characterized as "China's lost modernist" (see chapter 2). For decades, the general public and intellectuals in China considered the assassination of Mu justified. Until recently, few knew that Mu had been working as an underground Zhongtong agent and was mistakenly killed as a *hanjian*.[3]

After the war, the Nationalist government did not put many cultural *hanjian* on trial. From December 1945 to early 1948, cultural *hanjian* accounted for only about 2 percent of all the *hanjian* convicted in Shanghai, and they received lighter than average punishments.[4] Those who were convicted had mostly been involved in producing enemy or puppet propaganda. Assisting in the production of enemy propaganda constituted treason or similar offenses for reasons not difficult to fathom, and it remains a crime in various jurisdictions today. In 2006, an American-born convert to Islam, Adam Gahahn, became the first American to be charged with treason since the end of World War II, for affiliation with "an enemy of the United States, namely al-Qaeda" and "appearing in terrorist propaganda."[5]

During the War of Resistance, numerous newspapers in occupied areas were taken over by the Japanese, and to varying degrees became champions of Japan's "Great East Asian War." Promoted as the Daitoa Senso in Japanese and Dadongya Zhanzheng in Chinese, this war had the alleged goal of liberating Asian nations from Western imperialism. To strengthen cultural ties between China and Japan and to consolidate the Japanese occupation in China, the Japanese army and its Chinese collaborators planned numerous events to bring together literary figures from both nations. Promoting such messages and endeavors among the Chinese public certainly weakened the force of the resistance propaganda disseminated by the anti-Japanese United Front. In the postwar trials, therefore, well-known editors, including Tao Kangde from *China Weekly*, Zhang Ke from *Dadong Weekly*, and Liang Shi from *China Daily*, all publications sponsored by the puppet regime, were convicted of the *hanjian* crime.

Certain prominent individuals in journalism were convicted no less for their political dissidence than for their vocal support of Japan. Chen Binhe, *Shenbao*'s long-term editor, who continued his work after the Japanese takeover, became one of the most-wanted *hanjian*, partly for his left-wing connections and partly for his constant harsh criticism of the Chiang Kai-shek administration. A self-made "literary man" (*wenren*), Chen Binhe emerged in 1930s Shanghai as an eminent editor despite his lack of formal education beyond middle school.[6] As his career path repeatedly demonstrated, Chen's strengths lay in his resourcefulness and his abilities to work with people of diverse backgrounds and political positions.

Chen Binhe's Japan connections had enabled him to advance in his career, yet his attitude toward Japan had been ambivalent and shifting. In 1928 Chen met with a Japanese consular official in Shanghai, Iwai Eiichi, and became Iwai's informant.[7] With Iwai's support, Chen edited and produced the monthly *Japanese Studies* (Riben yanjiu, 1929–31). During this period, Chen made great efforts to become a Japan expert, making several field trips to Manchuria to study Japan's strategic planning and empire building. In 1931 Chen began his career at *Shenbao* as head of its editorial division. In this role, Chen appeared to be a patriot who consistently denounced Japanese military aggression and Chiang Kai-shek's policy of nonresistance. In addition, he invited influential educators and social activists to contribute editorials, making *Shenbao* a mouthpiece for the resistance.[8]

Chen's political consciousness and audacious personality as an editor were also reflected in his reforms of the *Shenbao* supplement *Free Talk* (Ziyoutan). Chen believed that urbanites in Shanghai spent more time reading the supplement than the newspaper itself and that editors had not paid enough attention to this section. *Free Talk* had been dominated by the "Mandarin Duck and Butterfly" genre, including martial arts fiction, detective fiction, and sentimental love stories. Chen Binhe eliminated almost all this sort of literature and replaced it with essays by writers of the New Culture generation and left-wing writers such as Li Liewen, Lu Xun, and Mao Dun.

Shenbao in this period played a leading role in directing public opinion against a state that appeared oppressive, corrupt, and indecisive in the face of foreign aggression, and its status owed much to Chen Binhe's vision and effort. In the summer of 1932, *Shenbao* published three editorials criticizing the Nationalist government for its corruption and for prioritizing military operations against the Communist party over resisting the Japanese. In response, Chiang Kai-shek temporarily suspended the circulation of *Shenbao* and threatened to ban the newspaper unless Li Liewen, Chen Binhe, Tao Xingzhi, and Huang Yanpei were fired. Chiang also required *Shenbao* to be placed under the supervision of the Nationalist Office of Propaganda. Shi Liangcai, the widely respected founder and owner of *Shenbao*, agreed to some of the terms but refused to subject the newspaper to the party's supervision. As a result, Shi was assassinated in 1934 by Dai Li's agents, and Chen Binhe was forced into exile in Hong Kong until 1942.[9]

For Chen, collaborating with the Japanese offered a chance to resume his career in journalism. By the time of his return to Shanghai, *Shenbao* had been taken over by the Japanese, and many individuals in the Wang Jingwei government were competing for the position of its editor in chief. Chen got this much-desired job thanks to his past connections with Japan and his impressive résumé. According to Jin Xiongbai, the chief editor of *Pingbao* and Zhou Fohai's close contact, Chen resumed his work for Iwai Eiichi at the same time. As the editor of a collaborationist newspaper, Chen did his part to keep the Japanese satisfied. Whenever Japan gained the upper hand in battles against the Allied powers, for instance, Chen would announce the news in *Shenbao* with red headlines, which were typically reserved for inspirational national news.

Chen's contemporaries and later scholars have struggled to figure out his convoluted political affiliations and allegiances. At least on the surface, Chen acted according to the dictates of circumstance rather than consistently following any particular leader or ideology. One scholar commented that Chen "had his own ways of dealing with the Japanese."[10] In actuality, Chen often took advantage of his good relations with the Japanese to shelter industrialists in Shanghai as well as the local community. In the eyes of most of the public, however, Chen's position and conduct indisputably made him a *hanjian*.

Indeed, Chen had formed strong connections with the Japanese in his own right, rather than through Wang Jingwei; they went back further and appeared more solid than Wang's own relations with the Japanese. In fact, *Shenbao* under Chen Binhe was not friendly to Wang Jingwei or his administration: it often mocked Wang's officials and his police force. Furthermore, Chen did not invest in both political camps for self-preservation, as many did at the time. Having foreseen a Japanese defeat, Zhou Fohai, a key member of the Wang Jingwei government, started to prepare for Chiang's return toward the end of the war. Chen considered it unwise for Zhou Fohai and Jin Xiongbai, among others, to play this dangerous game. He expressed his concerns as follows: "Japan is going to lose the war for sure now. But they still have millions of soldiers here, enough to wipe out all of you. If the Japanese decide to conduct a massacre before they retreat, that is because of people like you [who work for both sides]. If that moment comes, only I, Chen Binhe, stand a chance of stopping them. They believe that I am their real friend, unlike many people in the puppet regime. So my words will carry some weight."[11] Jin Xiongbai, himself a controversial figure who flirted with all sides, was never sure of Chen's ultimate political position and intent, but he acknowledged the force of Chen's words.

Most noteworthy and unforgivable about Chen Binhe in the eyes of Chongqing were his attacks on Chiang Kai-shek and his government. Chen went out of his way to report Chiang's contradictory comments and conduct over the preceding two decades. Criticisms so personal and meticulous, according to Jin Xiongbai, were rare even in regions under the Japanese and puppet control.[12] Following the outbreak of the Pacific War, for instance, Chen Binhe wrote an editorial criticizing the Chongqing administration and its recent policies.[13] Although Chen referred to this war as the "Great East Asian War," the editorial was not so much a pro-Japan propaganda piece as an expression of deep sympathy for the defenseless Chinese populace, the rank and file of the Nationalist army, and the Chinese Communist Party.

The whole editorial expressed disappointment with the entrenched problems of the Nationalist administration and its poor performance since the beginning of the war. Chen divided this editorial into several parts, analyzing Chongqing's military, political, diplomatic, and economic policies. In particular, Chen mocked Chongqing's faith in an impending swift rescue of China by its Anglo-American allies. The Chongqing regime, Chen commented, was filled with party mandarins pitted against one another and shameless officials who capitalized on China's war situation. All they had been doing was dreaming of a quick victory after which they could once again enjoy comfort and luxury in Shanghai and Nanjing.

Chen also astutely commented on China's marginal role in the British and American strategic plan for the Asia-Pacific region. Rather than advance China's own priorities, Chiang sent some of the best Nationalist troops to facilitate the Allies' defense of Burma and to cover the retreat of the British army. Chinese soldiers then became disposable pawns in the British and American maneuvers. Whether it was based on a hunch or intelligence information, Chen's evaluation of China's role in the Pacific War was right on target. Diaries and correspondence of the Allied commanders in Burma corroborate Chen's view. Even Chiang lamented the unequal alliance and the Allied mistreatment of China.[14] Chen had no access to these materials at the time, of course: he based his assessments of Chiang's military policies on what he considered misplaced priorities, the hostile natural and political environment in Burma, and Chiang's diversion of the Nationalist troops to the oppression of the Communists in northwest

China.[15] Chen's comments were a slap in the face for Chiang, who had struggled to boost public morale and burnish his image as a determined and reliable leader.

In addition to his political misconduct and dangerous opinions, Chen Binhe's decadent lifestyle made him a perfect target of the anti-*hanjian* campaigns. Chen was widely known for extravagance and philandering. One newspaper at the time referred to Jin Xiongbai and Chen Binhe as "two wealthy and generous customers of Yunlou," an exceptionally expensive Western-style restaurant on the eighteenth floor of the Shanghai Park Hotel.[16] Although Chen Binhe's salary as the editor in chief of *Shenbao* was not particularly high, he could always find ways to satisfy his taste for delicacies and luxury goods. Chen himself admitted that he had received considerable financial support from the notorious Sheng III, who monopolized the city's opium traffic during the war.

Chen was well aware of his reputation as a conspicuous cultural *hanjian* as well as the criminal charges that awaited him as soon as the war was over. In 1946, Chiang Kai-shek's Ministry of Central Propaganda ordered Chen's immediate arrest.[17] By then Chen had escaped Shanghai and was in hiding in eastern China, constantly changing identities and locations to evade arrest and prosecution. Chen Binhe eventually managed to reach Hong Kong and later Japan, where he remained until he passed away in the late 1960s. Chen's favorite daughter, who stayed in mainland China, had severed ties with her *hanjian* father because of pressures from work and her own family.[18]

To the authorities, Chen Binhe represented the most dangerous kind of cultural *hanjian*, who exerted influence through the mainstream media. The state was more willing to show clemency to other cultural *hanjian* if their collaboration was proved circumstantial and had limited effectiveness. Educators from schools and institutions sponsored or taken over by the puppet regime, for instance, appeared on the government-issued list of cultural *hanjian*, but many were pardoned if their superiors and colleagues provided positive character testimony and proof of their contributions.

Professor Chen Rong and Dean Qi Zhaochang from Jinling University in Nanjing were among the more fortunate ones.[19] They were identified as cultural *hanjian* for their involvement with a puppet institution founded on the campus of Jinling University during wartime. Jinling University was an American-founded university affiliated with the Methodist Church. In November 1937 the school board established an executive committee to handle emergency situations following the fall of Nanjing. The committee soon decided to relocate the majority of the faculty and student body to Chengdu, which was located in the free regions and close to Chongqing. The committee entrusted the preservation of the main campus and its facilities to a commission that would stay behind. This commission consisted of five members, including Chen Rong, Qi Zhaochang, M. S. Bates, and two other Americans, with Bates in charge. During the Nanjing Massacre in December 1937, the commission rescued numerous residents and provided food and lodging to refugees.

As the situation deteriorated in Asia in 1941, the three Americans left China, leaving Chen Rong and Qi Zhaochang in charge of the university. The two were ordered by the school board to "try their best to preserve the campus under any circumstances," and so they did. In March 1941, as the Japanese army occupied the campus, Chen and Qi led the faculty and students in a retreat to the middle school affiliated with Jinling University. Soon after, the Wang Jingwei government appropriated the campus for the foundation of a "Central University."[20] Its administrators invited Chen and Qi to deliver lectures. With their personal safety and the university property at stake, Chen and Qi acquiesced and lectured on agriculture and engineering, respectively.

When the two were faced with *hanjian* charges, Jinling University made great efforts to protect them. In October 1945, the university officially recognized the two professors' loyalty and wartime contributions to the institution. When he returned to China the following month, Bates immediately reported on Chen and Qi's wartime activities to the Ministry of Justice. Bates also provided the minutes of the executive committee's meeting in Chengdu in 1940 to prove that Chen and Qi had followed the orders of the committee and done their best under the circumstances of the occupation. These efforts paid off: the Capital High Court dropped the charges against Chen Rong and Qi Zhaochang.

These two professors were typical of those who had made compromises to preserve their institutions during the Japanese occupation. Yan Fuqing, another individual branded a cultural *hanjian*, had participated in the puppet Medical Education Committee, Sino-Japanese Cultural Association, and National Central Academy.[21] The Ministry of Education, in its official correspondence with the Ministry of Justice, testified that Yan Fuqing took these nominal positions under constant pressure from Chu Minyi, the head of Wang Jingwei's Executive Yuan.[22] The letter applauded Yan's ability to keep the property of the Shanghai Medical College intact. Yan, too, was exempted from prosecution.

Despite the vagueness of the term "cultural *hanjian*," the selective prosecutions show that the state had certain criteria for identifying the most dangerous *hanjian*. Individuals who challenged the official discourse of war and resistance undermined not only public morale but also the Nationalist regime of censorship and mind control. For the same reason, the Nationalist government undertook political rectification among ordinary teachers and students, especially those who had been educated in Japan. The Ministry of Education set up an Inspection Committee for Students Who Studied in Japan to register such students and make sure they were properly indoctrinated.[23] The committee required these students to read texts such as *Teachings of the Founding Father*, which included the core ideologies of the Nationalist Party, as laid out by Sun Yat-sen, and submit book reports regularly. To obtain employment in their home country, students had to pass an even stricter round of inspection and screening.

Similarly, the government set up a screening committee in each "recovered region" (*shoufu qu*) to scrutinize faculty and staff from all higher education institutions for possible *hanjian* activities during the war.[24] *Hanjian* suspects were to be handled by the judiciary. Those "who had probably collaborated but were yet to be exposed" (*shangwei faxian you funi xianyi*) might still lose their jobs, depending on decisions made by their home institutions.[25] In October 1946, the Ministry of Education issued the Resolutions for Screening Students Who Graduated from High Schools in Recovered Regions.[26] Students who had passed the college entrance examinations were permitted to attend college on a type of probation. Only after the screening committee confirmed their academic and political qualifications could they be formally enrolled.

Public opinion, for the most part, was supportive of the screening process and the punishment of cultural *hanjian*. In the view of ordinary citizens, although the educated elites could not physically fight the war on the Japanese side, they could "wreck the country and ruin the people" (*huoguo yangmin*) with pen and paper.[27] Readers of major newspapers singled out specific kinds of cultural *hanjian* and called for their arrest. One reader of the *Central Daily* (Zhongyang ribao) echoed the government's denunciation of *hanjian* among educators, whom he considered particularly harmful because they "poisoned the future generation of the nation."[28] Others pushed for the arrest and prosecution of *hanjian* in the publishing industry, whom they considered an overlooked category but one no less dangerous than *hanjian* from literary, news media, or art circles.[29]

This unforgiving attitude toward cultural *hanjian* largely resulted from the high moral expectations the Chinese had traditionally held for the literati class. For hundreds of years, scholar-officials had been the cornerstone of the Chinese imperial bureaucracy and standard-bearers of culture and morality. When the Qing emperor abolished the civil service examination in 1905, the main path by which educated elites could enter officialdom was cut off. Modernization called for the encouragement and appreciation of talents in the natural sciences and social sciences, making the traditional curriculum, based on Confucian classics, irrelevant, if not obsolete. The new generation of Chinese intellectuals, however, inherited from their Confucian predecessors a sense of social responsibility. In the 1910s and early 1920s, the May Fourth intellectuals charged themselves with the mission of awakening the masses, reforming Chinese culture, and rejuvenating the nation at a time when the state appeared weak and corrupt.

The greater the responsibility they shouldered, the greater the harm they could cause if they failed in their ascribed roles. While people demanded the punishment of cultural *hanjian*, those in cultural and arts circles launched a voluntary purge of their own to demonstrate their patriotism and defend their collective moral authority. The Shanghai Cinema and Play Association, for instance, convened a special committee to expose members who had collaborated during wartime. The committee distributed thousands of notices among actors, playwrights, and fans, soliciting anonymous accusations. This gesture won attention and support from the news media.[30] Writers, a more influential, self-conscious and divided group, conducted a similar intragroup purge by even more radical measures.

RESISTANCE-BASED MASCULINITY AND THE PURGE AMONG MEN OF LETTERS

The most vocal social force behind war mobilization and the punishment of *hanjian* had been left-wing writers. In 1938, representatives of writers and artists founded the National Resistance Association of Cultural Circles (Zhonghuaquanguo Wenhuajie Kangdi Xiehui), which grew in membership and influence throughout the war. This association was charged with a mission to "use pens as weapons" in the resistance cause. More than half of its leading members were either also members of the Association of Chinese Left-Wing Writers or consistent left-wing sympathizers.[31] Through posters, comics, films, and plays, they systematically disseminated messages of resistance and promoted unity among all levels of society throughout China.

Another focus of the association's work was to condemn collaboration with the Japanese. It developed varied strategies to denounce different types of *hanjian*. News reports and fictional pieces depicted minor *hanjian* as either the pitiful and gullible poor, whose minds could still be reformed, or fundamentally immoral opportunists who needed to be eliminated. Although members of the associations showed no mercy to peers and colleagues who had bowed to the Japanese, they were more tactful and patient toward prominent scholars and writers with national influence. As demonstrated in the case of the writer Zhou Zuoren, they alternated between threats and persuasion, and between contempt and pity.

As the famous writer Zheng Zhenduo later commented, Zhou's "betrayal" of China was the greatest loss to the Chinese literary world during the fourteen years of war.[32] Zhou Zuoren, along with his more left-leaning brother, Lu Xun, was a leading figure in Chinese vernacular literature and a cultural icon of the May Fourth generation. After the fall of Beijing in 1937, the president of Beijing University, Jiang Menglin, entrusted the university to Zhou Zuoren and three other professors who had decided to stay. In the subsequent years, Zhou managed to safeguard the university and even expanded its facilities and library collections. These achievements, however, came at the price of his political integrity. From 1939 onward, Zhou became increasingly involved with collaborationist regimes and became an advocate of pan-Asianism, an ideology that the Japanese army turned into a justification for its imperialism. Later explanations of what pushed Zhou into the enemy camp included his marriage to a Japanese woman and her impractical spending habits, his desire for recognition and status, and a mysterious assassination attempt on him in 1939.[33]

Zhou's friends and acquaintances in free regions made repeated attempts to prevent him from turning to the wrong side. As one of the few top intellectuals remaining in occupied areas, Zhou's choices and activities held great significance and were constantly reported and speculated on by newspapers. In May 1938, the National Resistance Association's official newspaper, *Resistance Literature and Art* (Kangzhan wenyi), published an open letter to Zhou, which was coauthored by Mao Dun, Yu Dafu, Lao She, Feng Naichao, Ding Ling, and fourteen other nationally known writers. This letter, written before Zhou took any puppet positions, was prompted by a rumor that Zhou had been compromised. The nineteen patriotic writers

FEMALE *HANJIAN* AND CULTURAL *HANJIAN*   123

scolded Zhou, a widely respected university professor, for "committing the greatest wrong and bringing shame to the cultural circles." They urged Zhou to redeem himself by coming to free China immediately and contributing to the resistance efforts, in which case he would be forgiven and treasured again by the people. Otherwise, the public would consider him "a main villain and traitor of the nation."[34]

When it was eventually confirmed that Zhou had taken part in the puppet regime, those who had tried to save him responded with disbelief and a great sense of loss, rather than denunciation. Zheng Zhenduo reflected on "how we had lost Zhou Zuoren," attributing Zhou's surrender to weakness in his character and a lack of confidence in China's capacity to defeat Japan.[35] Even after Zhou was arrested in 1945, Zheng pleaded for clemency from the Nationalist government on account of Zhou's academic achievements and linguistic skills. For his roles as a top official in the puppet regime and a spokesperson for Wang Jingwei, Zhou was sentenced to fourteen years' imprisonment (later commuted to ten years). For this relatively lenient treatment Zhou had to thank the influential friends and students who pleaded on his behalf, in addition to recognition of his efforts to preserve Beijing University.

Toward cultural *hanjian* who did not enjoy the kind of fame and connections that Zhou did, resistance intellectuals showed less sympathy. Patriotic writers took the initiative in exposing *hanjian* in their social circles. On August 13, 1945, two days before Japan's surrender, the National Resistance Association selected eighteen distinguished writers, playwrights, and literary critics to form a Committee for Investigating Literati Who Sided with the Enemy.[36] The committee aimed to expose "contaminated" editors and publishers, propagandists for the enemy, teachers who pushed for an education of enslavement, and staff members of all puppet-controlled, profit-oriented cultural enterprises. In the meantime, the association published an open letter of support to intellectuals in Shanghai who did not give in to the Japanese. Writers such as Xu Guangping, Zheng Zhenduo, and Li Jianwu were praised as exemplary intellectuals. The association also urged these politically upright writers to facilitate the investigation of cultural *hanjian*.[37]

The committee proposed several ways to penalize cultural *hanjian* in addition to prosecution by the state. It suggested that short biographies of cultural *hanjian*, with accounts of their wartime conduct, be disseminated in China and abroad; that they be excluded from all legitimate cultural associations; that their work be blacklisted by publishers; and that their employment in schools and for newspapers and journals be terminated.[38] This proposal won official endorsement and was implemented on November 3, 1945.[39] A majority of alleged cultural *hanjian* whom the state had forgiven were thus ostracized by their professional community.

In a political milieu that allowed extralegal investigation and slander in the name of nationalism, people with varying agendas rode the tide and pushed the anti-*hanjian* movement to extreme actions. Nothing accomplished the goal of defaming cultural *hanjian* better than the pamphlet *Criminal Histories of Cultural* Hanjian (Wenhua hanjian zui'eshi). This booklet was a collection of the rumored traitorous activities and scandalous lives of seventeen individuals, including the popular writers Zhang Ailing and Zhang Ziping, the poet Lu Yishi, the cultural official Hu Lancheng, the editors Tao Kangde and Wang Fuquan, and the scholar Liu Yusheng. All were eminent men and women of letters who had achieved wide recognition prior to the war. The editor of this collection, Sima Wenzhen, literally "Sima the literary detective," was determined to bring these individuals to the attention of the government and the general public:

> This little pamphlet aims to reveal the ugly side of the wartime literary world and uncover the inside stories of the "Great East Asian Literary Circle." I will also provide information on individual cultural *hanjian*. . . . [Accounts like this one] will remove their disguises and terminate their pernicious influence at this crucial stage of nation building. This pamphlet, therefore, serves as a mirror that reflects the true faces of demons and monsters [*zhaoyao jing*]. This little "magical weapon" will give them no place to hide.[41]

Sima compiled this pamphlet with the goal of facilitating the investigation of cultural *hanjian*. Yet to what extent do materials of this type provide evidence of *hanjian* crimes, and what do they reveal about the different dimension of the anti-*hanjian* campaigns?

The *Criminal Histories* shared common themes, content, and strategies with publications by similar titles. In postwar Shanghai and other recently liberated regions, a patriotic fervor filled the air, and anti-*hanjian* talk was ubiquitous. This political climate gave rise to a number of small-scale, short-lived presses with righteous-sounding names that published scandals and salacious anecdotes about public figures in the name of condemning *hanjian*. The *Criminal Histories*, published by the "Bright Dawn" (Shuguang) Press in Shanghai, was exceptional in that its compiler was not anonymous (though Sima Wenzhen was obviously a pen name). The *Hideous Histories of* Hanjian (Hanjian choushi) series was issued by the Great Harmony (Datong) Press. *Revealing the Faces of Female* Hanjian (Nühanjian lianpu) was published by the Great Righteousness (Dayi) Press. Both were anonymously edited.

These pamphlets were literary attacks that complemented the legal purge of *hanjian*. As the titles suggest, pamphleteers targeted both male and female public figures with accounts that catered to mass voyeurism. Only half of the targeted individuals were recognized and tried as *hanjian* by the Nationalist government. For these, the editors selected anecdotes about their political and moral misconduct, vividly conveying their crimes to a less-educated audience. Those whose activities did not warrant prosecution but still fit the popular notion of betrayal were still punished through defamation for their association with the Japanese or major *hanjian*.

This type of literature illuminated the gendered dimensions of the anti-*hanjian* campaigns. Historians have noted that abstractions of gender relations are commonly deployed to express the relationship between the rulers and the ruled or the unequal power relations between nations.[40] During the War of Resistance, wartime mobilization and anti-*hanjian* propaganda often employed such rhetorical strategies. For instance, when the World War I memorial peace statue in Shanghai was damaged by Japanese bombs, *Shenbao* published an article titled "The Body of the Goddess of Peace Is No Longer Intact."[41] Here, the war and the enemy who brought the war to Chinese soil were seen as masculine and violating, while China was represented by a figure of peace, feminine, innocent, and vulnerable.

Chinese war propaganda uniformly depicted *hanjian* as individuals lacking in masculinity. The Chinese characters for *hanjian* were constructed in a way that pointed to the illicit and emasculate nature of the crime. Newspapers and popular literature used the term *xianmei*, generally used to refer to women's acts of pandering to men, to portray the conduct of male *hanjian* in their relations with the Japanese. Individuals who had showed uncompromising attitudes toward the Japanese were widely celebrated and their manliness emphasized. Mei Lanfang, a Beijing Opera artist renowned for impersonating female roles onstage, refused to perform for the Japanese, cementing this refusal by growing his beard in 1941.[42] Even though Mei had gained fame for embodying elegance and femininity in theater, he "demonstrated his virtue" (*mingzhi*) and reasserted his masculinity at this moment of national emergency.

In this gendered context, the compilers of the *Hideous Histories* used sexual content and sensational stories to increase the circulation of their publications. This genre of literature targeted major political *hanjian*, artists and writers who maintained their Japanese connections during the war, merchants who had engaged in black marketeering, and so on. In the case of the merchants, the fact that they had prospered while the rest of the population was sliding into poverty was enough to constitute betrayal. A selection of the twenty-seven article titles in the fifth issue of *Hideous Histories* illustrates the range of individuals under attack and the bizarre content of the literature:

> Dirty Propaganda Plot of the Puppet Government
> Liu Haisu Has Achieved Nothing
> A Disgrace to the Legal System: Nie Chongyi
> Lu Ying, the Sex Addict
> Old Pervert: Zhou Yueran
> Sheng III Persecuted His Old Friend with a Lawsuit
> Devious Histories of Zhou Fohai
> The Details of the Arrest of Zhang Shankun
> Han Yuwen: Tycoon in the Rice Business yet a Minion of the Japanese
> The Exclusive Stories of the Fire in the Mortuary
> Ma Lianliang Is Still Active
> The Inside Stories of 1136 Yuyuan Road: Gathering Place of a Group of
> Clowns
> Violent and Abusive Huang Liewen, Puppet Head of Qingpu County
> The Self-Appointed Commander General Ou Daqing
> The Active Conspirator of 76 Jessfield Road: Fu Yewen
> Chen Yangwu: Head of the Puppet Department of Education in Zhejiang

Some but not all of the individuals named here were *hanjian* convicts. Among those who were not, the compilers focused on those with social connections to Japan. Cultural *hanjian* were particularly vulnerable to such scrutiny, as many members of the Chinese cultural elite in the early twentieth century had been educated in Japan and still maintained close contact with friends and colleagues there. This part of their identity and social life made them targets of the anti-*hanjian* discourse. The famous oil painter Liu Haisu, for instance, was branded a *hanjian* primarily because of his Japan connections.

Liu (1896–1994) was established as a despicable traitor through a selection of anecdotes about his public and private life. *Hideous Histories* reported that Liu once flew on a Japanese airplane, omitting to explain the context of his journey.[43] The Japanese arrested Liu Haisu while his works were on tour in Java and demanded that he join the art association sponsored by the puppet regime. Liu refused, agreeing only to hold several exhibits with Japanese endorsement. In exchange for this compromise, the Japanese escorted him back to Shanghai. Liu donated the income from his exhibitions to China's resistance forces. *Hideous Histories* ignored this gesture and used irrelevant anecdotes to reinforce the impression of Liu's traitorous nature. They also seized on the fact that some of Liu's colleagues had once admiringly called him a "traitor in art."[44] This label, which Liu originally cherished as a humorous recognition of his introduction of groundbreaking concepts and techniques to Chinese art, was now taken out of context and given a new political meaning.[45]

According to the anti-*hanjian* literature, traitors like Liu Haisu would never win respect from anyone because of their loss of Chineseness. The compilers reported, based on hearsay, that Liu once wore a Western suit to a social event hosted by Wang Jingwei. The guards at the event refused to let him in because "the invitation specified that all guests should wear Chinese-style long gowns."[46] Liu was "extremely embarrassed" by the situation.

Other anecdotes about Liu reflected a recurring theme in this genre: that a traitor would experience betrayal himself. Liu's third wife, Cheng Jiahe, whom the pamphlet referred to as his "third concubine," was reported to have cheated on him with a low-ranking official in the Wang Jingwei regime.[47] The use of *concubine* rather than *wife* created the impression that *hanjian* lived corrupt and immoral private lives and assigned the women in their lives to objectified and historically retrograde positions.[48] The account built on and reinforced the popular perception that the relationships and marriages of artists were transient, unstable, and immoral, in keeping with the "political fluidity" of these individuals.

Most stories in the *Hideous Histories* series offered no solid evidence. The pamphleteers solicited stories and anecdotes of *hanjian* from readers and then published them uncritically. As further illustration of the decadent lives of *hanjian*, the pamphlet included a collection of shorter anecdotes titled "Fragmentary Records of the Absurd Lives of *Hanjian*." All of these were contributed by readers. The titles included the following:

The Legislator Who Eats "Cunt-jujube" and Smells Bound Feet

Deng Zuyu Madly in Love with Huang Guichun, the Famous Courtesan

Wang Ruikai Chants Sutras in Front of Journalists

Jiang Kanghu Caught Smuggling Goods on Business Trips

"The Thirteenth Red" [stage name of a courtesan] Cries over Her
    Imprisoned Husband

Liang Hongzhi Hooked Up with "Spring of the Jade Chamber" [stage
    name of a courtesan]

Nothing Is Too Strange or Scandalous for the Puppet Ministry of
    Education

The pamphlet associated most male *hanjian* with prostitution, perverse sexual behaviors, and various forms of political corruption. Short entries revealing the sex lives of *hanjian* were particularly imaginative, with details that were impossible to know, and suggested that their perversions compensated for impotence. In such ways, *Hideous Histories* reinforced the connection between political betrayal and personal decadence.

Not only did such pamphlets use the alleged lack of masculinity of *hanjian* suspects as a political metaphor, but they also feminized certain individuals in a directly sexual sense. The authors alleged illicit relations between certain female impersonators in the Beijing Opera and Japanese military officers, calling one of the players, Zhao Xiaokun, "the female commander" (*mu siling*). Actors like Zhao were contrasted with Mei Lanfang and other female impersonators who had refused to perform for the Japanese. The author further commented that because so few performers had maintained their "virtue" or "purity" (*jianzhen*), Beijing opera theaters were dominated by "theatrical evil" (*juyao*), represented by actors like Zhao.[49]

With its juicy content and up-to-date news on the *hanjian* celebrities, the *Hideous Histories* series won a sizable audience. Its circulation and impact can be judged by the published letters from readers. In the second issue of *Hideous Histories*, one article revealed how Gu Jiren, a minor figure in the puppet Rice Control Commission (Mitonghui), was arrested as a *hanjian*.[50] Gu's position was too low to attract official notice: he was caught only because his aunt reported him to the authorities. According to *Hideous Histories*, his aunt decided to "sacrifice blood ties to the righteous cause" mainly because of their recent conflicts over inheritance rights. A month later, a new issue of *Hideous Histories* published a letter from Gu Jiren's aunt. She claimed that the series had wronged her, as she had demanded neither the division of family property nor the arrest of her nephew. Although the events in the Gu family will probably never be known, the letter shows that the *Hideous Histories* series was widely read enough for even commoners to be concerned about how they were depicted in such accounts.

FEMALE *HANJIAN*, DOUBLY CURSED

Advocates of war mobilization and anti-*hanjian* campaigns paid particular attention to women. Resistance intellectuals saw women as the wives and mothers of fighters—or of traitors. On October 30, 1937, *National Salvation Daily* (Jiuwang ribao) published a special issue on women's roles in the war. In the foreword, Shi Liang, the renowned female lawyer and patriotic activist, urged women to devote themselves to war relief, propaganda, and education.[51] Other contributors encouraged women to sacrifice their personal attachments to their husbands and sons to the national need for soldiers.[52] Such opinions reinforced the trend that Chinese intellectuals had set since the early twentieth century, liberating women from shackles of traditional practices and educating them to be qualified citizens of the nation. Women, in this liberal nationalistic discourse, were linked with the state and the nation rather than with men.[53]

While resistance intellectuals recognized the positive roles that women could play in national salvation, they also stressed women's distinctive capacity for criminal behaviors. In 1940, when disastrous floods ravaged south Hebei and caused famine and dislocation among the local people, a resistance pamphlet warned that a handful of female *hanjian* were purchasing Chinese children for the Japanese under the pretext of adoption.[54] The pamphlet suggested that these women were betraying their traditionally benign roles as mothers by sabotaging China's future citizens.

After the war, newspapers published petitions from readers advocating the investigation, arrest, and trial of female *hanjian*. In 1946, in an article published by the left-leaning journal *Democracy Weekly* (Minzhu zhoukan), the author evoked traditional beliefs that the fate of the state was connected to a gendered framework of virtue and depravity, as manifested in cosmological signs:

> If the state is to prosper, there are auspicious signs; and if the state is to meet its demise, there are evil and misfortune. Evil and misfortune come in different forms, such as abnormal astronomical phenomena,

earthquakes, floods, and the emergence of evil spirits as well as male and female wicked souls. . . .

People tend to focus on male *hanjian* and ignore female *hanjian*, since the latter appear to be gentle and physically weak. . . . What people do not know is that these female human-devils [*renyao*] are good at making connections with powerful figures, tricking others and spreading disaffection. They can do more harm than male traitors. . . . Using their beautiful appearance, they seek personal gain and superficial pleasure. They show no care for the fate of the nation. . . . Many male *hanjian* who have been arrested worked with female *hanjian*, and they are waiting for their female partners to rescue them.

The author urged the government to arrest and punish female *hanjian* first and counter their "pernicious influence."

The Nationalist government in fact punished many female *hanjian*, defined by their association with major male *hanjian* or Japanese nationals. Official purges and popular campaigns alike considered women unable to make political decisions on their own initiative. Some were put on trial as unofficial proxies for husbands who died before their trials. For instance, Wang Jingwei's wife, Chen Bijun, was sentenced to life imprisonment for "helping with the Japanese invasion and weakening Chinese resistance."[55] Ye Jiqing, Li Shiqun's wife, and She Aizhen, Wu Shibao's wife, were each sentenced to fifteen years' imprisonment. The two men were important members of 76 Jessfield Road, Wang Jingwei's intelligence headquarters in Shanghai.[56] Both women realized the true but unstated reason for their incrimination. They attempted to evade punishment by stressing their domestic roles and downplaying their involvement in the activities of 76 Jessfield Road, but to no avail.[57] Mistresses or suspected mistresses of *hanjian* were also put on trial if they had engaged in the political activities of the puppet regime.[58]

Among the female *hanjian* who were tried, few were intelligence agents in their own right. Yoshiko Kawashima, also known as Jin Bihui, who used her several different identities to gather intelligence for the Japanese army, was an exception. Despite not being of Han ethnicity—she was born into the Manchu royal family and raised in Japan—Kawashima was tried as a *hanjian*. Her life, wartime activities, arrest, and trial attracted enormous public attention.[59] Newspapers often referred to her as a female spy (*nü jiandie*), provoking lurid speculation as to how she had gathered intelligence on the Chinese war effort. On March 25, 1948, Kawashima was executed in

Beijing, but her legendary life and her role in the Japanese invasion of China made her a subject of continuous speculation and fascination.[60]

If the number of women actually tried as *hanjian* was small, popular anti-*hanjian* literature, especially the "hideous histories" genre, targeted a much larger group, most of whom never engaged directly in political or military collaboration with the Japanese. *Hideous Histories of Female Hanjian* contained articles on fifteen women, including the wives, mistresses, or suspected mistresses of major *hanjian;* female celebrities who were associated with Japanese officers or puppet officials; and two "*hanjian* daughters." The two daughters, Zhan Fangzi and Zhou Wenji, were so labeled because they had "assisted their fathers in collaborating with the Japanese."[61] Their cases raise the classic dilemma in Chinese historical and popular stories: what to do when loyalty to the state (*zhong*) and filial piety (*xiao*) are at odds. The pamphleteers conveyed a strong message that family attachments should come second to the good of the nation.

Female celebrities named in this pamphlet included Su Qing, a writer who was involved with Chen Gongbo; Wu Mingfang, a "social butterfly" who was involved with Japanese officers; Bai Guang, a movie star who was involved with Japanese officers; Li Qingping, a painter who was involved with Japanese officers; Li Lihua, an actress who spoke Japanese and starred in Japanese feature films; Yan Bingzhen, a translator for the Japanese army, who was involved with Japanese officers; and Li Xianglan, a Japanese actress with a Chinese stage name who frequently played Chinese girls in Japanese propaganda movies. The inclusion of Li Xianglan (or Yamaguchi Yoshiko, also known as Ri Koran, 1920–2014) was ironic, as she was a Japanese national and thus could not have "betrayed" the Han.[62]

Many women targeted by the compilers of these pamphlets were writers, artists, or actresses. For this reason, their names also appeared in *Criminal Histories of Cultural* Hanjian. These women had established themselves in society and demonstrated possible career paths for women in the Republican period. The "hideous histories" genre, however, denied their ability to make independent political or lifestyle choices, measuring them instead by the activities of their male partners. The pamphlets described them in unabashedly sexist, crude, and derogatory language. Circulated in the radicalized political environment of the postwar period, anti-*hanjian* literature marked a sharp departure from the more female-oriented literature and media culture of the early 1940s.

In wartime Shanghai, a new group of creative writers, artists, and producers came to prominence.[63] Since the Japanese and the puppet regimes

allowed no resistance literature, and Shanghai's residents resented war propaganda produced by Japan and the puppet government, literature and
arts that focused on romance, sexuality, and domestic issues grew in popularity. For instance, Zhang Shankun (1905–57), the manager of the China
United Production film company, produced family dramas and tragic
romances that would pass Japanese censorship.[64] Two women writers,
Zhang Ailing and Su Qing, gained popularity by depicting material
culture, ordinary people, and the unique landscape of the city. In her auto-
biographical novel *Ten Years of Married Life* (Jiehun shinian), Su Qing
revealed in detail the terrors of pregnancy, childbirth, and motherhood in
wartime. Zhang Ailing, in her renowned short story "Blockade" (Fengsuo), depicted a brief romance between two strangers made possible by
their meeting in a confined space during a street blockade.[65] The apolitical,
romantic subject matter, combined with their distinguished writing styles,
enabled Zhang and Su to survive and flourish under foreign occupation.

As Zhang and Su became celebrities, however, their lives became subject to public voyeurism, like those of film actresses and popular singers.[66]
As Haiyan Lee points out, with the popularization of the late Qing genre of
"scandal fiction," private lives became increasingly subject to public scrutiny and judgment.[67] Both Zhang and Su were young, independent, and
somewhat mysterious modern women, whose careers, marriages, and
political choices were constantly exposed to the public gaze.[68] Publishers
printed their photos on the backs of their books to attract readers, and
readers were as interested in the authors' private lives as in their literary
productions.

This golden period for women writers ended in August 1945 with the
return of the Nationalist government and the launching of the anti-*hanjian*
campaigns. Left-wing intellectuals and politically radical writers returned
to reclaim the reading space they had lost during the war to writers such as
Zhang Ailing and Su Qing. Individuals who had stayed in occupied Shanghai, including Zhang and Su, were vulnerable to suspicion of collaboration.[69] Not only were they faced with an increasingly competitive and
unfavorable market for their work, but the content of their writing, along
with their private lives, became the subject of ridicule and criticism.

Did they collaborate? Neither Su nor Zhang promoted the Japanese invasion, nor did either of them hold a position in the Wang Jingwei regime.[70]
Therefore, they were not targeted by the government. Nonetheless, both
were publicly attacked as "*hanjian* writers." One ostensible reason was that
Zhang and Su had published in journals that were viewed as politically

questionable. Zhang had published essays in the journal *Magazine* (Zazhi), which was famous for its political ambivalence.[71] Su Qing had founded the journal *Heaven and Earth* (Tiandi yuekan), which was sponsored by Chen Gongbo, the mayor of the puppet Shanghai Municipal Government.[72]

The themes, subjects, and bold content of Su and Zhang's writings also made them the targets of anti-*hanjian* pamphlets. Even before 1945, Su and Zhang had been criticized by their peers. Tan Zhengbi, another female writer, considered Zhang and Su's works too narrowly focused and thus not to be compared with those of earlier women writers, such as Xie Bingying and Feng Yuanjun, whose works reflected "the demands of the masses."[73]

Postwar anti-*hanjian* pamphleteers went further and attacked Su and Zhang for "using sexual content to attract readers."[74] They also focused on the respective relationships of Su and Zhang to Chen Gongbo and Hu Lancheng, major *hanjian* who were tried by the Nationalist government. Profit driven and politically justified, the tabloids and pamphlets constantly published news and rumors about the private lives of Su and Zhang, ridiculing everything from their writing to their clothing. Their stories illustrate the strategy of postwar literary campaigns against female celebrities as well as the opportunities for and constraints on women's work and writing in wartime Shanghai.

Su Qing's literary works drew on her personal struggles and frustrations. Su (whose original name was Feng Yunzhuang) terminated her education at the National Central University when she married and became pregnant. After a painful labor, she gave birth to a girl, disappointing her husband and her in-laws, who all wanted a boy. Suffocated by the dullness of life as a housewife, she began to write. Her first essay, "Giving Birth to a Girl," came out in a magazine and was well received. She then published several other short articles and adopted the pen name Su Qing in 1937. Her relationship with her husband, Li Qinhou, deteriorated over the next few years with the birth of their second daughter, Li's affair with a married woman, and Li's increasing resentment of Su Qing's work as a writer.[75]

In 1942, Su Qing divorced her husband and devoted herself to writing fiction and short essays. Her writings focused on familial relations, especially issues that hindered modern women from pursuing independent lives and careers. Su Qing's career peaked in the 1940s. Her most famous novel, *Ten Years of Married Life*, was reprinted seventeen times. Her collection of prose, *Washing Silk*, was reprinted ten times.[76] In 1943, she began publishing the monthly *Heaven and Earth* and established her own press.[77]

Su Qing's reputation was tainted by speculation about her relationship to Chen Gongbo. In 1942, on hearing Chen's praise for her recent works, Su published an article describing Chen as interesting and affable. Chen responded warmly and, knowing that Su was seeking employment, offered her a secretarial position. Before long, Su Qing voiced criticisms of the procedures for reviewing and annotating government documents. Chen suggested that Su should resign, commenting that "women were not suited to politics."[78] She did so, but he continued to pay her a salary. By the end of 1942, Su Qing had moved out of her husband's house, and Chen lent her money to rent a house and buy furniture.

When Su established *Heaven and Earth*, it was rumored that Chen Gongbo had given her funds to purchase twenty-five thousand sheets of paper, a tremendous quantity considering the shortage of supplies in wartime Shanghai. The postwar version of the story portrayed Su Qing riding grandiosely through Shanghai's main streets in a truck filled with bundles of white paper.[79] Her journal in general was apolitical, but it regularly published contributions by Chen and members of his circle, including Zhou Fohai and his wife and son. *Heaven and Earth* also carried advertisements for the puppet Central Reserve Bank and books written by Chen Gongbo and Zhou Fohai.[80]

During the postwar anti-*hanjian* campaigns, Su Qing faced severe attacks. Sima Wenzhen suggested that she had a sexual relationship with Chen Gongbo. *Criminal Histories* labeled her "the female counterpart of Zhang Jingsheng and the illicit imperial concubine of Chen Gongbo."[81] The comparison with Zhang Jingsheng was an attempt to frame her frank discussions of sexuality as pornographic writing. Zhang Jingsheng was a professor and sexologist of the 1920s who solicited readers' narratives about their sexual experiences and compiled them into a book, *Sex Histories* (Xingshi). This collection provoked enormous controversy in the media as well as the wrath of the authorities.[82] General readers in the 1920s regarded the collection as pornography, and numerous illegal publishers produced collections of pornography under the same title. Since Zhang Jingsheng endured much criticism and misunderstanding of his study, the comparison served to stain Su's work as similarly unworthy and scandalous.

Su Qing's own discussions of female sexuality were far less explicit. In *Ten Years of Married Life*, Su gave a detailed account of the protagonist's wedding night, sex life, pregnancy, and giving birth from a female perspective. After discovering her husband's affair with another woman, the newlywed protagonist is sexually awakened and looks for a lover in her college.

Despite the attacks on her work, Su Qing won critical approval and mass popularity in occupied Shanghai. Zhang Ailing commented that Su was her favorite contemporary woman writer because Su's style was that of "grand simplicity."[83] The sales of Su's fiction also attested to her popularity. Both *Ten Years of Married Life* and its sequel were reprinted multiple times. *Heaven and Earth* was an undeniable commercial success. Three thousand copies of its first issue sold out on the first day, and an additional printing of two thousand copies also sold out. Within twenty days of the first issue's circulation, the journal received 247 letters from readers and 123 unsolicited contributions.[84] Su's connection to prominent *hanjian* might have won financial support for *Heaven and Earth*, but it could not have generated such a popular response among readers.

The anti-*hanjian* literati, however, claimed that Su Qing "had no chance of prominence in literary circles" and that she occupied only "a temporary and minor position in the publishing industry" because of her dubious connections with editors and publishers.[85] Excoriating the popularity of *Heaven and Earth*, Sima Wenzhen voiced a certain embittered misogyny, nothing that "a woman unexpectedly beat so many men who also run their own journals—no wonder she does not know who she is."[86] *Hideous Histories of Female* Hanjian went one step further, spreading a rumor that Su Qing had blackmailed Chen by threatening to reveal a fake pregnancy.

The "hideous histories" genre also deployed insults adapted from popular slang. Pamphleteers employed slurs such as "evil spirits of cultural circles" (*wentan yaoguai*), "demon king" (*mowang*), and "literary devils" (*wenyao*). Sexist words with an uncultured origin were often used against female *hanjian*. For instance, "precious goods" (*baohuo*) refers to a self-important but undistinguished individual who is laughable in others' eyes. Other terms used to denigrate Su Qing included "wicked slut" (*yaofu*) and "female devil" (*nüyao*). Those who praised Su Qing's essays were called "collaborating literati" (*hanjian wenren*). Su Qing's writing and publishing career was referred to pejoratively as a "business" (*shengyi*).

Even some serious newspapers joined in the attacks on Su Qing. For instance, *Wenhui bao*, a left-leaning and reputable newspaper, disparaged Su Qing's works as "pornographic readings" (*seqing duwu*), the only attraction of which was the "lure of sexuality."[87] Many tabloids published speculations about Su's personal life, hairstyle, and outfits. During the occupation, Shanghai's newspapers portrayed her as a silent, dignified and elegantly dressed woman. After the war, however, as the "hideous histories" genre grew popular, many publications portrayed Su as a "literary prostitute," mocking her clothes and everyday behavior.[88]

Such accusations and insults put Su Qing under unbearable emotional and economic pressure. Writing was her only means of supporting herself and her three children. She attempted to defend herself in 1947 in the introduction to *A Sequel to Ten Years of Married Life.* Su admitted that she chose to write and publish her works in occupied Shanghai but denied that she was wrong for doing so. Instead, she claimed that the government was unreasonable for leaving its people behind in an occupied city while requiring absolute loyalty from them:

> My articles are my articles, no matter where they are published. It is said that artists should carefully protect their reputation. To be honest, I only care about filling my stomach. . . .
>
> I did not choose to publish under Japanese occupation. I think the important thing here is not whether I sold my articles, but whether by selling my articles I harmed the nation. Otherwise, [I sold my writings in occupied Shanghai] just like rice merchants sold rice and rickshaw pullers sold their service to passengers. If the nation does not deny the rights of its citizens to survive at the level of bare existence, I survived, and I do not feel guilty.[89]

Ongoing anti-*hanjian* campaigns doomed Su Qing's future as a popular writer. In 1947, a group of self-righteous activists prevented a bookstore from selling *Ten Years of Married Life,* saying that the book contained "poisonous elements." More than a thousand copies were returned by bookstores, causing Su Qing and the publisher enormous financial losses. Several reputable newspapers invited Su to work as an editor on the condition that she abandon her widely known pen name. She refused. As a result, she could only publish essays in tabloids, where, she complained, her contributions were relegated to placement next to news stories such as "Carpenter Raped a Minor."[90] Su Qing's literary output dwindled, and her income from writing fiction and contributing to newspapers and journals shrank dramatically in the following years.[91]

Su Qing continued to be haunted by her past after the establishment of the People's Republic of China in October 1949. The Communist government had championed the anti-*hanjian* campaigns and now turned the same legal and popular tools against alleged public enemies. Unlike many other writers, who left for Hong Kong, Taiwan, or elsewhere, Su Qing remained in Shanghai. She attempted to adapt herself to the changing political circumstances, learning Russian and becoming a revolutionary playwright.[92] She produced a series of historical and modern plays, including the highly regarded *Qu Yuan*. Reportedly because of Su Qing's "problematic past" (*lishi wenti*), she never received an award as the playwright of *Qu Yuan*, even though a number of awards were given to actors, directors, and musicians in productions of the play.[93]

Su Qing's ongoing friendship with her old acquaintances from Chen Gongbo's circle brought her additional trouble as the political atmosphere grew more radical. During the anti-rightist movement, Su Qing was arrested and imprisoned for more than a year for her past relations with *hanjian* and friendships with several rightists, including Hu Feng and Jia Zhifang.[94] She was attacked again during the Cultural Revolution, and her monthly salary shrank from three hundred yuan in 1951 to fifteen yuan in 1966. As a result, Su Qing lost her enthusiasm for playwriting. Shortly before her death in 1982, Su expressed the desire for a last look at the work of which she was most proud, *Ten Years of Married Life*, a book that had been banned for years. Her son-in-law borrowed a copy from someone who had secretly kept the book, reportedly fulfilling her final wish.[95]

Like Su Qing, Zhang Ailing reached the peak of her literary production and fame in the early 1940s and faced attacks immediately after the war. Zhang was labeled a "female *hanjian*" mainly because of her marriage to Hu Lancheng, a notorious cultural *hanjian* who served in the Ministry of Propaganda in the Wang Jingwei regime.[96] Zhang Ailing and Hu Lancheng were both targeted by anti-*hanjian* pamphlets, though Zhang was particularly ridiculed for her marriage, her writing, and random details of her life.

The pamphleteers recognized Zhang's literary achievements and subjectivity as a woman, and, in an inversion of traditional gender bias, mocked Hu Lancheng for riding to fame through his relationship to Zhang. However, Zhang was criticized for her alleged willingness to be Hu's "third concubine," on account of Hu's two previous marriages.[97] The word "concubine" (*qie*) was inaccurate at best, as the distinction between a formal wife and a concubine was not clear-cut under the Nationalist laws.[98] The use of *qie* here was intended to deprive Zhang of her status as an independent, modern woman and associate her indelibly with a traitorous paramour. The pamphleteer reserved some sympathy for Zhang, suggesting that there was still a possibility for her to redeem her reputation. The tone was didactic and condescending: "Whether or not Zhang still has a future in writing depends on how she behaves from now on."[99]

Criminal Histories launched additional personal attacks on Zhang. The editor, Sima Wenzhen, ridiculed her name, suggesting that Zhang Ailing sounded more like a dancing girl or a prostitute than a writer. He thus predicted that "she was destined to enjoy only a brief period of popularity, just like a dancing girl."[100] The suggestion that the career of a female writer and her popularity were as frivolous, and as morally suspect, as those of a dancing girl was revealing of the contemporary disrespect of apolitical women writers. As Sima put it, Zhang had once had the potential to become a great writer, but she had buried her future by allowing *hanjian* such as Hu Lancheng to drag her down.

The tabloids joined the campaign against Zhang. In March 1946, *Shanghai School* (Haipai) revealed the "exclusive news" that Zhang had been seen sitting in a jeep with heavy makeup, going to the theater with an American officer, under the headline "Zhang Ailing as a Jeep Girl."[101] This piece of salacious "evidence" ran counter to the accusation that Zhang was a *hanjian*, a crime constructed in the anti-Japanese context, since America had been China's ally during World War II. Because of the witch-hunt atmosphere and the profit-driven nature of the tabloids, however, few questioned the flawed logic of such attacks.

Zhang's public degradation invited further humiliation and mistreatment. In her later writings, Zhang recounted how an old acquaintance in Shanghai's literary circles took advantage of her status as a *hanjian*'s wife. In the semiautobiographical story *Little Reunion* (Xiao tuanyuan), Zhang shed light on her life in postwar Shanghai as Hu Lancheng's wife. Xun Hua, a character in *Little Reunion*, was based on a left-wing editor and playwright in Shanghai who had befriended Zhang and Hu Lancheng. In Zhang's story, Xun sexually harasses the protagonist, Jiuli, while her *hanjian* husband is in exile after 1945. Jiuli bitterly comments that "everyone can take advantage of a *hanjian*'s wife."[102]

Many readers continued to support Zhang for her unique style and their identification of her writing with the city of Shanghai. Between 1946 and 1947, Zhang wrote two screenplays and published two serialized novels, which were warmly received.[103] After late 1947, Zhang's published output diminished. This was partly because of her depression in the wake of her divorce from Hu Lancheng. Moreover, because of her relationship with Hu, her screenplay *Darling, Stay at Home* (Taitai wansui) was poorly reviewed by literary critics. Zhang Ailing left Shanghai for Hong Kong in 1952, eventually settling in the United States in 1955.

Zhang did not discuss the issue of collaboration except for a hint in her novella *Lust, Caution* (Se, jie), which was written in 1950 and made into a film in 2007. The novella is based on the failed assassination of a *hanjian* by a female underground agent. Zhang shows subtle empathy for the male protagonist, who is constantly tormented by his choice to collaborate, and for the female assassin, who betrays her mission after she comes to know her intended victim as an individual and develops feelings for him.[104] The film stirred heated discussion in mainland China and prompted people to reevaluate the label of *hanjian*. As for her own case, Zhang, an individual who always chose to ignore criticism and rumors, nevertheless felt the necessity of self-defense. In 1946 she wrote, "I have never talked about political issues in my work, and have never received any subsidies." Regarding her marriage to Hu Lancheng, she asserted that "there is no need to reveal my private life to the public, and I have no obligation to make personal confessions to anyone but my family."[105]

CONCLUSION

As the crisis of war deepened in the 1930s, progressive intellectuals in China gained a stronger voice and greater authority in mobilizing the people and pushing the government to resist the Japanese advance. At the same time, these events constrained writers and artists by making nationalism the only permissible theme for their work. As the famous writer Lao She stated: "During the War of Resistance, Chinese literati should not and cannot freely write about anything they want to. Rather, they should all devote themselves to the resistance cause. The national crisis calls for literati to throw away their personal lives and join a collective life centering on the nation and society. A writer should be like a new recruit in the army, leaving everything behind and giving himself to the nation."[106]

Here Lao She, like many other writers during wartime, reinforced the standard grand narrative of Chinese history that both political parties upheld. The notion that literary and artistic productions were frivolous, or even harmful, unless they adopted the correct political tone was reinforced during the Mao years.

Intellectuals and artists who deviated from this theme or failed to conform to political expectations ran the risk of being identified as cultural *hanjian*, especially if they failed to relocate to free China. Some, indeed, served the propaganda needs of the Japanese and the puppet regime and were therefore convicted of the *hanjian* crime. More found themselves in a political and moral gray area, which made them vulnerable to suspicion and accusations of *hanjian* activity. Certain individuals were singled out not necessarily because they were guiltier than others but because of other factors, including commercial interests. Su Qing herself speculated that those who owed her commissions and who pirated her works participated in the campaigns that aimed to destroy her socially.[107]

Su Qing and Zhang Ailing became targets of the anti-*hanjian* campaigns also because many left-leaning intellectuals sought to suppress the influence of female-dominated literature during and after the occupation. As Haiyan Lee argued, these women writers publicized the idea that "personal happiness, especially as it pertains to women, does not necessarily hinge on collective [future] happiness." Because this idea was not compatible with the political needs of either party, these female writers "induced criticism from the increasingly left-leaning critical circle" as well as from conservatives.[108]

The purge of female collaborators was not peculiar to China. In France during the *après-libération*, about twenty thousand women had their heads shaved for "horizontal collaboration," a euphemism for sleeping with the Germans, among other acts. The act of head shaving was usually carried out by the local community, as the women's actions were seen as moral transgressions rather than crimes.[109] What was distinctive about anti-*hanjian* campaigns in postwar China was that sleeping with male *hanjian* was as much stigmatized as sleeping with the Japanese. *Hanjian*, after all, had been excluded from the national and ethnic community, and women who knowingly associated themselves with *hanjian* were deemed guilty by association, a traditional legal rationale and practice. Common people's war wounds and postwar economic struggles further intensified the resentment towards *hanjian* and those who were close to them.

Condemnation of lost female virtue was not just for women. Allegations of promiscuity functioned by means of analogy to denounce all those who turned against their nation, men as well as women. Pamphlet editors employed scandals and salacious anecdotes about these individuals as corroboration of their alleged political betrayals. Gendered slurs made attacks on *hanjian* effective and appealing to a broad audience and shaped the ways that the public rendered moral judgments on enemies or suspected enemies of the state. Many rhetorical strategies and phrases in the "hideous histories" genre survived and are familiar to us today because they were taken up later during mass campaigns after 1949.

CHAPTER 5

PUNISHING *HANJIAN* BEYOND CHINESE BORDERS

THE REGULATIONS ON PUNISHING *HANJIAN* DEFINED THE CRIME as conduct that endangered one's own nation and people, on the assumption that the accused would be Chinese. In practice, however, the Nationalist government also applied the law to non-Chinese "traitors." The fall of the Japanese empire placed its former colonies at the mercy of the Allied powers, which competed for a strong presence and influence in postwar Asia. Chiang Kai-shek's government, motivated by a sense of national mission to reclaim lost territory, applied its legal definition of *hanjian* to individuals from Manchuria, Taiwan, Southeast Asia, and beyond. Using its newly gained judicial sovereignty to buttress its claim of jurisdiction over these individuals, the government sought to realize a vision of Chinese identity that transcended the physical boundaries of the Chinese nation-state.

Colonial arrangements and constantly shifting borders in Asia in the early twentieth century allowed certain groups to acquire a status that resembled dual citizenship. But the contested nature of their citizenship in fact rendered these people stateless and vulnerable to the power plays and exploitation by various nations. Though few in number, *hanjian* cases against such individuals raised serious questions about the legality and applicability of Chinese laws. The Nationalist government's insistence on jurisdiction over these groups was challenged by forces abroad and constrained by drastic political shifts at home.

Controversy over these cases resulted from different understandings of what constitutes nationality. Each modern nation-state had its own particular process of geopolitical and ethnocultural formation. For generations, political leaders in China had understood and articulated Chinese identity in ethnoracial terms, which were not constrained by temporal or geographic divides. This mindset is reflected in the frequent reference to the

Taiwanese and overseas Chinese as *tongbao*, literally "born of the same womb." The government and people in mainland China stressed the bloodlines and cultural roots they shared with Taiwanese and Chinese Vietnamese identified as *hanjian*, which made the alleged betrayal all the more unforgivable. The Nationalist government pushed for the extraterritorial application of its anti-*hanjian* laws, therefore, to realize the unity of civic and ethnic Chinese identity.

The policy of including overseas Chinese in the anti-*hanjian* campaigns illustrated the Nationalists' interference with the long-term process of Chinese diaspora. Its timing, however, could not have been worse. Over centuries, large numbers of Chinese, for a variety of reasons, emigrated to other countries and formed communities branded with unique values and practices.[1] Scholars have recently raised problems with the application of the term *diaspora* to these groups because it assumes a Chinese identity that transcends in-group differences and renders overseas Chinese perpetually foreign to local societies.[2] Chineseness can be seen as a process rather than a fixed quality, as individuals and collectivities might become, stay, or cease to be Chinese.[3]

The process of retaining or losing one's Chineseness was constantly affected by arbitrary government decisions as well as by unexpected calamities. The Nationalist anti-*hanjian* campaigns can be seen as a countermeasure against political, social, and circumstantial factors that threatened to take away the identity of Chinese people overseas. China's victory in World War II and its newly gained international prestige encouraged the Nationalist government to reach out to Chinese overseas. The Civil War and the Communist takeover, however, interrupted this effort and triggered a new wave of Chinese emigration on an unprecedented scale. This chapter shows how the anti-*hanjian* campaigns negotiated with colonial legacies and postwar political trends to reassert the Chineseness of its lost citizens, as demonstrated in the cases of Taiwanese and Chinese Vietnamese.

TAIWANESE *HANJIAN*

The term "Taiwanese *hanjian*" (*taiji hanjian*) needs to be understood in light of the shifting identities of people in Taiwan, as the small island welcomed different rulers from the 1600s onward. The Chinese character *ji* can mean nationality (as in *guoji*), native place (as in *jiguan*), or registry (as in *huji*). Taiwan, once part of the Qing Empire (from 1683 to 1895) and then a Japanese colony (from 1895 to 1945), was reintegrated into the Republic of

China with the Japanese surrender in 1945. After centuries of cohabitation among people of diverse origins and changing political allegiances, a unique, hybrid culture and distinct identity had developed among the Taiwanese. Taiwan, however, had never become an independent polity, nor had *taiji* constituted nationality in its full sense. The status of *taiji* conferred the legal and commercial privileges accorded to foreigners on Taiwanese who traveled to mainland China.

The term *taiji* also aroused suspicion, contempt, and sometimes envy among mainlanders, as it implied that someone was on a registry kept by the Japanese colonial government. The creation of the *taiji* category resulted from the cession of Taiwan to Japan following the defeat of the Qing Empire in the first Sino-Japanese War (1894–95). When the two governments signed the Treaty of Shimonoseki in 1895, they set a two-year period during which residents in Taiwan could decide whether to return to the mainland. On March 19, 1896, the Japanese Office of the Governor General (Zongdufu) granted Japanese citizenship to Taiwan residents who chose to stay but put them on a separate registry from ethnic Japanese from the home islands of Japan.[4] *Taiji* gradually acquired negative connotations, denoting the less civilized, crime-prone, second-class citizens on the island, the "others" of the Japanese immigrants in Taiwan.

When more and more people of *taiji* status started to visit mainland China after 1908, various issues regarding their citizenship surfaced. Many took advantage of loopholes in the travel-certificate system that the Japanese operated in Taiwan and the policy that those who came to China from Japan did not need to notify the Japanese consulates.[5] As a result, a large number of Taiwanese entered mainland China via Japan to conduct business and purchase property, without the knowledge of the Office of the Governor General. In 1935, more than fifteen thousand Taiwanese sojourned on the mainland, two-thirds of whom were concentrated in the Xiamen area in Fujian.[6]

Xiamen was not only an ideal place for the Taiwanese to travel and invest, but it was also a place from which the Japanese could solidify their control of Taiwan and expand further into mainland China and Southeast Asia. Separated by only a strip of water, Xiamen and Taiwan shared historical trade networks and kinship connections. Following the cession of Taiwan, Xiamen had become the main base for anti-Japanese activities, so the Office of the Governor General regarded Xiamen as strategically important for securing Japan's interest in south China. In addition, many Chinese emigrated southward to neighboring countries from Xiamen, which they continued to regard as their hometown, maintaining social connections and placing their investments there. Therefore, the city was vital to Japan's broader geopolitical considerations in Southeast Asia.

As more *taiji* people came to Xiamen, some discovered that they could benefit from their ambiguous citizenship status. Some Taiwanese successfully passed as Chinese to travel inland and purchase property, privileges that were denied to foreigners. To enjoy lower taxes and extraterritoriality, however, the same people claimed foreign (Japanese) citizenship. Frustrated with those who cheated the system, the Fujian government pushed the Office of the Governor General in Taiwan to come up with a solution.

Local residents in and around Xiamen also took advantage of the confusion resulting from *taiji*. Increasingly, opportunistic souls from Fujian, seeking the benefits that came with the *taiji* status, disguised themselves as Taiwanese. They could conveniently do so because they had a similar accent and physical appearance to the Taiwanese, and often shared the same kin.[7] In the 1910s, in response to the various problems involving *taiji*, the Office of the Governor General developed a set of criteria for determining eligibility for *taiji* status. These criteria, which included character, skills, and assets, allowing the Japanese to grant *taiji* status or de facto Japanese citizenship selectively. Only those who were seen as adding value to the Japanese empire and who would not tarnish its reputation were allowed to claim *taiji* status.[8]

Before 1945, the Taiwanese had no claim to Chinese citizenship. For decades there had been greater barriers than the strait separating Taiwan from the mainland. The island had been a Japanese colony since 1895, and it fought on the Japanese side during the Second World War. Its return to the Republic of China was a result of agreements made among the Allied nations, rather than a process of gradual decolonization or a well-coordinated indigenous movement. To prepare for Taiwan's reintegration, therefore, the Chinese state and media faced the daunting task of bringing the two peoples closer together. They opted for a friendlier label for people of *taiji* status, which was *Taiwan tongbao* (*taibao* for short), or "Taiwanese compatriots." Having surfaced during wartime, this term has since dominated the welcoming discourse toward the Taiwanese. After the war, mainlanders were fed an overflowing amount of information on Taiwan. On the heels of the civil and military officials who were appointed to administrative positions in Taiwan, representatives from different presses and newspapers rushed to the island for firsthand observations. These journalists introduced mainlanders to the different faces of Taiwanese people and society. The "treasure island," as they described it, was an affluent, beautiful, friendly place. A recurring theme of such reports was the innate Chineseness of Taiwan. *Dagong bao*, for instance, urged people to stop imagining Taiwan as a colony. The editor argued that the Taiwanese were essentially south Fujianese and Hakkas from Guangdong. Since "blood is thicker than water," there was no doubt that "they are truly patriotic."[9]

The call for mainlanders to treat the Taiwanese as compatriots grew in part out of practical needs for China's reconstruction and future development. *Dagong bao* made a meticulous assessment of Taiwan's resources, industrial basis, and strategic importance for building the Chinese navy. The writer urged the readers to "just think about how much our nation and our people will benefit from all the resources here once we take them over."[10] The author also stressed that such an arrangement was mutually beneficial, listing various ways in which the motherland could protect Taiwan and boost the island's future development.

Beneath the enthusiastic praises and welcoming gestures in the press, however, lay a sense of wariness. Although reporters all tried to appear politically correct by describing how the vast majority of "Taiwanese compatriots" longed to rejoin the national community, they also remarked on the influence of Japanese colonial rule on Taiwanese culture and identity. Concluding a tour around the island, journalists from *Wenhui bao* produced a detailed editorial that was overall balanced and rich in detail. Its title, however, based on an exaggerated anecdote of the ignorance of one Taiwanese person, was disheartening: "Experiencing Taiwan: Their Ignorance of the Past and Present of the Mainland" (Taiwan xing: Buzhi youqin, geng buzhi you han, taibaohai ba women dangzuo qingguoren).[11] Other publications, to varying degrees, lamented the legacies of Japan's isolationist policy and the education of enslavement it had imposed on the Taiwanese. Compatriots though they might be, these articles implied, the Taiwanese could not be fully trusted after all.

The integrationists among Taiwan's elites echoed the optimistic voices from the mainland, confirming Taiwan's allegiance to the Chinese nation. In particular, they emphasized the inner Chineseness of the Taiwanese people, which they had retained throughout Japanese rule. On July 31, 1945, when receiving important members of the national assembly and media representatives from Chongqing, Li Wanju, a leading figure of the Taiwan Revolutionary Alliance (Taiwan Geming Tongmenghui), delivered a speech titled "Taiwan has not been Japanized."[12] Li recounted how Taiwanese patriots had relentlessly resisted the "Japanese invaders" (*rikou*) during the past fifty years. Li's speech also highlighted a recent event in the Philippines in which more than six hundred Taiwanese soldiers had defected and fought against Japanese troops alongside Chinese guerrillas and American forces.

The mainstream media in Taiwan made similar attempts to influence the public on both sides. *Taiwan minsheng bao*, a newspaper affiliated with the Taiwan Revolutionary Alliance, published an extensive discussion on the political beliefs and regionalist views of the Taiwanese. The editorial admitted that Taiwan had been geographically and politically separated from its homeland for so long that mainlanders did not know their Taiwanese compatriots well. This lack of knowledge, in addition to the activities of a handful of Taiwanese *ronin* ("masterless samurai," a Japanese term used here to denote Taiwanese ruffians, which also implied that the Taiwanese were beholden to the Japanese yet rejected by them) and *hanjian*, accounted for an overall negative perception of the Taiwanese people among mainlanders. Speaking to a mainland audience, the author described a majority of Taiwanese as quiet, hardworking, caring, and always nostalgic for their motherland. By nature they were "a branch of Han descendants who had been placed under alien rule for the past half century." Their emotional attachment to their home country, the author testified, was not a bit weaker than that of people from the mainland.[13]

The Taiwan Revolutionary Alliance directed public opinion in such ways precisely because it had been founded with the guidance and support of the Nationalist government. In early 1941, resistance forces from Taiwan gathered in Chongqing and announced the foundation of the alliance. Representatives from the Nationalist Ministry of Justice, the Military Council, and the Legislative Yuan attended the founding ceremony. In addition, the Nationalist party's press organs and other media outlets in Chongqing published front-page stories and emotional editorials educating the mainlanders about Taiwan, its Chineseness, and its anti-Japanese endeavors in the past and present.[14] In January 1943, the Taiwan Revolutionary Alliance supported Chiang Kai-shek's plan of reclaiming Taiwan in his negotiations at the Cairo conference.[15] To demonstrate the close ties between Taiwan and the mainland, the alliance announced that "93.7 percent of the people in Taiwan retain Chinese bloodlines," a statistic that sounded attractive to Chinese people leery of miscegenation with the Japanese but which was impossible to prove.[16]

The leaders of the Taiwan Revolutionary Alliance, such as Li Wanju and Qiu Niantai, were handpicked by Chiang Kai-shek because of their prominent positions in Taiwan and close ties with Chongqing. Between 1943 and 1946, these individuals coordinated with the Nationalist government to push for Taiwan's nationalization. Emphasizing Chineseness was an important strategy in this endeavor. At the same time, these individuals tried to protect the rights and interests of the Taiwanese. As the cases of Taiwanese *hanjian* show, Taiwanese elites who had connections in Nanjing made courageous moves to shield their people from the kinds of purges that were unfolding on the mainland.

A primary spokesperson for the Taiwanese was Qiu Niantai. Qiu's words carried considerable weight because of his family background, his familiarity with Taiwanese politics and culture, and his participation in local resistance movements. His father, Qiu Fengjia (1864–1912), was a highly respected figure in Taiwanese history who continued to personify the pro-unity sentiments and forces in Taiwan. Qiu Fengjia led the futile yet heroic resistance to Japanese occupation following the cession of Taiwan in 1895. Fengjia named his son Niantai, literally "remembering Taiwan." Niantai himself was no less a patriot, as demonstrated by the anti-Japanese activities that he had organized at different stages of Japan's colonial expansion in Asia.

Qiu's allegiance and expertise on Taiwan affairs won him the trust of Chiang Kai-shek. On April 17, 1944, Chiang established a Taiwan Investigation Committee (Taiwan Diaocha Weiyuanhui), and appointed Qiu as a member. The committee conducted research and drafted blueprints for nationalization and reconstruction projects in Taiwan. After the Nationalist government established the Taiwan Provincial Administrative Executive Office (Taiwan Xingzheng Zhangguan Gongshu, or TPAEO), the committee continued to advise the central and local administrations on all types of issues.[17]

In addition to performing his official duties, Qiu devoted himself to building bridges between the mainland and Taiwan. He invited influential individuals in Taiwan on a special trip to the mainland to connect with important government figures and institutions, in addition to visiting historical sites.[18] Qiu had a deep understanding of and sympathy for Taiwan, an island that, in his opinion "had been isolated from the homeland and left floating on the sea" (*guxuan haiwai*), and for the people, who had no power over their own fate. He refuted any suspicion that Taiwanese lacked nationalistic consciousness. A small percentage of Taiwanese were indeed forced to fight for the Japanese, but even they were not willing to "take foes for parents" (*ren zei zuo fu*).[19] At the time of Taiwan's return and the nationwide anti-*hanjian* campaigns, Qiu felt responsible for advocating for fair treatment of the Taiwanese people by the central government.

The Nationalist policies regarding Taiwanese *hanjian* were inconsistent at best. The government had originally envisioned all laws and regulations issued in mainland China as applying to Taiwan, including the Regulations on Punishing *Hanjian*. The state could thus immediately replace colonial legal concepts and institutions with the Nationalist legal code and judiciary. Equally significant in this move was the assertion of Chinese jurisdiction over Taiwan. At the same time, Chiang Kai-shek allowed his representatives in Taiwan some flexibility. The TPAEO, headed by General Chen Yi, was granted the authority to enact provisions that addressed local problems and emergency situations.[20] To what extent the TPAEO could bypass legislative procedures and employ this authority, however, was never made clear. This lack of clarity soon had negative consequences.

The TPAEO, like the central government, saw the extermination of *hanjian* as a necessary step toward nationalizing this former Japanese colony. On January 16, 1946, the Nationalist garrison headquarters in Taiwan, on the orders of the Ministry of the Army, decreed that local people must report *hanjian* within two weeks. People were panicked as much as they were confused, for no one knew what constituted the *hanjian* crime. Taiwan had been part of what China considered the "enemy nation," and Taiwanese had had to fulfill their duties as citizens of that nation. One newspaper article commented that if the Regulations were to be interpreted at face value, everybody in Taiwan who had lived under the Japanese rule could be considered *hanjian*. Two days later, the TPAEO confirmed that indeed, the Regulations on Punishing *Hanjian* should be followed in Taiwan as in other Chinese provinces.[21] Soon afterward, the first group of five *hanjian* was arrested. When the two weeks were up, the common people had brought three hundred cases to the TPAEO or the Taiwan High Court.[22]

In launching the anti-*hanjian* campaign, the TPAEO had particular targets in mind. *Xinsheng bao*, the government-run newspaper, urged the public to expose individuals who had conspired with the Japanese military in plotting Taiwan's independence after Japan's surrender. Many in this group were powerful members of Taiwanese society who had benefited from Japanese patronage. Newspapers called them "scholar gentry in the service of the Japanese emperor" (*yuyong shishen*). In March 1946, the garrison headquarters arrested many of these individuals. Attacks on *hanjian* and the "scholar gentry" continued until October 1946.[23]

As with Chinese *hanjian*, the arrest and imprisonment of Taiwanese *hanjian* was supplemented by a total or partial revocation of their rights and credentials. In February 1946, TPAEO issued its Restrictions on the Political Rights of Taiwanese under Suspicion, which excluded *hanjian* suspects from local elections. Even if the court decided to drop the *hanjian* charges, anyone who had worked in the puppet regime or its institutions would have their political rights suspended for a designated number of years. In addition, former members of the Associations for the Devoted Subjects of the Emperor (Huangmin Fenggonghui), which the Japanese organized in 1941 to tighten its colonial control, were barred from holding any public office.[24] Later government correspondence revealed that these restrictions came out as administrative orders from the TPAEO, which did not consult with the Ministry of Justice.[25]

People in Taiwan found their subjection to mainland China's anti-*hanjian* laws unfair, but only a few were in a position to speak out. Between 1945 and 1947, Qiu Niantai pushed for a more just solution to the issue of Taiwanese *hanjian*. When the TPAEO announced the restrictions on the political rights of the Taiwanese elites, Qiu immediately protested. He accused such a policy of "giving preferential treatment to the Japanese over compatriots," for many universities and even government organs had retained their Japanese employees.[26] If this edict remained in effect, Qiu warned, no Taiwanese would qualify for public positions, people would grow discontented, and unrest would ensue. Qiu's predictions alarmed leaders and lawmakers in Nanjing, who had no knowledge of the restrictions in question. The Executive Yuan and the Ministry of Justice both reprimanded the TPAEO for ignoring legislative procedures and passing provisions that lacked any legal basis.[27] This political battle ended in victory for Qiu and the numerous local elites he tried to protect, at least for the time being.

In October 1946, Qiu pointed out the illegality of treating Taiwanese as *hanjian* and war criminals (*zhanfan*). He argued that the laws targeting Chinese *hanjian* were not applicable to people in Taiwan, where history had taken a different trajectory. Qiu reasoned as follows:

> Calling Taiwanese people *hanjian* and war criminals would be misplacing the blame and ignoring the nation's past. When the Treaty [of Shimono-seki] was signed, Taiwan was ceded, and people there were abandoned. People put up resistance to the Japanese occupation but to no avail. They had no choice but to be enslaved. Legally speaking, to call the Taiwanese

hanjian does not make any sense, as they were Japanese citizens. A Taiwanese person was not allowed to take any high position in the colonial administration, or to command a battle, or to plot an invasion. Taiwanese were too powerless to become war criminals.[28]

When Qiu wrote this petition, more than twenty Taiwanese individuals were being detained in Nanjing as either *hanjian* or war criminals. Courts in Guangdong, Fujian, Zhejiang, Jiangsu, Shandong, and Hebei were processing numerous cases involving Taiwanese *hanjian* and war criminals. The slow pace of the proceedings, intentionally or not, prolonged the individuals' sense of estrangement and agony.[29] Qiu requested that with the exception of those who had actively participated in massacres, the government should allow those arrested to return home on bail.

Qiu's actions were also fueled by his anger with the injustice of the anti-*hanjian* process. Most those whom Qiu considered actual *hanjian* were wealthy and resourceful enough to escape punishment. People who were arrested as *hanjian* on either side of the Taiwan Strait were mainly ordinary people without titles or assets. What they had done or failed to do during wartime had almost no impact on the outcome of the war. Furthermore, in Qiu's opinion, many Nationalist officials and soldiers were taking out their hatred of the Japanese on the Taiwanese people, regardless of their degree of involvement in Japan's colonial rule and expansion.[30] Qiu's protests and suggestions were reiterated by Taiwanese elites when they visited the Ministry of Justice in Nanjing.

Qiu's efforts paid off. In November 1946, the Nationalist government granted most Taiwanese exemption from prosecution for the *hanjian* crime. The anti-*hanjian* laws would apply only in cases where solid evidence or witness testimony offered proof of serious abuses of power or inhumane acts.[31] Laws governing war crimes were still considered applicable to the Taiwanese. Following this edict, the Taiwan High Court stopped accepting *hanjian* cases, and most *hanjian* suspects arrested in Taiwan were set free.

As *hanjian* were being exposed and arrested in Taiwan, many Taiwanese went through the same process on the mainland. For them, the central government's policy of exemption was not immediately applied. Xiamen saw the most systematic and draconian punishment of Taiwanese *hanjian*, primarily because of the high concentration of Taiwanese criminals, spies, and translators in the area. Between Xiamen's liberation in October 1945 and restoration of the judiciary in August 1946, the arrest and investigation of *hanjian* cases was handled by Nationalist intelligence and military officials. Under Dai Li's authorization, Juntong established a special committee on the "cleansing of *hanjian*" (*sujian*) in Jinmen and Xiamen. The committee was headed by Shen Jinkang, who had commanded Juntong's Xiamen office and the local police.[32] In the ten months before the judiciary took over *hanjian* cases, this committee arrested 231 *hanjian* suspects, half of whom were Taiwanese.

Initially, Juntong followed military orders in identifying Taiwanese guilty of the *hanjian* crime. When the Ministry of the Army in Nanjing ordered the exposure of *hanjian* in Taiwan, it also issued Resolutions on Handling Taiwanese Persons, a set of brief instructions on how to categorize and handle Taiwanese on the mainland:

> Taiwanese persons who served in the Japanese army are to be treated indistinguishably from Japanese soldiers and handed over to the government organ to which they surrendered.
>
> Taiwanese persons scattered in different places are to be grouped together, kept separate from the Japanese and *hanjian*, and kept under guard to prevent escape.
>
> Taiwanese persons who served as spies for the Japanese, harmed compatriots, or colluded with the Japanese in profiting from military supplies are to be prosecuted.
>
> Taiwanese persons who are proved innocent can choose to stay or return to Taiwan, though ideally they should be handed over to the TPAEO for resettlement.
>
> On their return journey, Taiwanese should depart in groups; and the TPAEO should be responsible for their registration and transportation.[33]

When these resolutions were issued in January 1946, Juntong had already arrested a large number of *hanjian*, many of whom were of *taiji* status. Days after the resolutions were announced, more than one thousand people registered to return to Taiwan. Not all made it back. When two departing passengers were identified by local residents as former detectives of the puppet police force, the Xiamen police started screening all outbound passengers for *hanjian* suspects. In the following months, while about four thousand Taiwanese sojourners departed for home, more than one hundred *hanjian* suspects and their families were detained by Juntong's *sujian* committee.[34]

To conclude its work up to August 1946, when the judiciary took over, the Juntong committee compiled reports of *hanjian* cases in a collection titled *Records of the* Hanjian *Criminals in Fujian and Taiwan* (Mintai hanjian zuixingjishi), or the *Records*. This collection provided detailed accounts of 166 *hanjian* trials, revealing important patterns in wartime collaboration in Xiamen and in the prosecution of *hanjian*. The prefaces and comments on individual cases reflected the polarized framework within which crimes were measured and moral evaluations were made. The committee applied the same dichotomy of loyalty or betrayal to *taiji hanjian* and *benguoji hanjian* (literally, "*hanjian* of our own nationality," or mainland *hanjian*) alike, though it had listed them as two separate categories.

Biographies of and comments on Taiwanese *hanjian* deployed peculiar vocabularies and criminal analyses. Lai Guomin, a Juntong agent who served on the committee, considered the evils done by Taiwanese *hanjian* "greater than those by *hanjian* from Fujian and other provinces." Seeing that Taiwanese *hanjian* accounted for half of the arrested, Lai called the Taiwanese "truly detestable" for relying on their Japanese masters to bully their compatriots.[35] Another agent classified the Taiwanese with the Japanese as two great evils that had haunted Xiamen even before the war. With the support of the Japanese consulate, he alleged, Taiwanese *ronin* "robbed and killed everywhere in Xiamen." The committee also called certain individuals "utter slaves of the Japanese," a phrase that was seldom applied to Chinese *hanjian*.[36]

The Nationalist government's policy of exempting Taiwanese *hanjian* in November 1946 did not alleviate the plight of those who had already been so identified.[37] By then the Juntong Committee had been dissolved, and the Fujian High Court took charge of the prosecutions based on Juntong's investigations. Since the *hanjian* crime was deemed inapplicable to Taiwanese defendants, the judiciary charged seventy-three of them with other crimes and found thirty-nine guilty. Ten were charged with various war crimes and transferred to a military tribunal in Shanghai.[38] Even if they were not convicted of the crime, all Taiwanese individuals arrested as *hanjian* were regarded as such by the government and the public. Media exposure of their identity and the publication of the *Records* contributed to their notoriety. These individuals came from a wide range of educational and occupational backgrounds. Cao Cifu, for instance, had served on the police force in colonial Taiwan before becoming a detective in Xiamen. Chen Yuqi's family had been involved in the opium business for generations. Lin Jiyong held a business degree from Meiji University in Japan. Huang Kuishan owned a clinic in Xiamen and had been practicing medicine.

The *Records* depicted all as having capitalized on the war and their Japanese connections to gain power, wealth, and social status. Some were accused of aggravating the suffering of the local people. Many Taiwanese in Xiamen took positions in the local puppet government, but this alone did not constitute a *hanjian* crime. Following the Resolutions on Handling Taiwanese Persons, Juntong allowed immediate bail for sixteen Taiwanese who had served in the puppet administration but were faced with no other charges.[39] Others, however, were accused of deliberately sabotaging the resistance movement or exploiting the local people. Their exemption from prosecution on account of their *taiji* status greatly upset the public and discredited the government's anti-*hanjian* work in general. The following profiles of Taiwanese *hanjian* illuminate what was at stake in these cases.

Hong Wenzhong was a Taiwanese born in Xiamen. Before the war, Hong ran a theater, which became a networking hub for Taiwanese sojourners in shady businesses sheltered by the Japanese consulate. After the fall of Xiamen in 1938, Hong served as a spy for the Japanese. Hong's main crime, which made him almost a personal foe of the committee, was his exposure and destruction of Juntong's underground office in Xiamen in 1940. At the time, the head of this branch office, Chen Qingbao, was disguised as manager of a shell company, with Juntong agents as its employees. One of the agents defected and went to Hong Wenzhong with loads of confidential information. Hong then led a group of Japanese detectives and Taiwanese *hanjian* to the office and caught the whole team by surprise. Four agents were executed shortly after, six were tortured to death, five escaped from prison, and twenty-one were imprisoned until the end of the war. This incident dealt a huge blow to Juntong's institutional pride, not to mention tremendous losses of personnel and resources.

The committee proposed to prosecute Hong for multiple war crimes. In addition to sabotaging the Nationalist intelligence network, Hong was found guilty of facilitating the enemy's assimilation policies, running gambling houses, supplying the enemy with equipment, and forcing locals into hard labor. The Office of the Procurator, to the disappointment of the committee and Hong's local victims, charged Hong only with regular criminal offenses, on account of his *taiji* status. Hong was sentenced to imprisonment for two and half years, whereas several of his Chinese accomplices received harsher punishment. The public in Xiamen was outraged, and

Hong's case was later cited to demonstrate the miscarriage of justice in cases involving Taiwanese *hanjian*.[40]

Lin Jiyong from Taizhong, Taiwan, was accused of manipulating the production and circulation of salt and opium. With an official position in the puppet administration, Lin turned one-fifth of the land in Jinmen into opium fields and forced the local people into planting this widely resented narcotic, making huge profits for the Japanese and for himself from the sale of the crop. The Committee detailed how Lin "relied on his *taiji* status to acquire a puppet administrative position on our territory," expressing a convoluted resentment toward Taiwanese *hanjian*. For the pain and shame he had inflicted on Chinese soil, "any member of the Chinese race would say that Lin deserved immediate execution."[41] The procurators originally charged Lin with regular criminal offenses. With the central government taking a more draconian approach to Taiwanese offenders in the aftermath of the February 28 Incident in 1947, Lin was transferred to the military tribunal in Nanjing to be tried as a war criminal.

Lin Shen was considered a Taiwanese *hanjian* for assisting the Japanese and informing on the resistance movement. In 1938, he was commissioned by the Japanese to supply labor for various transportation projects, for which he "manipulated innocent Taiwanese compatriots and trained Taiwanese labor for the Japanese." Soon afterward, the Japanese put Lin in charge of household registration, a position that enabled him to search for anti-Japanese elements (*kangri fenzi*) and solicit donations from local residents. In addition, according to local newspapers, Lin had forcefully occupied private property and was directly responsible for the death of several people. Residents in Xiamen "all wanted to eat him alive."[42] The Office of the Procurator, however, allowed him to go free on bail.

The accounts by Juntong and petitions by members of the Taiwanese elite, which held opposite positions on this issue, both reveal miscarriages of justice in the cases of Taiwanese *hanjian*. Many principal offenders escaped the law, whereas minor criminals were caught. The *taiji* status of certain defendants was not the fundamental reason for the uneven treatment of the accused; nor was it the main cause of public discontent. The complications with *taiji*, however, provided corrupt Nationalist officials with new ways to distort justice. Juntong felt the necessity of compiling records of these cases precisely because of the controversies and public distrust its work had caused. It complained about the difficulties in tracing the movable assets of defendants of *hanjian* and war criminals, which were estimated to be a handsome amount. The generous payments made to defense attorneys and the large amounts set for bail all spoke to the hidden wealth of the accused.

Some Nationalist officials openly attempted to profit from the process of "clearing *hanjian*."[43] Zhang Shenwei, the chief procurator in Xiamen, announced that out of the first 195 *hanjian* cases he had received from the Committee, he would allow bailouts for one hundred defendants, half of whom he promised to not prosecute. *Hanjian* defendants immediately rushed to his house and showered him with cash, gold, and luxurious gifts.[44] Zhang's blatant invitation to bribery cost him his career and also undermined public confidence in the local judiciary. In response, the local newspaper, *Jiang sheng bao*, disclosed the names of all *hanjian* suspects arrested in Xiamen, both Chinese and Taiwanese, and the current state of their cases, in order to make the process more transparent.

A less conspicuous problem with the investigation of Taiwanese *hanjian* was the use of torture, which was rare in the interrogation of Chinese *hanjian*. When the committee arrested Hong Wenzhong and Lin Guangming, a former Juntong agent who had defected, it was seeking vengeance for colleagues who died at their hands. Members of the committee admitted to using corporal punishment on Hong and Lin to obtain information, and more important, as a payback for what they had done to Juntong agents. Hong endured several rounds of torture without giving in, which simultaneously frustrated and impressed the committee. Lin Guangming, on the other hand, caved in before torture was even used. Although the committee maintained that the use of torture was unusual, the lack of supervision and established procedure certainly left room for abuse.

Outside Fujian, many more Taiwanese *hanjian* cases were still in limbo. As late as 1948, cases from Nanjing, Jiangxi, Beijing, and Tianjin showed that Taiwanese who had been charged with the *hanjian* crime with insufficient evidence were being detained by the courts without trial. In some cases, since the *hanjian* charge was no longer applicable, Taiwanese who had taken leading positions in Japanese-sponsored local organizations faced the charge of "transgression of Chinese sovereignty," which carried a ten-year prison term. In other cases, Taiwanese defendants were still tried as Chinese citizens for the *hanjian* crime.[45]

A watershed event, the February 28 Incident, prompted advocates from Taiwan to take up the issue of Taiwanese *hanjian* again. The takeover of Taiwan did not go as smoothly as the central government had planned or the local Taiwanese had wished. The lack of trust between the mainlanders and the Taiwanese doomed the process from the start. The

Nationalists' condescending attitude towards the Taiwanese, combined with policies that brought sudden changes to the political structure, customs, and language, further alienated a great number of Taiwanese who had lost privileges in the transition of power. Ethnic tension and resentment toward the Nationalist administration built up and erupted on February 28, 1947, when the police attempted to arrest a street vendor in Taipei for violating the state monopoly on cigarettes. This minor incident triggered large-scale protests that soon spread to other cities in Taiwan. The Nationalist veterans, under the command of Governor Chen Yi, crushed the protesters with gunfire. Following the incident, the Nationalists ushered in an age of "white terror" on the island that lasted for decades. This event has been commemorated as a turning point in Taiwanese history and has sparked extensive research and debate on both sides of the Taiwan Strait.[46]

Qiu Niantai was among those who urged the government to show leniency toward the Taiwanese. He observed that since the liberation of Taiwan, the Taiwanese people had felt increasingly marginalized by the mainlanders and alienated from Nanjing. He was eager to come up with a remedy. To Qiu, the incrimination of Taiwanese as *hanjian* and war criminals was a main cause of such ill feelings. He therefore suggested an amnesty for all convicted Taiwanese *hanjian* and war criminals to ease the tension and forestall further unrest.[47]

Dong Guoshu, who represented Taiwan in the National Assembly, also urged the central government to handle cases of Taiwanese *hanjian* with leniency and discretion, especially in light of the continuous tensions following February 28. Recapitulating the history of Taiwan in his petition, Dong emphasized that the Taiwanese people had proved themselves to be the "sons and daughters" of the Chinese race through their continuous wartime resistance activities. In Dong's analysis, Japan had deliberately created the impression that all Taiwanese were *hanjian* by keeping the law-abiding ones on the island and letting the criminal elements run wild on the mainland. In this way, Japan had pitted the Taiwanese and the mainlanders against each other.

According to Dong, although Taiwan had been recovered, the hearts of the Taiwanese had not, because of the unjust treatment they had received. In Southeast Asia, Taiwanese often encountered discrimination from Chinese diplomats, whose attitudes reflected that of the central government. More important, Dong saw the punishment of Taiwanese for the *hanjian* crime and the takeover of their property as the main impediments to reconciliation. Rather than prosecute *hanjian*, Dong suggested, the government should recognize patriotic Taiwanese who had resisted the Japanese.[48]

Accounts of Taiwanese veterans confirmed the sense of mistreatment and alienation they had developed since the liberation. In 1997, the Academia Sinica in Taiwan organized a meeting attended by more than sixty Taiwanese veterans who had fought in the Japanese army, who shared their experiences under Japanese and Nationalist rule. They had an overall negative impression of the Nationalist officials and soldiers they encountered, who treated them with insults and discrimination. Frequently branded as *hanjian*, these veterans bitterly resented the label, especially because, in their opinion, the Nationalists themselves were not patriotic at all.[49] One veteran recalled that a Nationalist party member and government clerk had studied English every day in the hope of emigrating to the United States.

Indifference, if not utter disdain, toward the Taiwanese seemed to saturate the Nationalist military at every level. The Japanese withdrew from the island of Hainan immediately after the war, leaving some eight thousand Taiwanese soldiers stranded there until 1946. The UNRRA (United Nations Relief and Rehabilitation Administration) found the Taiwanese starving, injured, and abused by the Nationalist soldiers who took over the island. The UNRRA exhausted its resources to arrange for the return of the Taiwanese soldiers, but the TPAEO replied that these *hanjian* should be left for dead in Hainan.[50] In collaboration with social organizations in Taiwan, the UNRRA managed to send the soldiers home. One soldier bitterly commented that the Nationalist troops were "greatly humiliated and defeated by the Japanese on the mainland, so they tried to take it out on us." Such a view was echoed by other Taiwanese veterans and the larger population.

When the Nationalist troops arrived in Taiwan, they were faced with a population who had held foreign citizenship for decades and still spoke a different language. Other than both once belonging to the long-vanished Qing empire, the only tangible connections between Taiwan and the mainland were made by Taiwanese who crossed the strait with ambiguous citizenship status. To prepare for a hasty reintegration of Taiwan, the government and integrationists on both sides championed the reunion of people "who were born of the same womb." This myth, however, was far from sufficient justification for the Nationalist government's punishment of the Taiwanese for their lack of loyalty in the past. The ill handling of Taiwanese *hanjian* by local Nationalist deputies further tarnished the government's image. The discourse of unity notwithstanding, mutual distrust and disdain haunted the encounters from the beginning. Central to this conflict was the mainlanders' perception of Taiwanese as *hanjian* in general.

The punishment of Taiwanese *hanjian* was also an essential part of what the historian Leo T. S. Ching calls the Nationalists' "neo-colonial policy towards Taiwanese," whom it claimed as its own citizens. To the Taiwanese, the elite class in particular, the issue was not merely one of political allegiance. Fifty years of Japanese rule had set Taiwan on a distinctive path toward modernity, which for Taiwanese intellectuals was epitomized by Japan rather than the distant West (or backward mainland China).[51] The nationalization of Taiwan was one and the same as de-Japanization. In that sense, the purge of Taiwanese *hanjian* was more important as a chance for the state to send a powerful political message than as a battle for justice.

HANJIAN AMONG CHINESE IN VIETNAM

As in Taiwan, the anti-*hanjian* cause in Vietnam was part of the Nationalist government's larger project of rebuilding a Chinese identity that transcended political boundaries. The Nationalist government recognized the immediate postwar period as a crucial time to reconnect with overseas Chinese, whose wealth and influence they saw as valuable assets for China's reconstruction. It pursued this cause by reinforcing the emotional and ethnic ties that had compelled many overseas Chinese to wholeheartedly support the defense of their motherland against the foreign invasion. The Nationalist government was most vigorous in reintegrating Chinese in Southeast Asia because of their geographic proximity, their number, and their wealth. The vision and plan of the Chinese state, however, were disrupted by other powers in postwar French Indochina as well as by the Vietnamese national independence movements. Moreover, the corruption and incompetence of Nationalist representatives in Vietnam alienated their *tongbao* there and undermined the anti-*hanjian* cause.

The Nationalist government's postwar maneuvers in Vietnam, as in Taiwan, aimed at interrupting the indigenization process by which immigrants gradually become natives in their language, customs, and identity. Vietnam—in particular Northern Vietnam, known as Annam to the Chinese—had been a familiar neighbor, protectorate, trade partner, and buffer zone for more than two thousand years. China had established an administration in this region as early as the third century, and Chinese immigrants had been finding their way to Vietnam for employment, business, and political asylum for centuries before modern times. In the tenth century, Annam regained its independence.[52] Ethnic awareness and identity grew among the Kinh (Viet) people while they defended and won back their homeland from the Chinese. This region became the cornerstone of the Vietnamese nation-state.[53] Some Chinese, despite the political reconfiguration in Annam, requested permanent resettlement there and married local women.

Major political changes in China and Vietnam in the mid-seventeenth century created tensions between the two that influenced the lives of Chinese immigrants. When the Chinese were experiencing the painful transition from the Ming dynasty (1368–1644) to the Manchu Qing rule, Vietnam was divided between the Trinh lords (1545–1787) in the north and the Nguyen lords (1558–1777) in the south. Directly bordering China, the Trinh lords accepted Chinese immigrants only under strict conditions and eventually forcibly assimilated them.[54] The Nguyen lords in the south, more distant from and less concerned with their relations to the Qing, welcomed the Ming loyalists who escaped from the Manchu rule, allowing them to maintain their ethnic and cultural identity.

Thus began the history of the Minh Huong (literally, "the Ming incense people"), a group of Chinese immigrants unique in their political background and ethnic claims. The meaning of the term has changed over time. According to the Dai Nam Chronicle, in 1679 about three thousand Chinese officers, soldiers, and their families landed at Thuan An in central Vietnam and settled there.[55] By the end of the seventeenth century, Chinese merchants and artisans had established villages and communities in the Dong Nai plain.[56] These communities, which they called Minh Huong *xã*, functioned as lineage organizations and initially consisted of ethnically Chinese men and their Vietnamese wives. Carrying on "the Ming incense" tradition acknowledged their shared Han ancestors and symbolized their allegiance to the Han-based Ming dynasty. In other words, the Minh Huong in Vietnam embraced an ethnically and culturally based Chineseness that went beyond the territorial and temporal bounds of any Han-based Chinese empire.

By the early nineteenth century, the Minh Huong people had been indigenized. The political connotations of the name faded, and it came to refer simply to those of mixed Sino-Vietnamese ancestry who still demonstrated a cultural affinity with China.[57] The Nguyen dynasty practiced divide-and-rule policies toward Chinese in Vietnam, which created separate communities and identities for Minh Huong and for *huaqiao*, or Chinese sojourners. Minh Huong were ordered to dress like Vietnamese and not leave for China.[58] *Huaqiao* at this time mostly came from neighboring Guangdong (Canton), and they relocated to Vietnam with the main purpose of profiting from the burgeoning maritime trade.[59]

The arrival of French colonialism dramatically complicated the bilateral relations between Qing China and Vietnam and the evolution of Chinese communities in Vietnam. By 1884, the French controlled Nam Ky (Cochin China) and had turned Bac Ky (Tonkin) and Trung Ky (Annam) into its protectorates.

Following China's defeat in the Opium Wars, waves of Chinese immigrants kept pouring into Vietnam, largely because of the welcoming policies of the new French colonial administration. The colonial government actively recruited Chinese labor for construction. Chinese in general enjoyed a wide range of rights under the colonial government, including trade, land ownership, and restriction-free travel to their home country. The Chinese population in French Indochina tripled between 1889 and the 1920s, reaching 158,000. Many Chinese sojourners of this period performed manual labor and service jobs, thus diversifying the socioeconomic profiles of Chinese in Vietnam. The number of Minh Huong people also grew under the French colonial government, but it did not keep pace with the number of *huaqiao*.[60]

Until the late 1920s, the French colonial government had dictated the issue of nationality for Chinese in Vietnam by drafting policies that best served its own needs. The government classified all those with Chinese fathers, and second-generation immigrants, as "foreigners," thereby recognizing that they were Chinese. The Minh Huong people, however, were singled out and offered the opportunity to choose between Chinese nationality and a new status known as "French Asian citizens." The French, however, deliberately made being Chinese more expensive. As a revenue-generating policy, it charged the Minh Huong people a fee if they opted to remain Chinese.[61]

With the rise of a modern Chinese state committed to rebuilding China, the nationality of Chinese in Vietnam became a pressing issue. On the establishment of the Nanjing government in 1928, Chiang Kai-shek immediately sought to reconnect with overseas Chinese by acknowledging their Chinese nationality. By the 1930s, China and France had gone through several rounds of negotiations and disputes regarding the citizenship of Minh

Huong and the rights of Chinese in Vietnam.[62] These disputes were partly over control and influence in Vietnam but also hinged on different understandings of the concept of nationality.

The Chinese Nationality Act of 1929 upheld the Qing government's principle of recognizing its subjects based on the "right of blood" (*jus sanguinis*), as opposed to the principle of "right of the soil" (*jus soli*) upheld by the French. Accordingly, the Nationalist government considered those born abroad to a Chinese father or a Chinese mother to be Chinese nationals. This rationale allowed the Nationalist government to extend its protection to Chinese outside the homeland.[63] Under the regime of extraterritoriality, such a rule also prevented overseas Chinese from escaping punishment for offenses committed in China. In response to the increasingly assertive Nationalist government, the French colonial government stipulated in 1933 that all Minh Huong people were to be recognized as subjects or protégés of France (*sujets ou protégés français*).[64] This announcement resulted from the practical desirability of subjugating Minh Huong to French authority and tax obligations. Regarding the issue of jurisdiction, the French responded forcefully, announcing that Cochin China was a territory of the French Union where Chinese law had no standing.

The Minh Huong's responses to the French mandate could not have been colder. To evade the tax obligations that resulted from their status as French subjects, some tried to pass as Chinese by listing themselves on the registers of various Chinese communities. Others, by petitioning the Consulate General of the Republic of China in Saigon, obtained certificates of provisional registration as Chinese. The 1930s saw a growth of nationalistic sentiment among Chinese in Vietnam. The vigorous modernization policies of the Nationalist state seemed to have brought hope to China, yet the imminent threat posed by Japan could doom the nation. The image of a victimized motherland striving for independence and strength induced empathy among overseas Chinese and an urge to support the nation from afar.

As the crisis of war deepened, the momentum of the national salvation movement spread among Chinese overseas, drawing them closer to China—both the ethnocultural concept and the nation-state. In Nanyang, or Southeast Asia, where Chinese communities had prospered and several world-famous Chinese tycoons emerged, the cry to save the nation echoed that in mainland China. Immediately after the Japanese army took control of Manchuria in 1931, patriotic Chinese merchants in Saigon and Cholon (today part of Ho Chi Minh City) organized a War Relief Committee, which collected from Chinese store and factory owners 10 percent of their daily food expenses, amounting to a donation of 1.3 million yuan to China's war effort.[65]

With the outbreak the War of Resistance against Japan in 1937, activists and community leaders in Cholon founded the National Salvation Commission of Overseas Chinese in Cochin China, which had soon established more than thirty branch offices all over Vietnam and boasted numerous corporate members as well as individual members.[66] In late 1938, the commission launched its own newspaper, the *National People's Daily* (Quanmin ribao) to report on the war and mobilize resistance among overseas Chinese.[67] As the title of the newspaper implied, overseas champions of China's War of Resistance saw themselves as an integral part of the nation.

A strong sense of Chinese identity and solidarity was apparent in the Declaration of the National Salvation Committee in South Vietnam (accompanied by a poster; see the photo below). In this emotionally charged document, members swore loyalty to "the highest leader of the nation," Chiang Kai-shek, and proclaimed their determination to support China's struggle for independence in various ways:

> At this moment of national survival, if we want to achieve victory and nation building, the only way is to fight on under one ideology, one government, and one leader. . . . Our soldiers are shedding their blood on the war front, and people on the home front should make their own contributions, so that we too can write a glorious page of history.
> Catching and punishing *hanjian* is essential to ensure our victory, so we shall make extra efforts on that score. We should accelerate our pace [of eradicating *hanjian*] by organizing the people and fortifying our defense.

The declaration concluded by stressing the shared ethnic roots of all Chinese, stating that "by doing so, we hope to comfort the spirits of our ancestors."[68]

Patriots overseas channeled their passion and concern for China into support for Chiang, whom they considered the most legitimate and capable leader to command China's War of Resistance. This meant renouncing alternative regimes and political figures who challenged the central government. In 1938, Hanoi came to international attention when Wang Jingwei made public his defection there.[69] Overseas Chinese in Southeast Asia were among the first to warn of Wang's collaborationist tendency. As early as 1938, Chen Jiageng, an influential entrepreneur and a member

Poster published by the National Salvation Committee in South Vietnam, 1937, showing a patriot striking down serpentine creatures labeled identified as *hanjian*. Academia Historica, Taipei, #020-019908-0017.

of the National Congress, proposed a bill titled "Seeking Peace with Japan Makes One a *Hanjian*," which directly targeted Wang's recent activities. In 1940, as the leader of the Association of Overseas Chinese in Southeast Asia, Chen denounced Wang immediately following his defection.[70] The National Salvation Commission, "in the name of the four hundred thousand Chinese in Vietnam," openly accused Wang Jingwei of betraying the nation.[71]

To respond to Chiang Kai-shek's call to punish enemies from within, the National Salvation Commission coordinated with the Nationalist Central Committee and the Chinese embassy in Vietnam to identify and extradite individuals suspected of being *hanjian*. As it demonstrated in the case of a Cantonese merchant, Yi Zicai, the commission was more draconian and determined in punishing "treacherous merchants" than the central government was. In September 1938, the commission exposed Yi's *hanjian* conduct to the Ministry of Foreign Affairs and called for his extradition and punishment. Yi was regarded as a *hanjian* because he was secretly working with Japanese intelligence, in addition to smuggling and selling Japanese products.[72] The commission had swiftly notified its local offices and other Chinese organizations to sever all economic ties with Yi. Now the commission expected the Nationalist government to punish Yi according to its own anti-*hanjian* laws.

Even though the Chinese consulate in Saigon confirmed Yi's collaborationist conduct, the government hesitated, weighing the diplomatic and political consequences of punishing people like Yi. Officials worried that an extradition request would be rejected by the French, who were trying to avoid friction with the Japanese at all costs, in which case the move would only harm the authority of the Chinese government. As a compromise, the central government decided to have the Guangdong provincial government confiscate Yi's assets in China and make Yi promise in writing that he would never smuggle Japanese products again. This result terribly upset the commission, which lamented that "the *hanjian* groups in Vietnam" would realize that the commission could do nothing to effectively punish them.[73]

Disheartened partly by Chongqing's indecision and partly by Japan's tightening grip over French Indochina, the national salvation movement in Vietnam diminished in scale and visibility after 1941.[74] Clandestine activities against the Japanese army and their local collaborators, however, never completely ceased. *The Chronicles of Overseas Chinese* recorded more than eighty-seven martyrs who were arrested for assassination attempts or spying for the Nationalist government.[75] From Chongqing, Chiang Kai-shek kept sending military personnel and intelligence agents to organize underground resistance activities. Many were captured and executed by the Japanese.[76]

At the same time, Wang Jingwei's government was competing with Chongqing for support and resources from the Chinese in Vietnam. Many prominent merchants and community leaders, openly or in disguise, worked with the Japanese army, which controlled the export of key commodities, including rice. Pro-Japanese guilds, professional associations, and social groups dominated wartime life in Vietnam between 1942 and 1945.[77] Deng Youya, a successful businessman and a prominent community leader in Haiphong, was among the collaborators. As the head of the surveillance system that the Japanese imposed on Chinese in Haiphong, Deng was among the most conspicuous *hanjian*.[78] In addition, Deng's business ties with the Japanese and the handsome amount of property he possessed made him a primary target of the Nationalist military on its arrival in Vietnam.

Following the withdrawal of the Japanese army, French Indochina quickly became a battleground where great powers fought among themselves and with Vietnamese nationalists.[79] Ho Chi Minh announced the establishment of the Democratic Republic of Vietnam (DRV) on September 2, 1945, with the dual goals of national independence and socialist revolution. The DRV enjoyed wide support from the Vietnamese populace, as the French colonial administration had lost its authority during World War II.[80] Ho blatantly condemned France for failing in its role as the "protector" of Vietnam, but France was determined to reclaim its control over Vietnam, with British and American backup.

To further complicate the political landscape, the Allied powers were vying for control over the region while still trying to maintain the balance of power. Having made great sacrifices for the war in Asia, the Chinese Nationalist government bargained for a stronger presence in Indochina. The Allies decided that the British army would liberate the areas south of the 16th Parallel, whereas the Nationalist army would liberate North Vietnam. In January 1946, the four Allied nations that participated in the Pacific War—the United States, Great Britain, China, and the Soviet Union—decided to distribute the fleet of the Japanese navy, consisting of 467 battleships and 2,114 merchant ships, evenly among themselves. The French request for a share of the booty was politely but adamantly rejected by the Chinese.[81]

Nationalist policies on Vietnam between late 1945 and 1946 were inconsistent, as the government tried to strike a balance between maintaining Vietnamese nationalist claims and staying out of French-Vietnamese conflicts. To carve out its sphere of influence in the region, the Nationalist government sent diplomats to London and Paris in support of the joint action by the Vietnamese and overseas Chinese against a British-French comeback. Print media in China denounced "renewed Western colonial ambitions."[82] Soon afterward, however, Chiang Kai-shek formed an anti-Communist alliance with the French against Ho Chi Minh's government in anticipation of a civil war with the Chinese Communists. As part of the compromise, the Nationalists agreed to withdraw their army from North Vietnam in 1946.[83]

Caught in the crossfire of French-Vietnamese conflicts, the Chinese communities in Vietnam became the scapegoats for the Nationalist government, which the Vietnamese regarded as having betrayed them. Between September 1945 and 1949, the DRV, the French, and ordinary Vietnamese took out their anger and hostility on the Chinese population with routine acts of violence. From September to November 1945 in the Saigon-Cholon area alone, the French military carried out more than three hundred attacks on Chinese Vietnamese and their property, resulting in 23 murders, 145 robberies, 28 cases of vandalism, and the destruction of 225 Chinese-owned homes. Areas under DRV control were no safer for the Chinese. In January 1946 alone, ten Chinese soldiers and twenty-two Chinese Vietnamese were killed by the local militia.[84]

All these unfortunate events happened at a time when Chinese Vietnamese were seeking reintegration into the political and ethnic community of China. The fact that Chiang Kai-shek attended the Cairo conference and participated in deciding postwar affairs in Asia boosted China's image among its lost children overseas. The Chinese communities also took pride in the liberation of northern Vietnam by Nationalist troops. In addition, they were drawn to China by the political instability and antagonism toward Chinese in Vietnam, from which neither the French nor the Vietnamese were willing to protect them. The Chinese consulate in Saigon reported in 1946 that many wealthy and well-educated Chinese in Cochin were not willing to participate in the upcoming national election in Vietnam and had recently applied for certificates granting them Chinese citizenship.[85]

The desire among overseas Chinese to reconnect with their national community was in perfect concord with the Nationalist government's vision of postwar Southeast Asia. With its military receiving the Japanese surrender in Vietnam and temporarily in charge of law enforcement, the Nationalist government made strong overtures to the Chinese there. In a letter to the Minister of Foreign Affairs, members of the Hanoi branch of the Nationalist Party emphasized the significance of overseas Chinese, particularly Chinese in Vietnam, to the project of revitalizing China: "China shares a border with Vietnam, and the two have maintained strong economic and cultural ties. Chinese in Vietnam, therefore, play important roles in maintaining China's security perimeter. Protecting and pacifying the Chinese in Vietnam is an essential part of our mission of national reconstruction [*jianguo*]." Having observed conditions in Vietnam firsthand, these Nationalists urged their government to negotiate with the French and grant citizenship to the Chinese in Vietnam. The Chinese separated from their home country would thus "be sheltered under our 'blue sky and white sun flag,'" rather than "treated as aliens or infants without a loving mother."[86]

In these endeavors, the Nationalist government's primary interest was the financial status of Chinese in Vietnam, who had traditionally dominated the service sector and thence expanded into trading, banking, and

manufacturing. By the early 1950s, there were 92 Chinese-owned big restaurants in Saigon-Cholon region, 826 eating houses, and 48 hotels. The
total value of Chinese investment in 1954 stood at US$80 million, 21 percent
of the total foreign investment in Vietnam at that time. One scholar estimated that ethnic Chinese businessmen controlled nearly 90 percent of the
non-European capital in Vietnam in the mid-1950s.[87]

The cash and capital of Chinese in Vietnam gave Chiang Kai-shek good
reasons to look after their interests in the turbulent time after the Pacific
War. On February 28, 1946, the Nationalist government signed the Chongqing Agreement with France, which gave the Chinese in Vietnam the right
to engage in mining, land transactions, and construction. In addition, the
recently restored French colonial government granted Chinese nationals
the status of "favored foreign resident," extending to them the same privileges enjoyed by the French, at the expense of native Vietnamese.[88] In
return, Chiang Kai-shek agreed to withdraw his army. This decision, however, left the Chinese under French control and surrounded by a hostile and
resentful Vietnamese populace.[89]

Central to the Nationalist government's political maneuvers in Vietnam
was its pursuit of punishing *hanjian*, which it considered necessary in order
to distinguish the loyal Chinese from those who had forsaken their Chinese roots. Prosecuting these individuals also meant nationalizing their
property and wealth, most of which had not been accumulated through
collaboration with the Japanese. Yet the anti-*hanjian* cause in Vietnam, as
the following cases show, turned out to be a diplomatic disaster for the
Nationalist government. Furthermore, it alienated the Chinese communities in Vietnam rather than reinforcing their Chinese identity.

The Chinese Ministry of Foreign Affairs estimated that 10 percent of the
Vietnamese population was Chinese by blood, which "undoubtedly" made
them Chinese citizens.[90] Following this line of argument, the Nationalist
government claimed jurisdiction over them and considered them subject
to Chinese laws, including the Regulations on Punishing *Hanjian*. General
Lu Han, the commander of the Nationalist First Front Army, liberated
northern Vietnam on behalf of the central government. As soon as Lu
arrived in Haiphong, he began to screen the Chinese community for
hanjian suspects. Deng Youya was among the first to be identified. Deng
was arrested and sent to the Yongning High Court in Guangxi, China, for
investigation and trial. The court found Deng guilty of "collaborating with
the enemy nation in manufacturing and selling military supplies" and sentenced him to three years in prison. In addition, all of Deng's property and

possessions were confiscated, except for a small amount for supporting his family.[91]

The case of Deng Youya was far from over, however. Poor coordination within the Nationalist government, competing diplomatic interests, and individual agency all affected the ensuing development of the case. The Chinese court in Guangxi was still processing Deng's case when the First Front Army withdrew from Vietnam as part of the Nationalists' deal with France. Before its departure, the army handed over Deng's property to the Chinese consulate in Haiphong. When the court in Guangxi reached a decision on Deng's case, it did not notify the Chinese consulate, and the latter had appropriated one piece of Deng's property for use by a Chinese newspaper, *Gangfeng ribao*. By 1948, Deng had managed to obtain his release from prison on medical grounds and left the mainland for Hong Kong. There he hired a French lawyer to sue *Gangfeng ribao* for trespassing on private property, on the grounds that he still held title to the property.

The battle over Deng's alleged *hanjian* crime, his property, and the fundamental issue of jurisdiction involved legal professionals and diplomats from China, France, and Vietnam. In January 1949, the Haiphong Court, with French backup, expelled *Gangfeng ribao* from the building, over loud protests from the Chinese consulate. The Chinese Ministry of Foreign Affairs supported the newspaper in appealing to the Hanoi High Court, but the result was most disappointing for China. The court argued that Chinese laws did not apply in areas under French jurisdiction and observed that France had never agreed to assist the Chinese in their anti-*hanjian* cause.

Deng and his family took advantage of these international disputes. On the advice of his French legal counsel, Deng avoided extradition to China by stressing his Minh Huong status. The French, after all, had recognized Minh Huong as subjects or protégés of France since 1933. In May 1949, Deng and his family forced entry into the disputed property, which had been sealed by the Chinese army and consulate. With only its diplomatic team left in Vietnam, the Chinese Nationalist government and judiciary agonized over this issue: "Debates over the nationality of Minh Huong were common in South Vietnam, but in North Vietnam, it was established that Minh Huong are considered Chinese. As this has been a divisive issue between China and France, we need to be extremely cautious and tactful in dealing with Deng's case. Our decision now will have important effects on future generations of Chinese overseas. The worst we can do is to maintain the status quo, leaving the status of Minh Huong unsettled [rather than let the French-Vietnamese alliance win this case]."[92]

The Nationalist government wrangled with the Vietnamese courts over Deng's case for another year, insisting that because he was born before 1933, he should not be considered a French subject. More important, the government stood by its claim that because the Nationalist military had liberated North Vietnam and maintained law and order there, it was entitled to handle criminal cases, including *hanjian* cases. The case of Deng Youya unfolded concurrently with the Civil War in China (1946–49). Between April 1949 and May 1950, when the Nationalist government was denied jurisdiction by the French and the Vietnamese, it also lost mainland China to the Communists and retreated to Taiwan. Given the circumstances, the Nationalists made remarkable efforts at nationalizing overseas Chinese, but it did so through establishing negative examples rather than by extending protection over China's "lost children."

Beyond international and domestic politics, what really killed the anti-*hanjian* cause in Vietnam was the conduct of representatives of the Nationalist government, who appeared unjust, arbitrary, and often utterly corrupt. The First Front Army, which enforced China's anti-*hanjian* laws in Vietnam, showed no empathy toward the Chinese in Vietnam and no respect for due process. The abuse of power and the distortion of justice were commonplace. The special commissioner, Wang Zhiwu, arrested hundreds of overseas Chinese, many of whom he tortured and blackmailed. Wang confiscated the sugar plantation of an individual named Huang Ju, for instance, sold the sugar harvest, and kept the profit.[93] Such deeds and transactions were conducted off the official record. Seeing the anti-*hanjian* cause as a quick money-making scheme, the Nationalists in Vietnam also took bribes for pardoning those who had been notoriously intimate with the Japanese. Wang Zhiwu reduced the sentence of Yang Xiulun for a sum of forty-five thousand yuan; Li Chengqiu pardoned Su Qingzhe, a dubious personality in the Chinese community, with whom he later co-owned a cinema and shared the profits. The same Li also appropriated Deng Youya's multiple automobiles and part of the revenue generated by Deng's hotel.

The Chinese in Vietnam could not have been more disappointed or outraged by the government they had supported. From the arrival of Nationalist troops in Vietnam to its withdrawal in June 1947, a stream of letters of grievance from Chinese in Vietnam reached the Nationalist government. As eyewitnesses to the corruption and cruelty of the First Front Army, the petitioners warned that not only the Chinese community but also the French, the Vietnamese, and even the Japanese were shocked by how the Nationalists treated those who were "born of the same womb." Ensuing investigations confirmed these accusations. Wang Zhiwu and Li Chengqiu did not dare to return to China with the First Front Army. The government charged them with corruption in 1949. By that point, however, it was too late to bring them to justice, to redeem the reputation of the government, or to win over the Chinese in Vietnam. The Nationalists were faced with a much greater crisis: they had lost mainland China to the Communists.

Conflicting French and Chinese claims and interests also obstructed the handling of another paradoxical category of *hanjian*, French *hanjian* (*faji hanjian*, or "French nationals who betrayed the Han race"). During its purge of *hanjian* on mainland China, the Nationalist government charged thirty-three individuals of Caucasian ancestry and foreign citizenship with the *hanjian* crime.[94] Some had acquiesced in Japanese rule by continuing to work and trade during the occupation, and others willingly collaborated with the Japanese. Almost two-thirds of them remained at large by 1949, when the Nationalist government lost the Civil War. Out of the twelve defendants who were put through investigation and trials, only one, a certain Glovge Emelionoff (as spelled in the court record), was found guilty.

The convict was a French citizen of Russian ancestry, who worked for the police bureau in Shanghai's French Concession and was in charge of foreign citizens' affairs. After the Wang Jingwei regime took over and reestablished the Shanghai municipal government on July 30, 1943, Emelionoff continued with his work. After the war, the Shanghai High Court tried him for assisting the puppet government and sentenced him to two and a half years' imprisonment.[95] Emelionoff and his lawyer appealed to Chiang Kaishek, pleading for dismissal of the case on the grounds that he was merely following the orders of the French consul. They argued that because Emelionoff drew his salary from the French government rather than from the Japanese or the puppet regime, he had no financial motivation to collaborate. In addition, Emelionoff considered his job entirely irrelevant to the war situation.

In 1947, the French government and public opinion in France pressured the Chinese ambassador to request the extradition of all French nationals charged with the *hanjian* crime, as well as a special pardon for Emelionoff. Through the ambassador, Qian Tai, the French proposed to exchange Chinese *hanjian* in Vietnam for *hanjian* of French nationality. The French Ministry of Foreign Affairs was diplomatic in its language. The ministry first expressed its respect for China's judicial independence and its reluctance to interfere with China's prosecution of French *hanjian*.[96] At the same time, it expressed its concern that these "French traitors in China" (*zaihua fajian*) would use their connections in France to blemish the image of the Chinese government and its legal system. "For the sake of Sino-French relations," the French minister of foreign affairs proposed the exchange of French and Chinese *hanjian*.

The minister of justice, Guo Yunguan, flatly refused the French request, using the language of international law to defend the Nationalist government's rights in the matter.[97] If a French national committed a crime in France and fled to China, Guo reasoned, France had the right to request extradition, but this principle did not apply in cases where the French had broken Chinese law on Chinese soil. Similarly, if a Chinese national committed a *hanjian* crime and fled to Vietnam, China had the right to ask for his or her extradition. Such a request was justified, and China needed to do nothing in return.

To make a stronger case, Guo compared China's legal purge of *hanjian* to trials of collaborators in France and to the international tribunals that prosecuted war crimes.[98] Guo maintained that France, of all nations, should understand the necessity of punishing traitors because it had experienced firsthand the harms they had done to resistance efforts. China therefore would "stand by the principles of international law" and reject any suggestion of an exchange.[99] While upholding China's judicial claims, Guo also asserted that the Chinese courts had shown particular leniency toward foreign nationals accused of war crimes or collaboration: for example, the Chinese court had withdrawn charges or granted acquittals in most cases involving French *hanjian*. By so doing, the Republic of China had demonstrated that it had the authority to prosecute French nationals if they had broken the law in China, but it had treated them with magnanimity instead.

CONCLUSION

The Regulations on Punishing *Hanjian*, as the legal basis of the anti-*hanjian* campaigns, was vague on the scope of its applicability. The Nationalist government, for the purpose of "resisting the Japanese and reconstructing the nation," imposed the anti-*hanjian* laws on foreign citizens in China and ethnic Chinese abroad. The categories of *hanjian* cases examined in this chapter raised challenges to the authority of the Nationalist administration, both within China and from other nations. As the cases of French *hanjian* show, the legal and diplomatic endeavors involved served partly to confirm China's judicial sovereignty, which it regained under the agreements made by the Allied powers.

To punish foreign nationals of Chinese descent for their wartime betrayal was an integral part of the Nationalist government's plan for postwar national reconstruction. This project was obstructed, however, by maneuvers by other powers, protests from local people, the lack of coordination within the Nationalist administration, and the shifting political landscape of mainland China. What truly destroyed the moral high ground of the anti-*hanjian* cause and alienated the overseas Chinese was the corruption and abuse of the Nationalists. The lack of empathy or emotional affinity shown by Nationalist representatives toward the Chinese in Taiwan or Vietnam reduced the persuasive power of the government's ethnically constructed discourse on Chineseness.

FROM CRIME TO EPITHET

THE YEARS BETWEEN 1931 AND 1949 WERE THE MOST VOLATILE in modern Chinese history. China defeated a formidable enemy against all odds and then was torn apart by a three-year civil war. Relentless warfare, dislocations, power struggles, and economic destruction reduced the announced goal of national rejuvenation to an empty slogan. Aggravating the sense of terror and division among the people was a politically charged and culturally rooted movement against *hanjian*. Although the war against Japan officially ended with Japan's unconditional surrender on August 15, 1945, the struggle against perceived enemies among the people continued, persisting until this very day.

That the anti-*hanjian* campaigns were initiated and sanctioned by the Nationalist government had important implications for its postwar political rivalry with the Communists. As numerous examples and opinion pieces show, the Nationalists undeniably mishandled the *hanjian* issue on the whole, despite the hard work of the judiciary and the government's promise to deliver justice. During the takeover of occupied regions and enemy property, the Nationalist government appeared inefficient, incompetent, and unethical. The trials of *hanjian*, conducted under the critical eyes of the public and the opposition party, exposed serious problems within the administration. Between 1945 and 1947, when *hanjian* trials were reported on a daily basis, a popular saying captured the public disillusionment with the recently restored government and its failure to deliver justice: "With gold bricks comes innocence; being penniless means no access to justice."[1] The prestige and confidence that Chiang Kai-shek's government had garnered by leading China to victory in the War of Resistance were quickly lost.

Postwar Chinese society was more divided than ever. Shrinking wealth and staggering inflation intensified the already fierce competition for employment and resources. Distrust and ill feeling were particularly strong between those who returned from free China and those who had stayed in

Japanese-occupied areas. Each group considered itself the greater victim and saw the other as having somehow benefited from the war. The nationalization of enemy and *hanjian* property did nothing to alleviate economic stress: rather, it further alienated the masses from the state and those with connections and privileges.

Moreover, during the long-drawn-out anti-*hanjian* movement, a rigid system of evaluating individuals' political nature with a simple dichotomy between loyalty and betrayal took root, with each quality associated with a pattern of conduct, expressions, personal traits, and lifestyle. In the tabloid-style press that gained popularity among general readers, betrayal was associated with wealth and decadence, feeding the belief that a few had prospered from the war at the expense of the majority. Now that the external invaders had been expelled, the alleged *hanjian* became the primary enemies, the "others" to the impoverished masses. During the anti-*hanjian* movement, Chinese collective identity and nationalism were articulated and reinforced through creating and naming a segment of the population as the outcast group.

More dangerous, this dichotomy between the loyal and the disloyal, the righteous and the corrupt, was given substance by a body of law that guided criminal justice in China for decades. The Nationalist anti-*hanjian* campaigns set the pattern for mass political campaigns that continued across the 1949 divide. China did not return to a peacetime legal system until three decades later, and is still striving to establish the rule of law. The CCP had been completely on board with the Nationalist anti-*hanjian* campaigns, from which it adopted important tools and rhetoric. The Communists consolidated their regime and exerted political control with laws similar to the anti-*hanjian* regulations, and they channeled the public's energy into ousting perceived enemies of the state. *Hanjian* was so ingrained in the memories of the Chinese people that after it ceased to be a crime, it remained a powerful epithet in popular vocabulary.

THE COMMUNIST CAMPAIGNS AGAINST *HANJIAN*

The CCP's position on the *hanjian* issue is of vital importance in understanding the longevity of the term and the nationalistic characteristics of the party. The word *hanjian* was from the beginning associated with the anti-Japanese war and sentiment in the institutional memory of the CCP. Terms such as "traitors and running dogs for the Japanese" (*riben hanjian zougou*), "*hanjian* deputies of Japanese imperialism" (*riben diguozhuyi hanjian*), and "traitors to the nation and the working class" (*gongzei hanjian*) frequently appeared in Communist resistance propaganda. Even though the CCP was the sworn enemy of the Nationalist Party and differed from its predecessor in its fundamental ideologies as well as its basis of support, the two parties shared a paranoia about and intolerance of internal enemies.

During the War of Resistance, the CCP aligned its laws and preventive policies against *hanjian* with those of its Nationalist ally to guard the areas under its control. The Communists also adapted their treatment of *hanjian* to their institutional needs and ideologies, so that such campaigns truly facilitated the party's wartime growth. The CCP was most unforgiving to *hanjian* suspects who were also its typical class enemies: former Nationalist bureaucrats and landlords. To broaden its base of support, the party identified *hanjian* who could be potentially converted to *qunzhong*, "the masses," placing them in reeducation and reform facilities such as "handicraft learning centers for self-renewal."[2] Such facilities boosted wartime production and provided unimportant *hanjian* a chance to redeem themselves, alleviating, to some degree, the harshly penal nature of the campaigns. In need of elite sympathizers and various kinds of talent, the CCP also showed more leniency toward professionals, technicians, and experts. In some areas, the party required partners of convicted *hanjian* to file for divorce, a policy in line with its general interventionist approach to marriage and family matters.[3]

The most revealing aspect of the CCP's effective and controlled use of popular energy in the punishment of *hanjian* was the organization of mass trials, which gave the legal process a truly participatory aspect. Such trials were mostly held for locally known and widely resented *hanjian*, and the audiences were filled with their emotional victims. The meetings were conducted by the local executive or judicial branch, with government representatives and local people together acting as prosecutors, jury, and judge. The public denunciation and execution in 1938 of Ji Sigong, a *hanjian* spy who had infiltrated the Communist army, was a case in point. Ji's criminal deeds were recited in front of a crowd of seven thousand people and a jury consisting of students and teachers. Ji was then shot to death.[4] Despite the seeming transparency of a public trial, such meetings afforded no guarantee of due process for the defendants, which was not the Party's priority in any case.

In comparison to the Nationalists, the CCP's handling of *hanjian* property, in particular, made the Party appear ethical, fair, and accountable. The lands of "extremely wicked *hanjian*" were to be confiscated, managed by the government, and leased to local peasants. Those deemed to have collaborated under duress were allowed to keep their land as a means to start anew, as long as they joined the resistance cause. In other words, land ownership depended on correct political consciousness and actions.[5] *Hanjian* wealth and possessions confiscated by the CCP benefited the public or went back to the original owners. In parts of Hubei under Communist control, for instance, *hanjian* property was used to fund the "resistance elementary schools."[6] In Rehe, the Communist Party confiscated two million yuan in local currency and large amounts of rice, firewood, clothing, and wheat, which it then distributed among the local victims of *hanjian*.[7]

The postwar trials of *hanjian* handled by the two parties showcased how they respectively positioned themselves before an impoverished population and a distressed society. The draconian measures taken by the CCP against *hanjian* had a socialist-revolutionary underpinning. In Chengde, Rehe, Communist cadres assembled more than fifteen thousand merchants, workers, and students to denounce *hanjian* who had bullied local people. Railway workers were the first to speak out, accusing Zhu Zhongxin, the head of a Japanese-controlled railway station, of embezzling a large portion of the workers' wages and penalizing them for alleged idleness. The local CCP stripped Zhu of his title and property and redistributed Zhu's wealth among his working-class victims. Following the example of the railway workers, merchants rose up to expose *hanjian* members of the Chengde Chamber of Commerce.[8]

A complete record of *hanjian* arrested and executed by the CCP is impossible to compile, as the party operated in a decentralized manner and the imminent war with the Nationalists curtailed its capacity to preserve data. We know from individual cases, however, that the proceedings against *hanjian* between 1945 and 1948 were swift and violent. In Xingtai, Hebei, a mass trial attended by forty-five thousand people concluded with the execution of two puppet county magistrates and two special agents on the spot. Two puppet mayors of Zhang Jiakou in Hebei met the same fate. Trials on a similar scale with the same outcome took place in several counties in Jiangsu and in many other provinces under CCP control.[9] Several locally notorious *hanjian* were rumored to have been punished by "death by a thousand cuts."[10]

The implementation of the anti-*hanjian* campaigns overall benefited the Chinese Communists as a means of garnering resources and a broader base of support. Its calculated treatment of different types of *hanjian* and their property boosted the reputation and power of the CCP as a reliable resistance force. In its rivalry with the ruling party, the CCP was adept at selecting the right targets and iron-fisted in punishing them. In numerous cases where the local members of the Nationalist administration and army became *hanjian*, the trials enabled the CCP to kill two birds with one stone.

The Nationalists could not afford to adopt the Communists' approach to redistributing *hanjian* property. As a result, their anti-*hanjian* campaigns appeared more retributive than restorative. As the central government, the Nationalists had to shoulder China's financial and personnel losses during the War of Resistance, which amounted to US$60 billion.[11] The Nationalist Party also had a much larger bureaucratic machine than the CCP that it was attempting to rebuild and revamp. From the perspective of the common people who were struggling to get back on their feet, however, it appeared that the money from convicted *hanjian* went straight to the government and in most cases, into the pockets of individual officials. The CCP's legendary weapon in winning the Civil War in China, namely popular support, came in no small part from the Nationalists' loss of it.

HANJIAN IN CHINA AND TAIWAN IN THE 1950S

The Chinese Civil War of 1946–49 ended with a Communist victory in mainland China and the retreat of the Nationalist administration to Taiwan. The confrontation of the two governments, each claiming to represent cultural orthodoxy and legitimate rule over China, gave rise to new meanings of the word *hanjian*. In the ideological and political battles being waged across the Taiwan Strait, *hanjian* continued to be a most dangerous criminal category. To consolidate its rule on the mainland, the CCP hunted for *hanjian* from the War of Resistance who had escaped the Nationalist purge, though some *hanjian* were incriminated mainly because of their affiliation with the Nationalists or the wrong faction of the CCP. In Taiwan, the wartime Regulations against *hanjian* remained in effect until the 1960s, yet Chiang Kai-shek used the word primarily to refer to the "Communist villains."

In the early 1950s, the Communists were pursuing *hanjian* who had been pardoned by the Nationalists or had served their short prison terms. Yuan Lüdeng, the economic *hanjian* discussed in chapter 3, was convicted of the *hanjian* crime again in 1953 and died in prison soon afterward. Su Qing continued to suffer political suppression for her past association with notorious *hanjian*. Less well-known *hanjian*, including Du Xijun, the puppet provincial governor of Hebei, and Ma Xiaotian, an important member of Wang Jingwei's intelligence network, were caught.[12] Lü Jinkang, a former Zhongtong agent who once surrendered to the Japanese but walked free by joining Juntong, at last paid for his *hanjian* deeds with his life.

In some cases, patriots under the old regime became "counterrevolutionary" *hanjian* under the new state. Yang Yushen was a former Nationalist Party member who had served in the Ministry of Education and been praised by the Nationalist government for refusing to surrender to the Japanese. In the 1950s, he was identified as a "Nationalist party stick" (*danggun*) and *hanjian*, for which offenses he was imprisoned for five years.[13]

Those newly identified as *hanjian* included CCP veterans with complex wartime affiliations and experiences, whom the party could not trust or decided to dispose of for political reasons. Pan Hannian, Yuan Shu, and Hu Junhe were all CCP underground agents who had infiltrated Wang Jingwei's intelligence network and social circles. All three were arrested in 1954–55 for being *hanjian*, spies, and counterrevolutionaries, and they remained in prison for more than two decades.[14] Because the CCP's apparatus was more efficient and far-reaching than that of its predecessor, its search for enemies among the people was more systematic and thorough. As an anonymous reader had cursed and correctly predicted in 1945, "Once a traitor, always a traitor."[15] Chinese historians have uncovered inconspicuous "minor *hanjian*" whose past was revisited and questioned in every wave of political movement from 1949 through the 1960s. Wang Wenyao, an ordinary worker, was repeatedly interrogated and purged for his *hanjian* conduct. Each time, as the political atmosphere intensified, the investigation "uncovered" evidence for more crimes Wang had committed, to which a mentally distressed Wang was forced to confess.[16]

The CCP prosecuted *hanjian* as a subcategory of the more encompassing "counterrevolutionary" crime. Between 1949 and 1953, the newly born People's Republic of China was constantly threatened by sabotage and by the escalating Cold War in Asia. Arson, murder, rape, and vandalism committed by local bandits, leftover Nationalist troops, and spies caused tremendous loss of life and public property. During this "state of emergency," the CCP, like the Nationalist Party during the War of Resistance, established a powerful umbrella agency, the Committee of the National People's Government (Zhongyangrenmin Zhengfu Weiyuanhui), to control all aspects of the government and military. This organ took charge of making, stipulating, and interpreting laws as well as supervising their implementation.[17] The committee's most important legislation in the early years of the PRC was the Statute on Punishing Counterrevolutionaries (the 1951 Statute).[18] This statute, which functioned as China's criminal law until the first formal criminal code came out in 1979, was intended to strike down all perceived enemies of the young People's Republic.

The 1951 Statute was inspired by the wartime version of the Regulations against *Hanjian* in its structure, wording, and core components, as a direct comparison reveals (see table 6.1). This book does not delve into the

TABLE 6.1. Comparison of the 1938 Regulations on Punishing *Hanjian* and the 1951 Statute on Punishing Counterrevolutionaries

	1938 Regulations	1951 Statute
Definition, principal crime, and punishment	Anyone who conspires with an enemy state and commits one of the following acts is considered a *hanjian,* and is to be sentenced to capital punishment or life imprisonment. (Article II)	Anyone who aims to overthrow the people's democratic dictatorship and sabotage the national cause is considered a counterrevolutionary (Article II)
	Plotting against the home country (Article II-1)	Anyone who conspires with a foreign imperialist power and betrays his home country shall be punished by death or life imprisonment (Article III)
Specific conduct exemplifying the principal crime	Instigating defection or collaboration among servicemen, government employees, or ordinary citizens (Article II-13)	Instigating insurrection among government employees, servicemen, or the people's militia (Article IV)
	Leaking, stealing, or secretly collecting political or economic information [on the resistance force](Article II-7)	Stealing or searching for state secrets or supplying intelligence to a domestic or foreign enemy (Article VI-1)
	Serving as guide for the enemy or assisting the enemy army in various ways (Article II-8)	Guiding enemy planes or enemy ships to bombardment targets (Article VI-2)
	Supplying, dealing, collecting, or transporting military supplies or materials for producing military supplies (Article II-4)	Supplying domestic or foreign enemies with weapons, ammunition, or other military materials (Article VI-3)
	Poisoning drinking water or food for the Chinese military or people (Article II-12)	Spreading poison or germs, or using other methods that cause major disasters to people, livestock, or agriculture (Article IX-2)
	Instigating financial chaos (Article II-10)	Disrupting the market or undermining finance under orders from a domestic or foreign enemy (Article IX-3)

well-studied topic of the CCP's campaigns against the counterrevolutionaries.[19] What is worth noting here is that the 1951 construction of the
counterrevolutionary (*fangeming*) crime bore little resemblance to the way
it was first defined by the CCP in 1934.[20] Rather, the 1951 Statue, which
many consider the beginning of the practice of legalizing political campaigns and turning political labels into criminal categories in the PRC,
drew heavily on the Regulations against *Hanjian*.[21]

Policymakers, jurists, and historians in China have noted the PRC's
departure from the pre-1949 legal code and practice. Indeed, immediately
after its establishment, the PRC abolished the Six Code system, which
served as the framework of Nationalist laws and procedures.[22] The CCP
laws claimed to serve the interest of the masses and thus departed from the
Nationalist laws in their ideological basis and functions. Nevertheless, the
Communists shared the Nationalists' approach of legitimizing violence for
the sake of regime consolidation. From the purge of *hanjian* to the elimination of counterrevolutionaries, one sees a continuous tendency of the
state in delegating the legal system to launch and facilitate political campaigns while simultaneously allowing mass participation in order to hijack
judicial authority.

While the PRC was hunting for *hanjian* along with other counterrevolutionaries, on the other side of the Taiwan Strait, Chiang Kai-shek was
reinventing the word *hanjian* in the context of anti-Communist discourse.
In 1951, "President Chiang" authored and published a political treatise, *The
Destined Demise of* Hanjian *and Failure of Invaders*.[23] Chiang clarified,
first, that the war facing China now was not between Taiwan and the
mainland; rather, it was a war between the Chinese people and Russian
imperialism. He admitted that Taiwan was small and its resources
extremely limited compared to those of the Chinese mainland under Communist control. He declared that the outcome of this national war would be
determined not by size or strength but on nationalism (*minzu zhuyi*), a
"spiritual force" now possessed only by the government and people in Taiwan. Chiang Kai-shek defined this spiritual force as follows:

> Nationalism is a belief based on the rationality and reasoning of human
> beings, and thus cannot be obliterated. Since the Spring and Autumn
> period [770–476 BCE], the differences between the Chinese and the
> barbarians have been drawn, and the dichotomy between the loyal and
> the traitorous has been established. . . . No foreign invasion, cultural
> enslavement, or shameless betrayal by *hanjian* could ever destroy this

national spirit or jeopardize human rationality. This spiritual force is what has enabled our Chinese race to stand strong amid external and internal crises and strive for rejuvenation.

By tracing this spiritual force in Chinese history, Chiang Kai-shek reinforced the genealogy of national crises and *hanjian* that Zhang Shizhao constructed at the dawn of the twentieth century. Chiang extended this historical narrative to include the War of Resistance against Japan, pointing out that not a single *hanjian* in remote or recent history had succeeded.

Finally, by identifying the Japanese and Russian imperialism together as the "most dangerous invasions China has experienced in the past two decades," Chiang Kai-shek concluded that "Mao Zedong and Zhu De are the greatest and most characteristic of all *hanjian*." Yet Chiang reassured the people in Taiwan and "our miserable compatriots on the mainland" that, as always in history, "*hanjian* are destined to be finished off, and despotism is destined to fall."[24] This new anti-*hanjian* discourse guided the large-scale suppression of Communist operatives in Taiwan in the 1950s.

The discourse and political movements in 1950s mainland China and Taiwan reveal that while retaining its nationalistic connotations, *hanjian* became a more malleable label, the meaning of which could change according to the context and the views of the user. Events and trends since the 1980s might seem to suggest that the term *hanjian* is now out of date. After all, the tensions of the Cold War and the possibility of a military solution to the Taiwan problem have faded: Taiwan has evolved economically and politically since martial law was lifted and the Nationalist dictatorship gave way to representative democracy. In the People's Republic of China, the policies of "reform and opening up" (*gaige kaifang*) have brought decades of steady economic growth and social progress. The term *hanjian* and the events that prompted its widespread use—external crises, internal divisions, mass movements, and political purge—should have been long ago cast away. This, however, is far from the case.

HANJIAN AS A POWERFUL EPITHET

The concept of *hanjian* is still relevant today, firstly because the War of Resistance still holds great significance to Chinese national identity and to contemporary Sino-Japanese relations. The grand narrative of the war and specific moments of suffering are not only reinforced in the writing of history; they also have become the subjects of literary and artistic production.

Film is perhaps the best medium for capturing all that is striking and grotesque with a war and to form collective memory. Since the late 1940s, countless films and documentaries have been made on the War of Resistance both in mainland China and in Taiwan. *Hanjian*, fictional or historical, are an eternal presence in such films. In works produced immediately after the war, *hanjian* who went unpunished were living reminders of war wounds and the evil opponents of good but powerless people. In *A Heavenly Dream* (1947), for instance, Gong, who has made a fortune by supplying the Japanese with constructional materials, buys himself an identity as an underground agent for the price of five hundred gold bars. Gong causes misfortune and agony for an upright architect, Ding, who has just returned Shanghai from Chongqing with his family. With no place to live and no means of supporting his pregnant wife and sick mother, Ding jumps from the top of a tall building he had designed.[25] Characteristic of the realist genre that emerged in postwar China, *A Heavenly Dream* condemns *hanjian* who walked free and continued to worsen social injustice.

By the 1950s, most actual *hanjian* who had worked for the Japanese had been executed or imprisoned. Yet *hanjian* on the big screen increased in number and demonstrated their evil deeds for all to see. For decades, *hanjian* had always played the antagonists to patriotic protagonists, leaving no middle ground. An archetypical portrait of *hanjian*—greedy, cowardly, greater villains than the Japanese—can be found in the classic patriotic film *Tunnel Warfare* (1965). Generations of Chinese have grown up watching reruns of this film on TV, and everyone remembers a line spoken by the *hanjian*, Tang—"Brilliant! Truly brilliant!"—applauding a Japanese officer's plan to eradicate the guerrilla resistance force.

Since the early 2000s, the portrayal of *hanjian* in film has become more diverse and nuanced, signifying a willingness of the general public to consider the varied motivations and dilemmas of wartime collaboration. Based on a prominent *hanjian*—Ding Mocun, a commander of Wang Jingwei's spy network—the character of Mr. Yi in *Lust, Caution* (2007) appears distressed and even mentally tormented by his work in the puppet government.[26] Li Zhao, a fictional police officer who translates for the Japanese in the blockbuster *Ip Man* (2008), is redeemed by protecting a patriotic Kung Fu master and becomes an unexpected hero. The moment when he shouts, "I am not a *hanjian*, but a translator!" marks the first time a *hanjian* was given the chance to defend himself. Similarly, in the spectacular film *The Flowers of War* (2011), Mr. Meng serves as a translator for the Japanese in order to save his daughter, who was deeply ashamed of her *hanjian* father.[27] *Hanjian* images as such prompt the audience to ponder the complicated circumstances of wartime collaboration and to imagine the characters' internal struggles between conscience and the will to survive.

The film *Back to 1942* (2012) addresses the sensitive issue of those who collaborated to avoid starvation, showing more sympathy for those who surrendered than to the Nationalist state. The choice between resistance and collaboration is represented by the two characters Shuanzhu and Lao Ma. Yet they are not set up as moral contrasts. Shuanzhu swears to protect the two children of his wife of one night, the widow Huazhi, yet loses them on the way out of the famine-stricken Henan. While searching for the children, he is caught by the Japanese and discovers that Lao Ma, previously a low-ranking Nationalist judicial clerk, now cooks for the Japanese. Lao Ma urges Shuanzhu to yield to the Japanese and join him. Shuanzhu, however, spits on the Japanese officer who lures him with a bun and is brutally killed. Common peasants at the time naturally resented the Japanese invaders. Shuanzhu's resistance, however, is not the product of conscious nationalism but rather the response to the Japanese officer's demand for a toy that he carries with him, the only reminder he has of his lost children. As for Lao Ma, anyone who watches the film can understand how he is driven to collaboration by the famine and the irresponsible government.

Yet the creation of more nuanced *hanjian* images on the big screen has done little to engender critical reflection on the word itself and its usage in the past and present. The term still retains all its negative force. Today it is so widely and casually used that it has become an Internet buzzword. Any unpatriotic opinion or action can be branded as *hanjian*. A Chinese student at Duke University who received this label for her alleged pro-Tibet independence speech and action during the 2008 Olympics torch relay is but one example. A search for the term *hanjian* in Chinese on Google on October 5, 2016 generated more than twelve million results in one-third of a second, only half of which are associated with figures from the War of Resistance.

The remaining hits are associated with more recent phenomena, opinions, and individuals from all political backgrounds and social circles. For example, Utopia (Wuyouzhixiang), the largest website for Chinese leftists, attacked the Nanfang Daily Group, the most outspoken news outlet in China and the most sympathetic to liberal democratic values, as "*hanjian* media" (*hanjian meiti*). In support of Utopia, a group of people from Hebei burned newspapers and magazines published by the group under a banner "Strongly Denounce the *Hanjian* Media!" Lee Teng-hui, the former president of the Republic of China and head of the Nationalist Party, has been considered a *hanjian* by many for his pro-Japan position as well as his support of the Taiwan independence movement. Even the Nationalist party called Lee a *hanjian* when he remarked in 2015, on the seventieth anniversary of the victory against Japan, that Japan was Taiwan's true motherland.[28] Other political figures among the many who have been labeled *hanjian* by their opponents are Chiang Kai-shek, Mao Zedong, Jiang Zemin (a former head of state of the People's Republic of China), Ko Wen-jo (the mayor of Taipei since 2014), and Ma Ying-jeou (a former president of the Republic of China). Nor are ordinary people safe from the charge. In response to the US air and naval patrols in the disputed area of the South China Sea, the "patriotic angry youths" (*fenqing*) in China denounced patronizing KFC and using iPhones as *hanjian* conduct.[29] The ubiquity of the word does not make it less harmful. Whenever it is used, it immediately puts a person on the defensive. Yet what can one do to disprove the charge of *hanjian*?

Some in China have even pushed for the reintroduction of anti-*hanjian* laws. In 2007, a member of the Chinese Academy of Social Sciences proposed the Resolutions on Punishing Those with *Hanjian* Speech and Opinion (*Chengzhi hanjian yanlun fa'an*) to the People's Congress, the legislative organ of the People's Republic of China. This proposal bore the signatures of six other well-established academicians and government officials, including the former vice president of the Chinese Academy of Social Sciences and the deputy director of the Bureau of Justice in Tibet.[30] It proposed that all those who took a revisionist approach in evaluating foreign invasions of China since the Opium Wars should be considered *hanjian* and sentenced to imprisonment for up to twenty years. This proposal targeted scholarly work that the petitioners saw as defending foreign imperialism, harming the national interest, and corrupting future generations' understanding of Chinese history. To make a stronger case, the signatories referred to the Verbotsgesetz 1947, an Austrian constitutional law that bans any printed work or media broadcast that denies or tries to justify crimes committed by the Nazi Party or its associated entities.[31] This proposal immediately attracted widespread discussion and criticism, including protests in front of the Chinese embassy in New York.

This attempt to write the *hanjian* crime back into law did not succeed. Yet as nationalism is gaining new momentum in China, there is ample opportunity for the word *hanjian* to regain its force. Mainstream newspapers, influential blogs, and casual online posts frequently raise questions and debates about *hanjian*, identify new *hanjian*, or caution the public against hidden *hanjian*. When disputes between China and Japan over the Diaoyu (or Senkaku) Islands escalated in 2012, anti-Japanese protesters took to the streets. They boycotted Japanese products and, in some violent cases, attacked Japanese retailers and restaurants. In the middle of the protests, an article titled "Beware of the Sabotage of Japanese Spies and *Hanjian*" was posted on one of the most influential Chinese blogs, epitomizing similar opinions and suggestions expressed at the time. The article starts with a sweeping charge against the Japanese that immediately brings people back to the time of war: "Japanese spies are all over the world, and the Japanese are capable of any evil deeds. They never stop sending spies to China or turning pro-Japan Chinese into *hanjian*. . . . Judging by the abnormal phenomena around the country now, the Japanese spies and *hanjian* are at work to sabotage the movement of protecting the Diaoyu Islands."

The article affirms the patriotism of most Chinese, using language that resonates with the resistance narrative of the past, and then calls for action against the spies and *hanjian*: "We have to believe that the most Chinese are patriotic and that those collaborating with foreign powers are few. To make sure that anti-Japanese activities are carried out in an orderly and robust fashion, we need to coordinate with local law enforcement and organize special squads. . . . All patriotic Chinese, unite! All anti-Japanese forces, unite! We have to believe in the central government and defeat Japan and *hanjian* through unity." The article concludes that "*hanjian* who speak for Japan are bound to meet a miserable end."[32]

Observing the Chinese public's responses to recent territorial disputes, foreign observers are struck by how Chinese patriotism continues to manifest itself with "unprecedented unity and consolidation."[33] A cornerstone of such unanimity is the living tradition of isolating and punishing *hanjian*. Moreover, Chinese have been conditioned from past national crises to act preemptively and forestall *hanjian* activity. This explains why the word appears most frequently at moments of diplomatic friction, territorial disputes, or foreign criticism of China. Yet *hanjian* is no longer applied solely in situations that involve "barbarians" or foreign intrusion, as it was in the past. Any speech or action that fails to conform to expectations for the display of nationalism or is seen to harm China's national prestige, as in the case of the Nanfang Daily Group, can be considered *hanjian* conduct. Not only has the historical memory of *hanjian* survived, but this constantly evolving term continues to define and shed light on Chinese nationalism.

APPENDIX A

Revised Regulations on Punishing *Hanjian*

Xiuzheng chengzhi hanjian tiaoli
修正懲治漢奸條例
August 15, 1938

ARTICLE I: All *hanjian* cases should be processed in accordance with this Act.

ARTICLE II: Anyone who conspires with an enemy state and commits one of the following acts is considered a *hanjian* and is to be sentenced to capital punishment or life imprisonment.

1. Plotting against the home country;
2. Plotting to disturb public order;
3. Forming an army or recruiting labor for military use;
4. Supplying, dealing, collecting, or transporting military supplies or materials for producing military supplies;
5. Supplying, dealing, or transporting grains or other items that could serve as provisions;
6. Providing financial support to the enemy;
7. Leaking, stealing, or secretly collecting political or economic information [on the resistance force];
8. Serving as a guide for the enemy or assisting the enemy army in other ways;
9. Impeding the work of government employees;
10. Instigating financial chaos;
11. Sabotaging communications or military infrastructure [of the resistance force], or military blockades;
12. Poisoning drinking water or food for the Chinese military or people;
13. Instigating defection or collaboration among servicemen, government employees, or ordinary citizens;
14. Allowing oneself to be enticed into collaboration by a criminal guilty of any of the above crimes.

ARTICLE III: Anyone who encourages, harbors or comforts any person who commits the *hanjian* crime is considered a joint principal party to the offense.

ARTICLE IV: Anyone who secretly shelters any person whom he knows or has reasonable grounds for believing to be engaged in committing the *hanjian* crime will be sentenced to life imprisonment or imprisonment for a minimum of seven years.

ARTICLE V: Anyone who intentionally frames others for any crime listed in this Act is to receive the sentence prescribed for the same crime.

ARTICLE VI: Anyone who attempts the *hanjian* crime without success is to suffer a penalty.

ARTICLE VII: Anyone who plans for or connives at any *hanjian* activity listed in Article II or Article III is to be imprisoned for a minimum of seven years. Anyone who plans for or connives at any crime listed in Article IV or Article V is to be imprisoned for one to seven years.

ARTICLE VIII: Any property or object obtained through committing the *hanjian* crime, or used for committing the crime, will be confiscated regardless of its original ownership.

ARTICLE IX: Anyone who is found guilty of any crime listed in Article II will have their property confiscated in its entirety.

For *hanjian* defendants who are wanted by the Nationalist Government yet remain at large, the state can declare the confiscation of their property.

For *hanjian* defendants whom the Nationalist Government has not ordered arrested, the highest military authority can approve the confiscation of a portion or the entirety of their property.

ARTICLE X: When confiscating *hanjian* property according to this Act, a proper portion will be left for supporting the families of *hanjian* defendants.

ARTICLE XI: Local administrative organs are entrusted to seize or confiscate *hanjian* property that is confiscated based on this Act. Such organs should compile detailed catalogs of confiscated property and items and send the catalogs to the highest military authority.

ARTICLE XII: Objects or property confiscated according to Article VIII will be transferred to the Nationalist army stationed nearby or to local administrative organs. The latter should send detailed catalogs to the highest military authority.

ARTICLE XIII: The responsible parties should make public announcements regarding *hanjian* property that has been confiscated or seized.

ARTICLE XIV: Anyone charged with the *hanjian* crime is to be tried by a military tribunal or the army. When a dispute over jurisdiction arises, the highest military authority should intervene and make a decision.

ARTICLE XV: Within five days after a verdict is reached for a *hanjian* case, the written judgment and the defendant's appeal (if applicable) should be sent to the highest military authority, along with all documents that serve as evidence in this case. If expedited processing is needed, the highest military authority is to be informed of the criminal facts, the laws applied, and the reasons for an expedited sentence before it approves it.

In the war zones, concluded *hanjian* cases and paperwork will be reported to the military commander of each war zone for approval. The commanders will evaluate the cases for approval and keep them on file for later report.

ARTICLE XVI: For cases sent for its approval, the highest military authority reserves the right to review, dispatch a person to audit the retrial, or transfer the case to another authority.

ARTICLE XVII: Relevant parts from the Criminal Code and the Criminal Procedure Law are applicable to *hanjian* cases if they do not contradict this Act.

ARTICLE XVIII: Anyone who has committed the *hanjian* crime yet turns himself or herself in before the crime is exposed will be processed according to the Regulations on *Hanjian* Who Voluntarily Surrender (*Hanjian zishou tiaoli*).

ARTICLE XIV: This Act takes effect on the day of its promulgation.

APPENDIX B

Resolutions on Preventing
Hanjian Activities and Espionage

Fangzhi hanjian jiandie huodong banfa dagang
防治漢奸間諜活動辦法大綱
Stipulated by the Ministry of Internal Affairs, 1939

ARTICLE I: These resolutions are drafted and implemented for the purpose of preventing *hanjian* activities and espionage for enhancing national security.

ARTICLE II: Local law enforcement is responsible for preventing *hanjian* and spies from sabotaging resistance efforts. In counties and villages without a standing police force, heads of villages and mutual surveillance units will take charge.

ARTICLE III: All people of the Chinese nation, regardless of age and gender, are responsible for investigating and exposing *hanjian* and spies.

ARTICLE IV: Localities are allowed to organize voluntary groups and police to supervise, command, and facilitate the surveillance against *hanjian* and spies. The structure of such groups, as well as the training and management of their members, shall be approved by local governments at different levels and reported to the Ministry of Internal Affairs.

ARTICLE V: All those who are engaged in preventing *hanjian* and spy activities shall, under all circumstances, obey the officers in charge and follow orders strictly.

ARTICLE VI: To prevent *hanjian* activity and espionage, special attention will be paid to the following groups and activities:

A. Suspicious groups or individuals:

Those who are generally ill-behaved;

Those who do not have regular jobs and frequently take part in social gatherings;

Those who are unemployed yet are often quite occupied;

Those who are without jobs or property yet are living comfortable lives;

Those who are employed yet are more engaged in activities that few know about;

Those who have been poor yet suddenly make a fortune;

Those whose household profiles are unclear;

Those who have suspicious visitors;

Those who interact with individuals with complicated backgrounds;

Those who have an inconsistent style of dressing or carry particular marks;

Those who overdress for their activities and overspend for their social status;

Those who seem anxious or disturbed in their expressions and speech;

Travelers or visitors with suspicious backgrounds;

Travelers with abnormal luggage;

Those who come out in the dark of night or the early morning to meet with others in public places;

Pedestrians with faces covered by hats or sunglasses;

Pedestrians who often look back to see if they are followed;

Pedestrians who appear to be in a panic;

Monks, beggars, rickshaw pullers, and peddlers who do not fit into their respective groups;

Those who suddenly have an increasing quantity of telegraphs or correspondence;

Those whose words are unpatriotic or sympathetic to the enemy;

Those who suddenly bequeath gifts or money to people who are not their close acquaintances;

Those who are dressed in the Chinese way but do not seem Chinese in their speech, habits, or behaviors;

Those who frequently interact with foreigners;

Nationals of the enemy state;

All other individuals who do not appear normal.

B. Suspicious activities:

Holding gatherings without approval or without state surveillance

Hosting weddings, funerals, or birthday banquets that are of an unusual format;

Intentionally leaking confidential information of political or military importance;

Spying on national defense mechanisms or plans for the enemy;

Colluding with the enemy;

Being used by the enemy;

Disturbing the social order and provoking panic;

Sabotaging the financial order;

Stirring up student protests;

Stirring up strikes;

Damaging important transportation lines or infrastructure of other types;

Taking photos or making drawings of government or military headquarters, strategic regions, roads, bridges, and other strategic points without permission;

Other suspicious activities.

C. High-risk locations:

1. Train stations, bus stations, and airports;
2. Docks, ports, and places along the coasts or riverbanks where people can easily get on or get off;
3. Entrances and exits of cities and arterial roads;
4. Parks and libraries;
5. Theaters and other public entertainment centers;
6. Hotels, clubs, dormitories, youth associations, hospitals, and factories;
7. Places where poor people and refugees gather;
8. Suspicious residences, stores, and houses;
9. Suspicious news agencies, post offices, and other social organizations;
10. Offices and schools with members of mixed backgrounds;
11. Temples and monasteries;
12. Places where nationals of the enemy nation cohabit or associate;
13. Other places with suspicious visitors or layouts.

ARTICLE VII: Constant attention and caution should be exercised toward individuals, activities, and places listed in Article VI.

ARTICLE VIII: Suspicious individuals shall be followed and questioned. Those who seem particularly dangerous must be arrested and taken to offices in charge of local security.

ARTICLE IX: Local residents who are informed of *hanjian* activities and espionage should immediately report to the offices in charge.

ARTICLE X: Responsible authorities should immediately and secretly carry out investigations and interrogations when a *hanjian* or spy case is brought in. Those who are innocent should be set free. Those who are guilty should be taken to the local garrison headquarters.

ARTICLE XI: Local governments should keep clear household records at a time of emergency. Changes to household numbers should be reported to the local police in a timely manner. Withholding such information is not allowed.

ARTICLE XII: Local stores, schools, office buildings, hotels, clubs, public residences, youth clubs, hospitals, factories, social organizations, theaters, teahouses, restaurants, brothels, temples, stations, docks, and other places are not allowed to accommodate suspicious-looking strangers. Those who break this rule will be punished severely. If those sheltered turn out to be *hanjian* or spies after investigation, the hosts will be charged with the same offense.

ARTICLE XIII: Local law enforcement should pay close attention to suspicious households and be ready to investigate at any time.

ARTICLE XIV: Local law enforcement should work with village heads to identify unemployed wanderers, keep a registry, and help them get settled and get employed, so that they will not be used by the enemy. Wanderers who do not comply or do not behave should be monitored or detained for penal labor, depending on how potentially dangerous they are.

ARTICLE XV: Offices in charge should reward those who help discover or investigate *hanjian* or spy cases.

ARTICLE XVI: Hoaxing and extortion in the name of preventing *hanjian* and spy activities are strictly forbidden. Those who frame others will be punished by law.

ARTICLE XVII: Anyone who clandestinely colludes with the enemy, *hanjian,* spies, or bandits will be severely punished.

ARTICLE XVIII: Local governments and offices in charge shall draft specific policies regarding the prevention of *hanjian* and spy activities and rewarding informants. Such policies shall be kept on file by the Ministry of Internal Affairs.

ARTICLE XIX: *Hanjian* and spy cases processed by local governments and garrison headquarters shall be reported to their superiors in a timely manner, so that these cases will reach the Military Council and the Ministry of Internal Affairs for approval.

APPENDIX C

Regulations on Handling *Hanjian* Cases

Chuli hanjian anjian tiaoli
處理漢奸案件條例
December 6, 1945

ARTICLE I: For cases involving *hanjian*, if the circumstances are not addressed by this Act, other laws or regulations are applicable.

ARTICLE II: Anyone is to be prosecuted for the *hanjian* crime if:

1. He or she took a position at the third level [*jianrenzhi* 简任职] or above of the civil administration of the puppet regime; or if he or she was the head of the fourth level of the puppet administration [*jianrenzhi* 荐任职];

2. He or she took a "specially appointed position" [*teren*] in the puppet regime;

3. He or she took any civil or military service position in the puppet regime and is accused of having infringed upon other people's property or other rights from that position;

4. He or she worked in the military, political, or intelligence branches of the Japanese army or the puppet regime;

5. He or she served as the principal of a postsecondary school or similar important position in an organization sponsored by the puppet regime;

6. He or she took a high-ranking position in financial or industrial organizations affiliated with or sponsored by the puppet regime;

7. He or she worked as the editor, director, or manager in any press, newspaper, or magazine in the occupied areas that produced propaganda for the puppet regimes;

8. He or she worked for movie studios, radio stations, or any other media or cultural organizations that produced propaganda for the puppet regimes;

9. He or she was a core member of the puppet party committee, New Citizens Association (Xinminhui), Harmony Association (Xiehehui), puppet Council, or other key puppet associations;

10. He or she participated in any cultural, financial, industrial, professional, autonomous, or social organizations in the occupied areas and is accused of having infringed upon other people's property or other rights from that position.

ARTICLE III: A *hanjian* as defined by Article II will receive a properly reduced punishment if he or she proves to have assisted the resistance forces during wartime or benefited the people in other ways. Such reduction of his or her punishment does not apply to the deprivation of civil rights.

ARTICLE IV: Among items of *hanjian* property that were obtained through embezzlement or misappropriation, those that were originally state owned or publicly owned shall be retrieved, and the rest shall be confiscated by the state or returned to the original owner. If all or a part of the aforementioned property cannot be retrieved, the market value of *hanjian*'s personal property should be assessed and the amount used to compensate the victims of his or her crime. If a *hanjian*'s personal property is insufficient for this purpose, all will be confiscated except for a portion necessary for the support of his or her dependents.

ARTICLE V: Military tribunals are responsible for trying military personnel who are at the same ranks as *hanjian* in the puppet regime; the Supreme Court and other civil courts are responsible for trying all other types of *hanjian* according to the Law of Procedure for Special Criminal Offenses [*Tezhong xingshi anjian susong tiaoli*].

ARTICLE VI: The principles on reducing punishments for *hanjian* who voluntarily surrender are applicable to those who turn themselves in after August 10, 1945.

ARTICLE VII: Upon recovering office space in previously occupied areas and resuming work, courts of all levels shall take over *hanjian* cases from political or military branches that have processed such cases during wartime. Any property confiscated by the political or military or other branches shall be transferred to the courts.

ARTICLE VIII: If necessary, the Supreme Court and advanced courts shall dispatch qualified personnel to localities where *hanjian* crimes were committed, to investigate and try cases that local courts are unable to settle.

ARTICLE IX: Prosecuting attorneys shall be responsible for investigation.

ARTICLE X: Local governments and army shall facilitate the arrest and punishment of *hanjian*.

ARTICLE XI: This Act takes effect on the day of its promulgation.

NOTES

Introduction

1. Zhang Shizhao, "Hanjian bian," 158.
2. On the unique and complex historical construct of the Han, see Mullaney et al., *Critical Han Studies*.
3. Shaila Dewan, "Chinese Student in U.S. Is Caught in Confrontation," *New York Times*, April 17, 2008; Grace Wang, "Caught in the Middle, Called a Traitor," *Washington Post*, April 20, 2008.
4. Nora, "Between Memory and History," 7–24.
5. The Chinese Ministry of Education has ordered history textbooks to be revised to extend the War of Resistance to fourteen years by setting the starting point at the Japanese invasion of Manchuria in 1931. He Haiwei, "Zhongguo xiugai jiaokeshu: 'banian kangzhan' bian 'shisinian kangzhan'" (Chinese textbooks to be revised: Now the "eight-year War of Resistance" has become the "fourteen-year War of Resistance"), *New York Times* (China edition), January 12, 2017. The concept of the fourteen-year war was first raised by President Xi Jinping of the People's Republic of China in a 2015 speech marking the seventieth anniversary of China's victory in this war.
6. Qin Xiaoying, "Why Ignoring China's Commemoration of War against Japan Is a Foolish Mistake," *Huffington Post*, www.huffingtonpost.com/qin-xiaoying/china -commemoration-war-japan-_b_8063576.html, accessed August 31, 2016.
7. Zhang Gang, "Kangzhan zhuti dianying zhanbo xian gaochao" (Screening of films on the War of Resistance has aroused much interest and discussion). *Meiri xinbao* (Tianjin), August 31, 2015.
8. See Mitter, *Forgotten Ally*; Schoppa, *In a Sea of Bitterness*; Esherick and Combs, *China at the Crossroads*.
9. Rousso, *The Vichy Syndrome*, 1–7; De Ceuster, "The Nation Exorcised."
10. Mitter, *Forgotten Ally*, 6.
11. Ibid., 5.
12. See the Communist Party's "Ten Tenets on Resisting Japan and Saving the Nation" (Kangri jiuguo shida gangling), issued on August 25, 1937, and the Nationalist Party's "Programs on the War of Resistance and National Reconstruction," in Peng Ming, *Zhongguo xiandai shi zilia xuanji*, 159–61, 194, 239.
13. Meng and Cheng, "Chengzhi hanjian gongzuo gaishu," 110. As late as March 1947, the Supreme Court issued a wanted list of 303 *hanjian*. "Zuigao fayuan tongji dapi louwang hanjian," *Shenbao*, March 9, 1947.

14. Liu Tong, "Guomin zhengfu shenpan riben zhanfan gaishu: 1945–1949," 72.
15. Jacobs, "Preparing the People for Mass Clemency," 152–72.
16. Zhang Yushu, *Kangxi zidian*, 255, 260.
17. Sartre, "What Is a Collaborator?" 41–64.
18. On the use of *zhunhanjian*, see Zhonggong Zhongyang Wenxian Yanjiushi, *Mao Zedong xinwen gongzuo wenxuan*, 313. The Nationalist government issued the *Fangzhi hanjian jiandie anjian tiaoli* (Resolutions on preventing *hanjian* and spy activities) to identify *hanjian* suspects. See appendix B.
19. There was less political stigma associated with collaboration in Southeast Asia, where the Japanese invasion marked "a foreign occupation of a foreign occupation." So the betrayal was not really of one's own nation, but of the foreign colonial regime that had been established there. Lawson, "Wartime Atrocities and the Politics of Treason in the Ruins of the Japanese Empire, 1937–1953," 7.
20. Lottman, *The People's Anger*, 41.
21. Deák, *Europe on Trial*, 28–30, 78, 101.
22. Virgili, *Shorn Women*.
23. Fu, *Passivity, Resistance, and Collaboration*; Brook, *Collaboration*.
24. Treat, "Choosing to Collaborate," 82.
25. Deák, *Europe on Trial*, 55.
26. Brook, "Hesitating before the Judgment of History," 104.
27. Deák, *Europe on Trial*, 112.
28. Ibid., 52–54.
29. The CCP, as a governing authority of border areas of China during the war, also presented itself as an authentic resistance state.
30. Chen, "Dadongya zhanzheng hou Chongqing zhi dongxiang" (Policy trends in Chongqing following the outbreak of the Great East Asian War), *Shenbao*, October 11, 1942.
31. Mitter, *Forgotten Ally*, 203.
32. See, for example, Brian Martin, "Resistance and Cooperation: Du Yuesheng and the Politics of the Shanghai United Committee," in Yeh and Henriot, *In the Shadow of the Rising Sun*, 187–208.
33. Lottman, *The People's Anger*, 41.
34. Zanasi, "Globalizing *hanjian*"; Musgrove, "Cheering the Traitor."
35. Brook, "Hesitating before the Judgment of History," 111; Treat, "Choosing to Collaborate," 99.

Chapter 1: From Epithet to Crime

1. Eichensehr, "Treason in the Age of Terrorism," 1448.
2. US Const. Art. III, § 3.
3. Brook, "The Shanghai Trials, 1946," 134.
4. Cihai Bianji Weiyuanhui, *Cihai*, 2:2027.
5. Wu Mi, "Qingdai guanshu dang'an suojian 'hanjian' yici zhicheng ji qi bianhua."
6. Liu Xiaoyuan, *Frontier Passages*, 6–13.

7. Li Man, "Rumour, Hanjian 漢奸, and Identity," 171. The text in which *hanjian* appears is Hu Zhen, *Zhouyi yanyi.*

8. "Li Chenshi zhi Guangzhou lühu tongxianghui he Guang-Zhao Gongsuo xinhan" (Mrs. Li Ze's letter to Shanghai Guangzhou Sojourners' Association), August 28, 1946, SMA Q117 (2–89). For Li Ze's case, see chapter 3.

9. Yang Sichang, "Zhaocai shuixi shanhou shu," 181.

10. Hevia, *Cherishing Men from Afar*, 30–52.

11. On ethnic composition and relations during the high Qing period, see Crossley, *The Wobbling Pivot*, 44.

12. See, for instance, *Qing shilu*, vol. 7, chapter 20, 53.

13. Wu Mi, "Qingdai guanshu dang'an suojian 'hanjian' yici zhi cheng jiqi bianhua."

14. *Xuanzong Chenghuangdi shilu*, vol. 338, 138.

15. Lin, "Mina hanjian zhaogao," 47.

16. Zhang and Yang, *Qingdai yeshi*, 177.

17. Here my interpretation departs from that of Frederic Wakeman in his seminal article on the topic. Wakeman, "*Hanjian* (Traitor)!" 299.

18. Zou Rong, *Gemingjun*, 34.

19. Zarrow, *China in War and Revolution*, 54–74.

20. Zhang Shizhao, "Hanjian bian," 158. Zhang praised as "Han heroes" Yue Fei of the Southern Song dynasty; Hong Xiuquan, who led the Taiping Rebellion (1851–64) against the Qing; and anti-Manchu revolutionaries such as Tang Caichang and Lin Shutang.

21. Zhang's long list of *hanjian* included Zeng Guofan (1811–72), Li Hongzhang (1823–1901), and Zuo Zongtang (1812–85), all model Confucianist Han officials in the Qing court who had suppressed local rebellions. For biographies of the three, see Zhao, *Qingshigao*, chapters 405, 411, 412.

22. For the story of Guan Gan, see Ban Gu, *Han shu*, chapter 54, "Biographies of Li Guang and Su Jian," 2450–59. Jie was one of the Hun tribes in Central Asia that intermittently harassed the Chinese dynasties. Zhang Bin was a Han Chinese who became the strategist for the Jie leader Shi Le, who founded the later Zhao dynasty (319–51). See Fang Xuanling, *Jin shu*, chapter 105, 2707–56. Shi Jingtang founded the short-lived later Jin dynasty (936–47) with the help of the Khitans, at the price of ceding sixteen prefectures in north China, strategic points in defending China proper against nomadic states to the north. Shi was often blamed for the military vulnerability of the subsequent Song dynasty (960–1279) and its eventual fall to the Mongols. Wu Sangui, Shang Kexi, and Geng Jimao were all Ming generals who surrendered to the Manchus and helped them conquer China proper. Zhao, *Qingshigao*, chapter 474, "Biographies of Wu Sangui, Geng Jingzhong, and Shang Zhixin."

23. Zarrow, *China in War and Revolution*, 56.

24. According to the rhetoric of the republic, the Chinese race included the Han, the Manchus, the Mongols, the Tibetans, and the Hui. This rhetoric was reflected in the five-color national flag, a symbol of the cohabitation and harmony of the five peoples. Harrison, *The Making of the Republican Citizen*, 98–103.

25. Fitzgerald, *Awakening China*, chapters 2–3; Liu Xiaoyuan, *Frontier Passages*, prologue.

26. Zarrow, *China in War and Revolution*, 302–3.

27. *Shanghaishi meishangye tongye gonghui jie Tiexue chujiantuan jinggao benye jianshang fanmai rimei youguan wenshu* (Records of the Shanghai Coal Association and its response to the threatening letters from the Iron and Blood *Hanjian*-Elimination Team), August 1932–August 1937, SMA (S304)-1-158. This file shows that this team had sent out similar warnings before.

28. On the National Products Movement, see Gerth, *China Made.*

29. "Xinshuyu: Hanjian," *Xinsheng* 60, May 26, 1935.

30. Guomin Zhengfu Junshi Weiyuanhui, *Mingmo hanjian liezhuan*, n.p., March 1936, SMA (K827)-117872.

31. Chan, "Official Historiography and Ideological Indoctrination in High Qing," 254.

32. Guominzhengfu Junshiweiyuanhui, ed. *Mingmo hanjian liezhuan*, preface by Chiang Kai-shek, 1–3. In this excerpt, Chiang referred to the Han as *wozu*. In this context *wo* means "our," and the character *zu* by itself can mean either race or ethnicity.

33. Paine, *The Wars for Asia*, 95; Shi Jiashun, *Liangguang shibian zhi yanjiu.*

34. Yu Renlin, *Gujin hanjian maiguoshilu*, 3.

35. *The Great Qing Code*, 34–35.

36. Ibid.

37. This code replaced the *New Criminal Code of the Great Qing*, promulgated in 1910, and served as the criminal code until 1928. Mühlhahn, *Criminal Justice in China*, 60–61.

38. Hung, *Outlines of Modern Chinese Law*, 284.

39. For instance, acts of "external aggression" during wartime would lead to five to twelve years' imprisonment. Capital punishment would apply if the defendant handed over important military facilities to an enemy nation, instigated native troops to surrender, or spied for the enemy. Ibid.

40. Second Historic Archives, ed. *Zhonghua minguoshi dang'an ziliao huibian*, vol. 5, 292.

41. Mühlhahn, *Criminal Justice in China*, 65.

42. *Zhonghua Mingguo xingfa* (The Criminal Code of the Republic of China) in *Zhonghua minguoshi dang'an ziliao huibian*, vol. 5, 473.

43. *Weihai minguo jinji zhizuifa* (Emergency Law on Crimes Endangering the Republic), in *Zhonghua minguoshi dang'an ziliao huibian*, 5:291–92.

44. Zanasi, "Globalizing *Hanjian*," 745; Brook, "The Shanghai Trials, 1946," 132.

45. Article 85 of the Constitution states: "The power of interpreting this Provisional Constitution shall be exercised by the Central Executive Committee of the Nationalist Party." Chinese Ministry of Information, *China Handbook, 1937–1945*, 95.

46. See War Measures Act Conference, *The Japanese Canadian Experience.*

47. Linz, "Legitimacy of Democracy and the Socioeconomic System," 65.

48. *Chengzhi hanjian tiaoli* (Regulations on Punishing *Hanjian*), September 7, 1937, Article 2; *Xiuzheng Chengzhi hanjian tiaoli* (Revised Regulations on Punishing *Hanjian*), August 15, 1938, Article 2. Both versions can be found in Zhang Yuanjie, *Chuli hanjian anjian tiaoli qianshi*, 13–14, 43–45.

49. Jia Kaiji, "Zhongguo suqing hanjian" (China is now eliminating traitors), in Bing Ying, ed. *Hanjian xianxingji*, 19. This article was originally published in English in the *Shanghai Evening Post*, date unknown. See also Liu Jixing, "Kangzhan chuqi beichusi de hanjian dacaizi."

50. Jia Kaiji, "Zhongguo suqing hanjian," 4.

51. Yu Jun, "Hanjian zai quan zhongguo huodong zhe" (*Hanjian* are active all over China), in Bing Ying, *Hanjian xianxingji*, 4–8.

52. *Chengzhi hanjian tiaoli*, Articles 2, 4, 7; *Xiuzheng chengzhi hanjian tiaoli*, Articles 2, 4, 7.

53. *Chengzhi hanjian tiaoli*, Article 10; *Xiuzheng chengzhi hanjian tiaoli*, Article 11.

54. The Resolutions can be found in Qian Qinglian, *Chengzhi hanjian fa*.

55. Ibid., Article VI.

56. Li Zonghuang, *Xianxing baojia zhidu*, 3.

57. See, for instance, Yang Ji'an, "Minguo shiqi xianggan bianjie baojia zhidu de shishi jiqi xiaoneng," 11–15.

58. Zhang Yuanjie, *Chuli hanjian anjian tiaoli qianshi*, appendixes, 14–45.

59. For a contemporary review and critique of military tribunals for nonmilitary defendants, see Sun, "Lun dui feijunren de junfa shenpan," 1–2. The principle of *xingluanguo, yongzhongdian*, or "harsh law for a time of turbulence," was first established in the *Rites of Zhou*. This principle was reiterated in Ban, *Han shu*, chapter 23, 148.

60. "Guofang Zuigao Weiyuanhui zuzhidagang" (Outline for organizing the Supreme Council of National Defense), *Geming Wenxian* 79 (1979): 482–83.

61. Mitter, *Forgotten Ally*, 205.

62. Ordinance no. 1891 of the Ministry of Justice, 1939, *Jiangsu canjia weizuzhi beijianju renyuan jiashu xiang quanguo sifa xingzheng huiyi huyu qing shifang yuanyu an* (Petition to the National Judicial and Administrative Conference for correcting the wrongful cases by family members of those accused of serving in puppet organizations), cited in SHA 7 (8931).

63. *Feichang shiqi weichizhi anjinji banfa*, July 24, 1940, Article 2, in Zhang Yuanjie, *Chuli hanjian anjian tiaoli qianshi*, 23.

64. "Zhongjian weiyuanhui mishuchu han wei funi xiangdi zhi dangyuan ying yifa chengban" (The Central Supervision Commission on punishing party members who collaborated with the enemy), in *Xingshi tebie faling: Hanjian*, 11–12, SMA Q (187)-1-204.

65. See, for instance, "Xingzhengyuan chaofa Guangdongsheng lincanhui jianyi chengban huaqiao fudi *hanjian* yi'an" (Guangdong Provisional Council's decision on punishing Chinese of other nationalities), in *Xingshi tebie faling: Hanjian*, 27; "Xingzhengyuan guanyu Shandongsheng lincanhui lizhong chengjian jianyi yi'an chaofa yuanling" (The Executive Yuan's decision on Shandong Provisional Council's suggestions on punishing the disloyal and rewarding the loyal), ibid., SMA Q (187)-1-204.

66. Xiao, *Zhongguo gongchandang kangri zhanzheng shiqi dashiji*.

67. He Deting, "Kangri genjudi sujian yanjiu," 178.

68. Ouyang, *Kangzhan shiqi Shaan-Gan-Ning bianqu chujian fante fazhi yanjiu*, 214.

69. Zhang and Han, *Zhongguo geming fazhishi*, 284.

70. See, for instance, *Suzhongqu di'er xingzhengqu susong zanxing tiaoli* (Provisional procedural law of the Second Administrative Region of the Central Jiangsu Border Area), September 1943. Quoted in He Deting, "Kangri genjudi sujian yanjiu," 176.

71. *Chuli hanjian anjian tiaoli*, Article 2. In the next three years, the Nationalist legislature made frequent revisions to this version of the Regulations. *Xingshi tebie faling: hanjian*, 5–7, SMA Q (187)-1-204.

72. There were five levels in the civil administration of the Nationalist government and Wang Jingwei's regime. Officials of the third level and above included the chairman of the government, the heads of its five branches, legislators, ministers, directors of ministerial bureaus, mayors, and other officials. Liu Shanshu, "Wenguan kaoshi zhidu jianjie," 510.

73. Two accomplished politicians, Wang Kemin and Liang Hongzhi, had established regional puppet regimes sponsored by the Japanese. Brook, "The Creation of the Reformed Government in Central China, 1938," in Barrett and Shyu, *Chinese Collaboration with Japan, 1932–1945*, 79–101; Taylor, *The Struggle for North China*. See also Boyle, *China and Japan at War*, chapter 5.

74. Barrett, "The Wang Jingwei Regime, 1940–1945," in Barrett and Shyu, *Chinese Collaboration with Japan, 1932–1945*, 102–15.

75. Boyle, *China and Japan at War*, 23.

76. Treat, "Choosing to Collaborate," 93–95.

77. Mitter, *Forgotten Ally*, 204.

78. Ordinance no. 1978 of the Ministry of Justice, 1940, *Jiangsu canjia weizuzhi beijianju renyuan jiashu xiang quanguo sifa xingzheng huiyi huyu qing shifang yuanyu an*, cited in SHA 7 (8931).

79. Van Schaack and Slye, *International Criminal Law*, 784.

80. Brook, "The Shanghai Trials, 1946," 138.

81. Xie, *Zhanshi sifa jiyao*, 125. In reality, depending on their location and the circumstances of their arrest, *hanjian* were handled by different parties with no consistent standards. For a case study in Shandong, see Lawson, "Wartime Atrocities and the Policies of Treason," chapter 7.

82. "Tezhong xingshi anjian susong tiaoli" (Procedures for processing special criminal cases), in *Zhonghua mingguo guominzhengfu gongbao*, January 12, 1944.

83. On the importance of *weijun*, or military collaborators, in particular, see Lawson, "Wartime Atrocities and the Policies of Treason," 279.

84. *Weizuzhi huo qi suoshu jiguan tuanti renzhi renyuan houxuan ji renyong xianzhi banfa* (Restrictions on the candidacies and qualifications of former puppet staff), September 12, 1946, 31–32, SMA Q (257) 1–49.

85. *Shanghai shizhengfu guanyu chengzhi hanjian faling* (The Shanghai Municipal Government and anti-*hanjian* statutes), December 11, 1948, SMA Q (1) 1–77.

86. See *Weizuzhi huoqi suoshu jiguan tuanti renzhi renyuan houxuan ji renyong xianzhi banfa*, November 27, 1946, 33–34, SMA Q (257) 1–49.

87. Ordinance no. 4200 of the Ministry of Justice, August 13, 1946.

88. Ordinance no. 1096 of the Ministry of Justice, September 1946, in SMA (154) 1963, 28.

89. *Benshi geyehui lianming yaoqiu zhengfu xiugai chengzhi hanjian tiaoli di shiwutiao de yaoqiu* (A petition to revise Article XV of the Regulations by the United Association of Shanghai Professionals), February 20, 1946–April 9, 1948, SMA Q (201) 1–333.

90. Ibid.

91. *Guanli gejiguan tuanti zhengyong riji jishu yuangong banfa* (Regulations on employing Japanese technicians and personnel in government and organizations), 42–43, SMA Q (257) 1–49.

92. "Qiu Niantai's petition to the Legislative Yuan," in Hou, *Guoshiguan cang Er'erba dang'an shiliao*, 14–15.

93. Ordinance no. 1739 of the Ministry of Justice, May 28, 1940; Xie, *Zhanshi sifa jiyao*, 415–17.

94. By 1937, the SBA had around 1,400 members. Xu Xiaoqun, *Chinese Professionals and the Republican State*, 219.

95. Ibid., 102, 252.

96. Shi Liang, "Funü zai Kangzhan zhong de renwu." Shi Liang had been sympathetic to the CCP and later became the first minister of justice of the People's Republic of China. The campaigns against "counterrevolutionaries" took place when she was in office.

97. *Ren Tianqiang deng guanyu lunxianqu lüshi funi ji zhanqu lüshi denglu shixiang de jianyi* (Suggestions regarding the issue of collaborating lawyers and registration of lawyers in war zone), SHA (7)-2966.

98. *Zhanqu lüshi qianyi houfang zhixing zhiwu banfa* (Resolution for relocating lawyers to the free regions), in Xie, *Zhanshi sifa jiyao*, 418–19. The Ministry of Justice promised to reimburse members of the SBA at the rates offered to midlevel government clerks.

99. *Shanghai lüshi gonghui huiyuan jiuji banfa* (Methods of reliefs to members of the SBA), Ordinance of the Ministry of Justice, February 17, 1941, in Xie, *Zhanshi sifa jiyao*, 418.

100. These penalties were based on Article 9 of the Regulations of Bar Associations and Article 35 of Articles for Lawyers (*lüshi zhangcheng*), *Shanghai lüshi gonghui funi lüshi ziliao* (Profiles of collaborating lawyers provided by the Shanghai Bar Association), 1, SHA (Q190)-1-13802.

101. "Tiaozheng Shanghai lüshi gonghui, zuo chengli jieshou weiyuanhui" (Receiving committee of the SBA established yesterday), *Zhonghua ribao*, December 30, 1940.

102. Xie, *Zhanshi sifa jiyao*, 418.

103. *Shanghai lüshi gonghui funi lüshi ziliao*, 3, SMA (Q190)-1-13802.

104. *Hu Yuanjun Hu Yuansheng lüshi shiwusuo xinhan* (Letter from the law office of Hu Yuanjun and Hu Yuansheng), January 4, 1941, ibid., 5–6.

105. Chen was the chief judge of the Supreme Court under the Reformed Government, and Wu joined the committee of its National Audit Office. "Letter from the Shanghai Bar Association to Shanghai First Special District Court regarding the collaboration of Chen Yijiong and Wubin," ibid., 34–37.

106. Ordinance of the Ministry of Justice, January 28, 1939, in Xie, *Zhanshi sifa jiyao*, 415.

107. "Funi lüshi minglu" (A list of collaborating lawyers), in *Shanghai lüshi gonghui guanyu chengbao diaocha funi qingxing ji qing xunyu zhiding shenqing falü rikan you falü xiaoli han* (Letters from the SBA regarding the investigation of the collaborating lawyers), 1–4, SHA (Q190)-1-13770.

108. On the late Qing legal reform and the codification efforts of the reformers, see Philip Huang, *Code, Customs, and Legal Practice in China*.

109. Between 1923 and 1926, Dong also worked as the vice president of the Commission on the Abolition of Extraterritoriality. Cavanaugh, *Who's Who in China*, 3:398; He, Yang, and Wang, *Zhongguo geming shi renwu cidian*, 710.

110. Chen Tong, "Zai falü yu shehui zhijian: minguo shiqi Shanghai bentu lüshi de diwei he zuoyong," 55–69. On average, lawyers charged hundreds of yuan for taking a case, but Dong's minimum fee was several thousand yuan.

111. Hua Yougen, "Dong Kong yu jindai zhongguo lifa" (Dong Kang and the legislation of modern China), 73–87.

112. Du Han, *Dong Kang zhuanji ziliao* (Biography of Dong Kang), originally published in *Dafeng xunkan*, 4 (1947): 123, SHA (34)-812.

113. *Shanghai Gaodeng fayuan chengsong panguo hanjian Liang Hongzhi, Fu Shishuo, Yan Jiazhi, Cai Pei dengxiaozhuan* (Short biographies of the *hanjian* Liang Hongzhi, Fu Shishuo, Yan Jiazhi, Cai Pei, et al., sent by the Shanghai High Court to the Ministry of Justice), June 1948, SHA 7 (4)-363.

114. *Gedi minzhong shangsu jianju hanjian goujie diren zuixing anjian* (Letters exposing local *hanjian* from the people of various places), 96, SHA 7 (4)-248,

115. Ordinance of the Ministry of Justice on February 26, 1947, *Shanghai lüshi gonghui guanyu chuli diaocha funi lüshi wenti de xunling laiwang hanjian*, 7, SHA (Q190)-1-13876.

116. *Beiping ziyou renquan baozhang weiyuanhui Ling Wei chengsong sifa guan kaoshi jige renyuan zhong zhi weiyuan renyong wenti de yijianshu* (A petition by Ling Wei from the Liberty and Human Rights Association in Beijing), 1947, SHA (7)-210.

117. *Qianxian Ribao* (Frontline daily), May 1, 1945.

118. Zhang Yuanjie, *Chuli hanjian anjian tiaoli qianshi*, preface.

119. Yu Qichang, "Chengzhi hanjian tiaoli zhi zheng dangshiyong," 1.

120. Ibid.

121. Li Zuyin, "Chengzhi 'wugao' de fashiguan," 5.

122. *Jiangsu canjia weizuzhi bei jianju renyuan jiashu xiang quanguo sifa xingzheng huiyi huyu qing shifang yuanyu an*, August 1947, SHA 7 (8931).

123. Ibid.

124. Chen and Yuan were among the few Chinese board members of the Shanghai Municipal Council, the self-governing body that administered the International Settlement and was dominated by Western businessmen. Chen fled Shanghai before the Japanese entered the International Settlement and thus escaped being forced or enticed to serve on the Japanese-controlled municipal council.

125. "Yin Rugeng: 'Si de yuanwang'" (Yin Rugeng: "I do not deserve to die"), *Xin Shanghai*, June 1946.

126. *Ren Tianqiang deng guanyu lunxianqu lüshi funi ji zhanqu lüshi denglu shixiang de jianyi*.

127. "Ordinance from the Shanghai High Court regarding the investigation of four lawyers suspected of collaboration, on January 28, 1947," *Shanghai lüshi gonghui guanyu chuli diaocha funi lüshi wenti de xunling laiwang hanjian*, 11, SHA (Q190)-1-13876.

128. "Correspondence between Shanghai Bar Association and the Shanghai High Court," ibid., 12. For instance, Ling Qihong and Gong Wenhuan were accused of serving in the puppet Dadao government and on the Clearing the Villages committee, respectively, whereas investigation showed that they had only practiced in the puppet courts.

129. "The Traitor Act," *China Critic*, September 1945, 64.

130. In 1934, the National Bar Association founded a commission of forty-one persons to take charge of rectifying wrongful cases. Shi Bifan, "Guomindang tongzhi shiqi ziyou zhuyi renquan yuandong pingxi," 78–84.

Chapter 2: Arbiters of Justice in a Lawless State

1. Yu Jun, "Hanjian zai quanzhongguo huodongzhe" (*Hanjian* are active all over China), in Bing Ying, *Hanjian xianxingji*, 4–7; Bing Ying, "Qianfang de hanjian" (*Hanjian* on the battle front), in *Hanjian xianxingji*, 8–10, originally published in *National Salvation Daily*.

2. Torture was reported in the case of the disguised monks in Changshu and the case in Songjiang. Bing Ying, "Qianfang de hanjian," 7–8; Ding Shi, "Yige hanjian de gongzuo" (A typical *hanjian*'s work), in Bing Ying, *Hanjian xianxingji*, 23, originally published in *Xinbao*.

3. Bing Ying, "Qianfang de hanjian," 8.

4. "Bai'e shaofu tongdi panxing ernian liuyue" (White Russian woman was convicted of collaboration and received two years' imprisonment), *Shenbao*, March 14, 1947.

5. Bing Ying, "Qianfang de hanjian," 10.

6. "Pinglu jinzhong dengdi di dapi pusha weizuzhi renyuan" (Enemy in Pinglu and central Shanxi arrested and killed puppet officials and staff in big groups), *Kangzhan ribao*, September 5, 1942.

7. *Junweihui diaocha tongji ju linian xingdong chengguo tongjibiao* (Statistics on Juntong's operations and results by year), 1938–45, Academia Historica, Taipei, 148-020100-0005.

8. Chiang Kai-shek first required these individuals to turn themselves in for their *hanjian* crimes. When none of them did so, the Ministry of Justice put their names on the wanted list. Xie, *Zhanshi sifa jiyao*, 125. See also *Guomingdang zhengfu mingling tongji zhi hanjian zuifan* (*Hanjian* criminals wanted by the Nationalist government), 1938–August 1945, SHA 7 (4)-206.

9. Fu Xiao'an was assassinated by his cook who secretly worked for Dai Li. Wakeman, *The Shanghai Badlands*, chapter 8.

10. Wakeman, *Spymaster*, 237.

11. Famous incidents included Shi Jianru's assassination of Deshou (the Manchu governor of Guangdong) in 1900, Xu Xilin's assassination of Enming (the governor of Anhui) in 1907, and Peng Jiazhen's assassination of Liang Bi in 1912. Ibid., 168–82.

12. Wakeman, "*Hanjian* (Traitor)!" 300.

13. Wakeman, *Spymaster*, 158.

14. Disan Zhanqu Jinxia Hanjian Anjian Chuli Weiyuanhui, *Mintai hanjian zuixing shilu*, 1947.

15. Ibid., 111.

16. On the inner workings of Shanghai's underworld and Chiang Kai-shek's relation to gang bosses, see Martin, *The Shanghai Green Gang*.

17. Wakeman, *The Shanghai Badlands*, 123.

18. Introduced by Dai Li, Du met with Chiang Kai-shek in 1931 and later worked with Chiang in monopolizing the opium trade and suppressing Communist activity in Shanghai. During the Japanese occupation, Du left for Hong Kong and then went to Chongqing. During Du's absence, Juntong continued to recruit from Shanghai's lower classes and the underworld. Wakeman, *Spymaster*, chapter 17.

19. Ibid., 238–47.

20. Guofangbu Qingbaoju, *Zhongyi jiuguojun zhi*, 14.

21. *Huxi tebie jingcha zongshu guanyu qingnian tiexue chujiantuan wenjian* (Reports by the Western Shanghai Area Special Police Force on the Iron and Blood Youth *Hanjian*-Elimination Team), May 1941, 45–48. SMA (R119)-1-278.

22. In establishing the WASP in February 1941, the Wang Jingwei government and the Shanghai Municipal Council made a joint decision to control this area and to protect the International Settlement and the French Concession. See Wakeman, *The Shanghai Badlands*, 104.

23. *Huxi tebie jingcha zongshu guanyu qingnian tiexue chujiantuan wenjian*, 20–26.

24. Ibid., 4–10, 13.

25. Ding, "Kangzhan shiqi Juntong Shanghaiqu de chujian xingdong," 56–59.

26. Martin, "Resistance and Cooperation," in Yeh and Henriot, *In the Shadow of the Rising Sun*, 198.

27. Chen, *Yingxiong wu ming*, vols. 3–4.

28. Disan Zhanqu Jinxia Hanjian Anjian Chuli Weiyuanhui, *Mintai hanjian zuixing shilu*, 108–10.

29. *Huxi tebie jingcha zongshu guanyu qingnian tiexue chujiantuan wenjian*, 7.

30. Chiang founded and chaired the Sanqingtuan partly to revitalize the Nationalist Party, which had been plagued by corruption. He integrated the Sanqingtuan into the party in September 1947. See Zhou Shuzhen, *Sanqingtuan shimo*.

31. *Huxi tebie jingcha zongshu guanyu qingnian tiexue chujiantuan wenjian*, 38.

32. Ibid., 12, October 19, 1940.

33. Letters from the law offices of Yu Hualong, Jiang Zongpan, and Gao Danhua, November 11–December 13, 1940. Ibid., 13–16.

34. For instance, *Jiuwang ribao* (1937–41) published several special issues on *hanjian*. See "Xiaomie hanjian zhuanji" (Special issue on eliminating *hanjian*), *Jiuwang ribao*, September 10–11, 1937.

35. *Shanghaishi meishangye tongye gonghui jie Tiexue chujiantuan jinggao benye jianshang fanmai rimei youguan wenshu* (Documents on the Shanghai Coal Association and their responses to the Iron and Blood *Hanjian*-Elimination

Team), August 1932–August 1937, SMA (S304)-1-158. This file shows that the team had sent out similar warnings before.

36. Ibid., 1.

37. Wright, *Coal Mining*, 99–101, 117–60.

38. Coble, *Facing Japan*, 50–55.

39. Coble, "Chinese Capitalists in Wartime Shanghai, 1937–1945," in Yeh and Henriot, *In the Shadow of the Rising Sun*, 52.

40. *Shanghaishi meishangye tongye gonghui jie Tiexue chujiantuan jinggao*, 3.

41. Ibid., 10.

42. Since the first Opium War (1839–42), foreign powers had imposed extraterritoriality on China, which gave foreign consuls legal jurisdiction over their own subjects. This policy was successively adopted by Great Britain, the United States, France, Austria-Hungary, and fourteen other nations. China had made constant efforts to abolish extraterritoriality since 1902 but did not achieve this goal until 1943. See Wesley, *The End of Extraterritoriality in China*, 1–25.

43. "Geguo chengchu funi renyuan fagui" (Laws and regulations on treason from different nations), Academia Historica, Taipei, 020-010-117.

44. Zanasi, "Globalizing *hanjian*," 731–51.

45. "Shoudu gaodeng fayuan chengsong panguo hanjian Chen Gongbo Chu Minyi deng panjueshu ji xiaozhuan" (Indictments and brief biographies of the traitorous *hanjian* Chen Gongbo, Chu Minyi, et al., sent by the Capital High Court), February 1946, SHA 7 (4)-305, 13–17.

46. *Chen Gongbo deng hanjian zuixing gezhong anjuan wenti yu Jiangsu gaodeng fayuan jianchating de laiwang wenshu* (Correspondence with the Jiangsu High Court concerning the *hanjian* case of Chen Gongbo and others), February 1946, SMA (Q1)-6-47.

47. Zanasi, "Globalizing *hanjian*," 731–51.

48. Ibid., 732; Treat, "Choosing to Collaborate," 94.

49. "Shoudu gaodeng fayuan chengsong panguo hanjian Chen Gongbo Chu Minyi deng panjueshu ji xiaozhuan," 13.

50. Ibid.,17, 8.

51. The Qingxiang Yundong was launched in rural areas under occupation, with the goal of consolidating military, economic, and ideological control. Second Historical Archive, *Riwang de qingxiang*.

52. "Shoudu gaodeng fayuan chengsong panguo hanjian Chen Gongbo Chu Minyi deng panjueshu ji xiaozhuan," 17.

53. Ibid.

54. "Decision made by the Central Political Conference of the Wang Jingwei government," quoted in "Shoudu gaodeng fayuan chengsong panguo hanjian Chen Gongbo Chu Minyi deng panjueshu ji xiaozhuan."

55. Chen Gan, *Chen Gongbo shiji*, 12.

56. Musgrove, "Cheering the Traitor," 3–27.

57. *Zhoubao*, April 13, 1946.

58. At the request of the Ministry of Defense in 1948, the Capital High Court shared the photos, brief biographies, and indictments of major *hanjian*. Most were

208 NOTES TO CHAPTER 2

arrested by Juntong, and the rest were arrested by the Nationalist garrison headquarters in Shanghai and the local army. "Shoudu gaodeng fayuan chengsong panguo hanjian Chen Gongbo Chu Minyi deng panjueshu ji xiaozhuan."

59. Wakeman, *Spymaster*, 206.

60. Qin, *Zhonghua minguo zhongyao shiliao chubian: duiri kangzhan shiqi*, 6:1625.

61. *Remin jianju hanjian ji nichan jubao chuli shishi banfa* (Resolutions on the People's Report on *Hanjian* Crime and Handling the Exposed *Hanjian* Property), Academia Historica, Taipei, 062–1763.

62. Ibid.

63. "Yulu geyuan banli hanjian anjian qingxing biao" (Progress report on *hanjian* cases brought to courts in Shandong and Henan), March 1947, Academia Historica, Taipei, 151–1707.

64. "Sifabu ling gedi gaoyuan jiasu shenpan hanjian anjian" (The Ministry of Justice's edict on accelerating the pace of trying *hanjian* cases), *Shenbao*, February 18, 1947.

65. Mitter, *Forgotten Ally*, 263–79.

66. White and Jacoby, *Thunder out of China*, 177.

67. Lo, "Lishi qingjing yu kangzhan shiqi 'hanjian' de xingcheng," 818.

68. See, for instance, "Guangdong gaodeng fayuan shouli hanjian anjian baogaobiao" (Progress report on *hanjian* cases processed by the Guangdong High Court), February–March 1946, Academia Historica, Taipei, 151–1828.

69. "Yulu geyuan banli hanjian anjian qingxing biao."

70. Xie, *Zhanshi xifa jiyao*, 132. The National Advisory Council was an institution organized by the Nationalist government to "convey public opinion" and to advise on the resistance cause. Shi Bolin, "Lun kangzhan shiqi guomin zhengfu de zhanshi zhengzhi tizhi," 25–41.

71. *Ding Guitang hanjian an ji Ding Guitang Kangbian shu* (The *hanjian* case of Ding Guitang and Ding's letter of self-defense), January–December 1947, SMA (Q186)-2-20675.

72. The CMCS was created in Shanghai in 1854, when France, Great Britain, and the United States decided to take control of the customs service in order to protect their trade interests from local rebellions. This arrangement persisted for ninety-six years. The three powers and the Qing government agreed that its inspector general (IG) should be a British or American national appointed by the Qing government. Chihyun Chang, *Government, Imperialism and Nationalism in China*, introduction.

73. Chang Chihyun, "Zhongguo haiguan de guanyuan shencha he zhanhou fuyuan," 190–91.

74. *Ding Guitang hanjian an ji Ding Guitang Kangbian shu*, 31. Among other things, Ding promoted the use of Chinese language in the CMCS to make information more accessible to Chinese merchants and to prepare for the future nationalization of the CMCS.

75. Ding acted as the deputy inspector general until the arrival of Lester Knox Little, appointed as IG by Chiang Kai-shek. Chang, "Zhongguo haiguan de guanyuan shencha he zhanhou fuyuan, 194.

76. Ibid., 189–219.

77. *Ding Guitang hanjian an ji Ding Guitang Kangbian shu.*
78. Chang Chihyun, "Zhongguo haiguan de 1949."
79. *Wang Xuechen, Xi Rungang, Mi Jia deng hanjian an* (The *hanjian* cases of Wang Xuechen, Xi Rungeng, Mi Jia, et al.), November 1945, SMA (Q1)-6-48. Wang Xuechen was successively the chief editor of the *Shanghai Digest* and the *Shanghai Daily Digest*, which were popular for their coverage of political news and political figures. See the online archives at Shanghai Archives Information Network, http://202.136.215.235:9080/shcbq/shby/200509020008.htm.
80. *Wang Xuechen, Xi Rungang, Mi Jia deng hanjian an*, 30.
81. Ibid., 35.
82. *Zhou Feicheng, Wu Jie, Du Mengsheng hanjian an* (The *hanjian* cases of Zhou Feicheng, Wu Jie, and Du Mengsheng), November 26–December 7, 1948, SMA (Q188-2-661); *Zhou Feicheng yapian an* (The opium case of Zhou Feicheng), November 1948, SMA (Q186)-240701.
83. *Zhou Feicheng, Wu Jie, Du Mengsheng hanjian an*, 3.
84. The addresses given were inside the middle school affiliated with Fudan University. Ibid., 6.
85. *Zhou Feicheng, Wu Jie, Du Mengsheng hanjian an*, 2–4.
86. *Hunansheng gaodeng fayuan disan fenyuan jianchachu hanjian an bu qisu shu* (Dismissed *hanjian* cases received by the procuracies of the third branch of the Hunan High Court), 1946–48, SHA 7 (4)-1170.
87. Chiang's order on January 6, 1946, cited in *Gedi minzhong shangsu jianju hanjian goujie diren zuixing xinjian* (Accusation letters against *hanjian* from various regions), 6.
88. Sima, *Zhongguo xin wenxue shi*, 86.
89. Ordinance no. 5601 of the Ministry of Justice, October 8, 1946, in Xie, *Zhanshi sifa jiyao*, 135, SHA 7(4)-248.
90. *Xiang zuigao fayuan jianchashu, shanghai gaodeng fayuan fachu xunling zhengming Li Zufan, Tang Chengbo, Shen Nengyi deng Juntong ju gongzuoyuan bingfei hanjian* (Letter of proof to the Supreme Court and Shanghai High Court regarding the identity of Li Zufan, Tang Chengbo, etc.), August 23, 1947–November 1, 1948, SHA 7(4)-229, 37. Li was the commander of the Fifth Front Army during the War of Resistance.
91. Ibid., 26–35.
92. Ibid.
93. For more information on the Grand Charity Hall, see Cao, "Riben qinhua jigou," 113–37.
94. Sheng was the third nephew of Sheng Xuanhuai, a late Qing reformist official who became a successful industrialist in Shanghai. Sheng III frequently appeared in popular anti-*hanjian* literature. See, for instance, "Bangzhu diren duhua zhongguo de Sheng laosan" (Sheng III helped the enemy to poison Chinese people), *Hanjian choushi*, 2:1.
95. Meyer and Parssinen, *Webs of Smoke*, 145.
96. On Du Yuesheng and the Shanghai Green Gang before the war, see Martin, *The Shanghai Green Gang*. The establishment of the Wang Jingwei government

threatened Du's control over Shanghai's underworld. Martin, "Resistance and Cooperation," 190.

97. *Shenbao* had been covering the Japanese-sponsored opium regime from Hong Kong. See, for instance, "Quanhu tuhang baiershijia, duhua zhengce bianben jiali" (With 120 opium stores in Shanghai, Japan intensified its poisoning policy), April 20, 1939; "Ben niandu chaohuo yapian, jiangchuang zuigao jilu" (Opium confiscated by the Shanghai Municipal Police this year has broken the record), May 6, 1939.

98. Shanghai Municipal Archives, *Riben diguo zhuyi qinlüe Shanghai zuixing shiliao huibian*, 479.

99. Dai believed that as a former Communist, Wang knew how to deal with the underground Communist movements in Shanghai. Wakeman, *Spymaster*, 146–49.

100. *Shanghai gaoyuan jianchachu diaocha Luo Hongyi nichan'an* (Shanghai High Court's investigation into *hanjian* Luo Hongyi's property), September 1946, SMA (Q188)-2-15.

101. In his letter of accusation and during the later investigation conducted by the court, the informant Fang Mianfu provided extensive evidence on Luo's property and wartime conduct. *Shanghai gaoyuan jianchachu diaocha Luo Hongyi nichan'an.*

102. *Shi Xixia, Wu Mingfang hanjian an* (The *hanjian* case of Shi Xixia and Wu Mingfang), SMA (Q187)-2-779.

103. Ibid. Wu Mingfang escaped before the investigation, and her name remained on the list of wanted criminals issued by the Shanghai High Court. In 1948, the court received an anonymous report of Wu's whereabouts, although it was not clear whether she was eventually arrested. She appears in several pieces of popular anti-*hanjian* literature. *Hanjian choushi*, 2:6.

104. "Bai'e migaoren panxing shiwunian" (The White Russian sellout has been sentenced to fifteen years in prison), *Shenbao*, March 23, 1947.

105. "Gailiang sifa chuyi" (A tentative proposal for reforming the legal system), *Dagong bao*, November 8, 1942.

106. Ju, *Weishenme yao chongjian falü tixi*. This publication came out during the annual conference of the Chinese Law Association in September 1946. Ju Zheng had published an article on the topic two years before. Ju, "Zhongguo faxi zhi chongxin jianli," 124.

107. Jiang, *Zhongguo falü kanbujian zhongguo*, chapter 4.

108. Ordinance no. 4263 of the Ministry of Justice, August 15, 1946, in Xie, *Zhanshi sifa jiyao*, 132.

Chapter 3: The Political Economy of the Anti-*hanjian* Campaigns

1. "Shall Traitors Go Free?" *China Critic*, October 4, 1945.

2. For instance, Hsu Yuan-duk stated that "all of us have accounts to settle with the traitors." Ibid.

3. *Chuli hanjian anjian tiaoli*, Article IV.

4. For a brief review of such debates and discussion, see Feng Bing, "Kangzhan shenglihou guomin zhengfu chengjian zhong de caichanxing yunyong," 137–45.

5. *Chuli hanjian anjian tiaoli*, Article IV.

6. "Xiuzheng Chuli hanjian anjian tiaoli," April 29, 1947, cited in Feng, "Kangzhan shenglihou guomin zhengfu chengjian zhong de caichanxing yunyong," 142.

7. "Moshou hanjian caichan zhuoliu jiashu shenghuofei wenti" (Questions about confiscating *hanjian* assets and supporting *hanjian* dependents), *Shenbao*, June 29, 1946.

8. "Zhixing moshou hanjian caichan ying zhuyi shixiang" (Key guidelines on confiscating *hanjian* assets), SMA (Q 187) 1–352, 9.

9. See, for instance, "Bugan wei hanjian zhi zi" (Unwilling to be a *hanjian*'s son), *Zhanshi texie*, 1938, SMA (D2) 0-69-151.

10. For instance, Gu Jiren, an official of the puppet Rice Control Committee, was exposed by his aunt, who was praised for *dayi mieqin*. *Hanjian choushi*, 2:8.

11. *Zhongyang xintuoju Suzhewanqu diwei chanye qinglichu qingsuan nichan guize* (The principles of settling enemy and *hanjian* property, drafted by the Jiangsu-Zhejiang-Anhui Enemy and Puppet Property Liquidation Committee), in *Chuli diwei chanye faling* (Regulations on processing enemy or puppet property), 48–50, SHA (Q187)-1-270, 1945–48.

12. Ibid. The Central Trust of China was affiliated with the Central Bank. Established in 1935, it was the first state-owned trust company in China. Among other functions, it purchased and sold commodities for the government. Chinese Ministry of Information, *China Handbook, 1937–1945*, 400–401.

13. *Fagei mibao nichan jiangjin guize* (Rules for granting rewards to informants), SMA (Q 187)-1-352, 18.

14. Some regulations, such as the *Zhongyang Xintuoju Suzhewanqu diwei chanye qinglichu qingsuan nichan guize*, made no mention of possible victims of *hanjian* or the original owners of *hanjian* property. Article IX of the regulations required all proceeds from the sale of *hanjian* property to be deposited into the Central Bank, after leaving allocations for *hanjian* dependents, the judiciary, the informants, and the processing committee itself. *Chuli diwei chanye faling*, 48–50.

15. *Jiasu chuli diwei chanye banfa* (Resolutions for accelerating the processing of enemy and puppet property), Article 3-3, in SMA (Q187)-1-270, 36. The increased value was calculated according to the market price and nature of the property.

16. *Xingzhengyuan jiaoyi chuli diwei chanye anjian shiyong falü yiyi* (The Executive Yuan's clarifications regarding applicable laws on processing enemy property), 10, SHA (7)-6513. Cui Meiming, "Dajieshou yu Shanghai minying gongye," 43–46, 55.

17. *Jiasu chuli diwei chanye banfa*, Article 3-2.

18. During wartime, *fabi* continued to circulate in free regions. After the Wang Jiangwei regime established its own central bank on January 6, 1941, it began issuing its own currency, *zhongchuquan*. Chiang warned Shanghai's banks that accepting the "puppet" currency would be considered a *hanjian* crime. This threat had little effect when the Wang Jingwei government forcefully pushed for the use of *zhongchuquan*. Coble, *Chinese Capitalists in Japan's New Order*, chapter 1.

19. *Zhongyang Xintuoju Suzhewanqu diwei chanye qinglichu qingsuan nichan guize*.

20. *Sifa xingzhengbu xunling: Ling zhi moshou hanjian caichan zhuobo sifa buzhufei fanwei yingzhi zhaoyou* (Ministry of Justice's Ordinance on Subsidizing the

judiciary with Confiscated Property), in *Chuli diwei chanye faling*, 24. The 8 percent was taken after allocations for the *hanjian*'s dependents, the informants, and direct victims had been deducted.

21. *Beizhan fenju kouliu dichan wujian qingce* (A list of confiscated items kept at the Beizhan branch office), in SMA (Q131)-5-209, December 23, 1945.

22. *Jieyong jieshou diwei fangdichan shougou chuzu banfa* (Resolutions on Borrowing and Receiving Enemy and Puppet Property for Rent or Sale), Article XI, in *Chuli diwei chanye faling*, 4–7.

23. *Xingzhengyuan dianzhi waixian hanjian caichan chuli yaodian wuxiang dian* (The Executive Yuan's five solutions to *hanjian* property in surrounding prefectures), in *Chuli diwei chanye faling*, 6.

24. If the local government needed funds to maintain or remodel the property, it was permitted to use up to 20 percent of the deposited amount. Ibid., 6–7.

25. See *Shanghaishi fangdichan zhi* (Gazetteer of Shanghai's real estate), chapter 3, available on the official website of the Shanghai Gazetteers Compiling Office, www.shtong.gov.cn/node2/node2245/node64514/node64523/node64587/node64593/userobject1ai58319.html, accessed April 17, 2015.

26. *Shanghai gaodeng fayuan jianchachu kouya hanjian fangwu weituo zhongyang xintuoju diwei chanye qinglichu baoguan qingdan* (A list of houses confiscated by the Shanghai High Court and to be processed), SMA (Q187)-1-2, 30–32.

27. *Shanghai gaoyuan tingzhang Liang Mi Zhuyong Beijingxilu 1186 hao fangwu qingju qianrang yian* (Correspondence regarding Liang Mi's forceful occupation of 1186 Beijingxi Road), ibid., 41.

28. Ibid., 41–43.

29. "Linsen Zhonglu 1803 hao Zhu Boquan nichan baoguan qingxing" (The current condition of *hanjian* Zhu Boquan's house on 1803 Linsen Road," SMA (Q1)-6-45, December 1947.

30. *Miu Bin hanjian an* (The *hanjian* case of Miu Bin), SMA Q (188)-2-696.

31. Ibid. The American embassy requested the temporary use of the house from Song Ziwen, then head of the Executive Yuan; Chiang Wei-kuo asked for it to accommodate part of his regiment. See also Zhang and Shen, *Guomin zhengfu zhiguan nianbiao*.

32. *Shifu guanyu moshou weizuzhi ji funi renyuan zhi fangwu caichan yinggai guigong yu jingchaju laiwang wenjian* (Correspondence between the Municipal government and the police regarding the confiscation of enemy and *hanjian* property), 47–48, September 25, 1945, SMA Q (131)-5-226.

33. "Sifa xingzhengbu xunling 4884 hao: fengling jieshou diwei chanye ji wuzi ying saoshu jiaoyou chuli jiguan chaming chanquan" (Ordinance no. 4884 of the Ministry of Justice regarding the Handover and Ownership of Enemy and *Hanjian* Property), September 1946, SMA (Q187)-1-2.

34. Henriot, "Shanghai Industries under Japanese Occupation," in Yeh and Henriot, *In the Shadow of the Rising Sun*, 21.

35. Coble, "Chinese Capitalists in Wartime Shanghai, 1937–1945," in Yeh and Henriot, *In the Shadow of the Rising Sun*, 52.

36. The statistics are from *Caizheng pinglun* (Financial review), January 1946, quoted in Cui Meiming, "Dajieshou yu Shanghai minying gongye."

37. "Hanjian yapian dawang: Sheng ni you'an chu sixing" (The *hanjian* and drug king Sheng You'an was sentenced to death), *Shenbao*, March 22, 1947.

38. "Meiguang huochai gongsi Fu Yung Kong hanjian an" (The *hanjian* case of Fu Yung Kong from the American–Far Eastern Match Co.), February 1946, SMA (Q6)-7-53.

39. Cochran and Hsieh, *The Lius of Shanghai*, 165–80.

40. Coble, "Chinese Capitalists in Wartime Shanghai, 1937–1945," 52.

41. Henriot, "Shanghai Industries under Japanese occupation," 32.

42. Ibid., 30.

43. Chen Binhe, "Dadongya zhanzhenghou Chongqing zhi dongxiang" (New developments in Chongqing since the outbreak of the Great East Asian War), *Shenbao*, October 11, 1942.

44. Martin, "Resistance and Cooperation: Politics of the Shanghai United Committee," 201–5.

45. Ibid., 204.

46. By referring to Wen, Lin, and Yuan as the "three elders," the postwar media acknowledged their seniority and leadership in the business world while also hinting at their conservatism and inclination for self-presevation. See, for instance, "'Haishang san lao' de zuize" (The guilt of the "three elders of Shanghai"), *Hanjian choushi*, 2:20.

47. Representing Du in Shanghai, Xu Caicheng used his connections with the Japanese military to start the Minhua Company. Martin, "Resistance and Cooperation," 204.

48. *Chengzhi hanjian tiaoli*, Article II, sections 4, 5, 6, 7 and 10; *Chuli hanjian anjian tiaoli*, Article II, sections 6, 10.

49. Zheng Zhenduo, "Chujianlun" (On eliminating *hanjian*), *Zhoubao*, September 15, 1945.

50. Duan Ruicong, "Jiang Jieshi yu kangzhan shiqi zong dongyuan tizhi zhi goujian," 34–53.

51. "Zhongdian cheng jianshang" (Treacherous merchants deserve harsh punishment), *Dagong bao*, November 3, 1942. The National Mobilization Commission established a task force to investigate *jianshang*.

52. In 1947, the government expenses were three times more than the budget. See Wenshi Ziliao Wenyuanhui, *Wenshi ziliao cungao*, 18–22.

53. Li Chengji, "Ruotao sixiong reshang guansi," 92–97.

54. *Riwei Nanjing zhengfu jingji hanjian minglu* (List of economic *hanjian* attached to the puppet Wang Jingwei government), SHA (7) 4–1982.

55. "Wen Lanting deng guanyu choubei Shanghai wupin zhengquan jiaoyisuo de laiwang hanjian" (Correspondence between Wen Lan-ting and others regarding the establishment of Shanghai Stock and Goods Exchange), March 24–April 24, 1920. Reprinted in *Dang'an yu shixue* 4 (2001): 10–19.

56. Huang Huiying, "Wen Lanting de shoushen he gaipan," 61–62.

57. Masui, *Kankan saiban shi*, 150.

58. The National Commerce Control Commission was a result of negotiations between the Wang regime and the Japanese, who decided to allow the former to be a little less financially dependent. Coble, *Chinese Capitalists in Japan's New Order*, chapter 4.

59. Huang, "Wen Lanting de shoushen he gaipan," 61.

60. Coble, "Japan's New Order and the Shanghai Capitalists," 152.

61. Masui, *Kankan saiban shi*, 147.

62. During Wen's retrial in 1947, the Nationalist party dispatched Ji Xizong to testify that Wen took the puppet position under orders from Chongqing.

63. Masui, *Kankan saiban shi*, 148.

64. Ibid.

65. Ibid., 147.

66. Ibid.

67. Another defense lawyer, Sha Yankai, emphasized Wen's frugal lifestyle by noting that he had been a vegetarian for decades. See Wu Mengqing, *Shanghai zongjiaozhi*, 128–29; Masui, *Kankan saiban shi*, 149.

68. Of the five Chinese members on the board prior to the takeover, Guo Shun, Chen Tingrui, and Yu Qiaqing had left for Hong Kong, and Xi Yushu had secluded himself from all political affairs. Yuan Ling, *Yuan Lüdeng zibai shu*, 19–21.

69. Ibid.

70. "Gaoyuan gengshen: Yuan Lüdeng chengren cuole" (Yuan Lüdeng admitted during the retrial that he had done wrong), *Shenbao*, April 19, 1947.

71. Yuan claimed that the Japanese army once planned on purchasing rice in and around Shanghai at two hundred yuan per *picul*, or half the market price, in addition to terminating rice rationing. Yuan agreed to serve on the Rice and Grain Control Commission so that the Japanese would raise the purchase price and resume the rationing system. Yuan Ling, *Yuan Lüdeng zibai shu*, 19. On the rice rationing system, see Henriot and Yeh, *In the Shadow of the Rising Sun*, 127.

72. Masui, *Kankan saiban shi*, 153.

73. Chinese emperors had often announced amnesties as gestures of benevolence to counterbalance the harsh criminal law. The Great Amnesty (Dashe) was usually announced at the beginning of a reign, on the emperor's birthday, or on another auspicious occasion. By announcing an amnesty several times after the War of Resistance, Chiang Kai-shek deployed a traditional style of rule based on strict codes and occasional measures of appeasement. Fang Zhanhong, "Da Hanjian Yuan Lüdeng shoushenji," 31–33.

74. "Wen Lanting bingzhong jiuyiyu Honghui yiyuan" (Wen Lanting hospitalized at Honghui hospital), *Shenbao*, February 13, 1947.

75. *Hanjian choushi*, 2:20.

76. Shanghai Huobaoshe, *Bujian lumi*, 23.

77. Masui, *Kankan saiban shi*, 141. Newspapers reported that Qian had worked toward the establishment of the puppet Central Reserve Bank under instructions from Zhou Fohai. Qian was held primarily responsible for forcing people in occupied areas to exchange *fabi* for *zhongchuquan* at an exploitative rate of two to one and for disturbing the financial order by flooding the market with 46 trillion *zhongchuquan*. The court pronounced the same sentence for him as it did for

Zhou Fohai. "Gaoyuan pan Qian Dakui sixing" (The high court has sentenced Qian Dakui to death), *Shenbao*, January 17, 1947.

78. Cochran and Hsieh, *The Lius of Shanghai*, 260–63.

79. Quoted in Di Han, "Jujian qijie sheng zhong tan chengjian zhenxiang" (The truths about the anti-*hanjian* campaigns), *Xiaoxi* 6, April 1946.

80. Yang, "Juntong jieshou Shanghai nichan ji Deng Baoguang, Chen Naichang weirenmin Baoquan caichan de qingkuang" (Juntong's takeover of enemy and *hanjian* property in Shanghai and protection of people's property), in Wenshi ziliao weiyuanhui. *Wenshi ziliao cungao xuanbian*, 718–27.

81. Wen-hsin Yeh, *Shanghai Splendor*, chapter 7.

82. Wakeman, *Spymaster*, 249, 289, 372. For a while, this army was in dire need of funds and provisions. Li Ze, together with Guo Shun, the manager of the Yong'an Company, supported the army for three months until its financial situation improved.

83. Shu served under Liu Zhennian, a Shandong-based warlord who recruited talented youths into his army, including Shu Yueqiao and several Communist Party members. One can reasonably assume that Shu was exposed to Communist theories and influence early in his life. See the online database of Shangdong Provincial Archive, http://sd.infobase.gov.cn.

84. *Xinxin gongsi jingli Li Ze hanjian de choushi* (The hideous history of *hanjian* Li Ze, manager of Xinxin Company), 4, SMA Y15 (1–134); "Li Ze funi zhengju zai zhenchazhong" (The evidence for Li Ze's *hanjian* crime is under examination), *Shishi xinbao*, January 9, 1946.

85. Xia Hua, "Shu Yueqiao jun fangwen ji" (An interview with Mr. Shu Yueqiao), *Shishi xinbao*, January 7, 1946.

86. "Xinxin zhigong yifeng gongkaixin" (An open letter signed by Xinxin employees), *Zhoubao*, October 8, 1945.

87. "Xinxin gongsi zhigong gei gejie renshi yifengxin" (A letter from Xinxin employees to the Shanghai public), *Shidai ribao*, January 3, 1946; "Xinxin gongsi zhigong jianju hanjian Li Ze" (Xinxin employees denounced Li Ze as *hanjian*), *Wencui*, January 3, 1946.

88. "Benshi da jianju an: Xinxin gongsi babai yuangong jufa zongjingli Li Ze tongdi" (Major *hanjian* case in the city: Eight hundred employees from Xinxin Company exposed the *hanjian* conduct of their manager, Li Ze), *Wenhuibao*, January 5, 1946.

89. "Lijie dangzu chengyuan minglu" (A list of the CCP representatives at Shanghai General Labor Union), available on the website of the Shanghai General Labor Union, www.spcsc.sh.cn/renda/node5902/node6688/node6689/node6777/userobject1ai1268524.html, accessed July 16, 2012. See also "Han Chengwu (1923–1982)" on the website of the Shanghai Gazetteer Compilation Office, www.shtong.gov.cn/node2/node2245/node4471/node56386/node56418/node56420/userobject1ai43065.html, accessed July 16, 2012.

90. Li Chengji, "Ruotao sixiong reshang guansi;" Chang Kai, *Zhongguo gongyunshi cidian*, 928.

91. "Xinxin gongsi zhiyuan jinri zhaodai jizhe" (Xinxin employees met with the press today), *Wenhuibao*, January 7, 1946.

92. "Xinxin gongsi zongjingli jiudai, shimin jianju hanjian diyipao" (The first strike against *hanjian* proves effective: The manager of Xinxin Company just arrested), *Daying yebao*, January 8, 1946.

93. Si Nong, "Xinxin gongsi jingli Li Ze beibu miwen" (Exclusive particulars on Li Ze's arrest), *Tiebao*, January 8, 1945.

94. Wang Chunying, "Zhanhou jingji hanjian shenpan: yi Xinxin gongsi Li Ze an weili," 132–46.

95. Wenshi ziliao weiyuanhui, *Wenshi ziliao xuanji*, 129:144. *Daying yebao*, among other newspapers, released the news of Guo Shun's escape in winter 1945. "Xinxin gongsi zongjingli jiudai, shimin jianju hanjian diyipao."

96. "Bi Gaokui yajie Nanjing, Li Ze jiang gongkai shenxun" (With Bi Gaokui dismissed and sent to Nanjing, Li Ze's open trial starts), *Wenhui bao*, January 24, 1946.

97. "Bi Gaokui chezhi, Shu Yueqiao huo Jiang zhuxi fuhan" (Bi Gaokui was dismissed from office, and Shu Yueqiao received a reply from Generalissimo Chiang), *Dagong bao*, January 15, 1946.

98. "Jushuo shi jiu'an, Bi Gaokui chezhi" (Bi Gaokui dismissed from office, supposedly for failing in an old case), *Wenhui bao*, January 16, 1946. Before his dismissal, Bi was responsible for interrogating Li Ze and had apparently attempted to minimize Li's crime.

99. "Xiaoyaofawai de hanjian: Shouchi jintiao tuyan tianxiaren ermu" (*Hanjian* at large: Li Ze tries to hide his crime by bribery), *Qianxian ribao*, January 7, 1946.

100. "Li ni Ze jinchen shoushen: sanrilai Li qinshu xiyan xiangui" (The vicious Li Ze was interrogated this morning: His family has been buying dinner for important guests for three days), *Qianxian ribao*, January 10, 1946.

101. Si Nong, "Xinxin gongsi jingli Li Ze beibu miwen."

102. Gen Qing, "Li Ze an xiawen ruhe?" (What's next in Li Ze's case?), *Xinxin gongsi jingli Li Ze hanjian de choushi*.

103. *Xinxin gongsi jingli Li Ze hanjian de choushi*, 10.

104. Li Chengji, "Ruotao sixiong reshang guansi."

105. "Hanjian Li Ze panxing sannian" (The *hanjian* Li Ze sentenced to three years' imprisonment), *Wenhuibao*, June 9, 1946. According to this article, Li Ze's witnesses suggested that he had sold iron to the Senda Iron Factory, not to the Japanese.

106. "Li Ze an yuding bari xuanpan" (The court will reach a decision on Li Ze on the 8th), *Shenbao*, June 4, 1946.

107. "Juntong de zhengmingxin" (A letter of support for Li Ze from Juntong), April 4, 1946, SMA (Q118) 12-31-27.

108. "Huang Ruitang de Zhengming xin" (A letter of support from Huang Ruitang), April 1946, SMA (Q118) 12-31-24.

109. Ping Xin, "Chengjian xinlun" (New perspectives on punishing *hanjian*), *Zhoubao*, October 15, 1945.

110. "Li Ze beipuhou, jingbei bu kaishi zhencha" (The police have started to investigate Li Ze's case), *Dagong bao*, January 9, 1946.

111. *Xinxin gongsi jingli Li Ze hanjian de choushi*. It is unknown who sponsored the publication and circulation of the pamphlet. The articles selected were from

newspapers of diverse political positions, and the pamphlet focused on the case of Li Ze rather than the "capitalist class" in general.

112. Shu Yueqiao, "Sishen Li Ze yougan" (Some words on Li Ze's fourth trial), *Xiaoxi* 7, April 30, 1946.

113. *Xinxin gongsi jingli Li Ze hanjian de choushi*, 19.

114. Ibid. On the case of Yang Naiwu and Xiao Baicai, see Alford, "Of Arsenic and Old Laws," 1180–1256.

115. See, for instance, "Li Ze an zuo xuanpa: jinchu tuxing sannian" (The court gave Li Ze a mere three-year sentence), *Shidai ribao*, June 9, 1946; "Li Ze zuo panxing sannian: Yuan jianju ren renwei pande taiqing" (Plaintiffs consider Li Ze's sentence too light), *Wenhuibao*, June 9, 1946.

116. "Li Ze an zuo xuanpa: jinchu tuxing sannian."

117. "Li Chenshi zhi Guangzhou lühu tongxianghui he Guang-Zhao Gongsuo xinhan," August 28, 1946, SMA Q117 (2–89). On the rise of Guangdong group and its activities on the eve of the fall of Shanghai, see Goodman, *Native Place, City and Nation*, 54–62, 287–91.

118. Luo, *Sanguo yanyi*, chapter 25.

119. "Shanghai gongshangjie guanyu Li Ze bei zhikong wei hanjian shi zhi guominzhengfu jiang zhuxi de kuaiyou" (An express mail to Generalissimo Chiang from Shanghai's industrialists regarding the case of Li Ze), SMA (Q118) 12-31-23.

120. "Tilanqiao jianyu menqian, yiqun song jianfan de jianshu" (*Hanjian*'s family members bring delicacies to Tilanqiao prison), *Qiaoshengbao*, July 10, 1946.

121. "Li Ze ruyu yilai, xinshui zhaozhi, caichan rugu" (Li Ze retains his salary and possessions after going to prison), *Lianhe bao*, July 18, 1946.

122. Li Chengji, "Ruotao sixiong reshang guansi."

123. These included Zhou Bangjun, who was the chair of the "Anti–Britain and America Association" (Fanyingmei Xiehui), and Jiang Kanghu, who was the head of the puppet Examination Yuan. *Xinxin gongsi jingli Li Ze hanjian de choushi*, 33.

124. "Li Ze zuo jiudai hou, Xianshi gongsi quanti zhigong qunqi xiangying" (Following Li Ze's arrest, employees from the Xianshi Company take action), *Daying yebao*, January 8, 1946; "Kangyuan zhiguanchang zhigong jianju Xiang Kangyuan" (Employees from the Kangyuan Can Factory exposed Xiang Kangyuan's *hanjian* conduct), *Daying yebao*, January 10, 1946.

125. "Kangyuan Zhiguanchang zhigong jianju Xiang Kangyuan."

126. "Li Chenshi zhi Guangzhou lühu tongxianghui he Guang-Zhao Gongsuo xinhan."

127. "Hanjian yu dixia gongzuo" (*Hanjian* and underground work), *Dagong bao*, January 16, 1946.

Chapter 4: Engendering Contempt for Female *Hanjian* and Cultural *Hanjian*

1. Sima Wenzhen, *Wenhua hanjian zui'eshi*.

2. *Chuli hanjian anjian tiaoli* (Regulations on Handling *Hanjian* Cases), Article II, SMA Q (187)-1-204.

3. See Field, *Mu Shiying: China's Lost Modernist*. Since the 1970s, scholars have found evidence to prove that Mu worked for Zhongtong and that his assassination was the result of a lack of trust and coordination between various intelligence offices that reported directly to Chiang. Sima Changfeng, *Zhongguo xin wenxue shi*, 86.

4. This estimate is based on reports from major regional newspapers such as *Shenbao* and *Dagong bao*. From December 22, 1945, to early 1948, *Shenbao* reported on more than five hundred trials of *hanjian*. Ten were cultural *hanjian*. Most of the convicted cultural *hanjian* were sentenced to prison terms of less than ten years. See also *Nanjing gaodeng fayuan xiang sifa xingzhengbu chengsong wei jiaoyubu ji fushu jiguan xuexiao zhuyao renyuan mingdan* (List of personnel in the puppet Ministry of Education and its affiliated institutions), SHA (7)-4-458.

5. "American Charged with Treason," *CBS News*, October 11, 2006, www.cbsnews .com/news/american-charged-with-treason/.

6. Before entering the world of journalism, Chen acquired several teaching and administrative positions in higher education through his connections with influential figures, including Huang Yanpei, a highly regarded educator and the founder of the China Democratic League. On Chen Binhe's early life and connections, see Cai, "Buxue youshu de Chen Binhe," 70–77.

7. Cai, "Buxue youshu de Chen Binhe," 72; "Short Biographies of Chen Binhe," Shanghai Archives online, www.shtong.gov.cn/node2/node2245/node4522 /node10080/node10082/node63754/userobject1ai54025.html, accessed May 5, 2010.

8. The contributors included Tao Xingzhi, a famous educator; Zhang Naiqi, the manager of the Zhejiang Industrial Bank; and Yang Xingzhi, a prolific political essayist. Cai, "Buxue youshu de Chen Binhe," 72.

9. Ibid., 73; Wakeman, *Spymaster*, 179–81. While in Hong Kong, Chen founded *Gangbao* with the patronage of the anti-Japanese and anti-Chiang General Chen Jitang, a Guangdong-based warlord. Jin Xiongbai, *Wang Zhengquan de kaichang yu shouchang*, chapter 95.

10. Zhou Fohai once asked Jin Xiongbai to probe Chen's political views and true identity, as he was troubled by Chen's overly close relations with Japan. Jin, *Wang Zhengquan de kaichang yu shou chang*, chapter 95, 212; Boyle, *China and Japan at War*, 169–90;

11. Jin, *Wang Zhengquan de kaichang yu shouchang*, chapter 212.

12. Ibid., chapter 95.

13. Chen Binhe, "Dadongya zhanzheng hou Chongqing zhi dongxiang," *Shenbao*, October 11, 1942.

14. Mitter, *Forgotten Ally*, 242.

15. Chen, "Dadongya zhanzheng hou Chongqing zhi dongxiang."

16. Jin, *Wang Zhengquan de kaichang yu shouchang*, chapter 208.

17. "Wenhua hanjian Chen Binhe zhongxuanbu hanqing tongji" (Order from the Ministry of Central Propaganda to arrest Chen Binhe, the cultural *hanjian*), *Shishi gongbao*, July 31, 1946.

18. Cai, "Buxue youshu de Chen Binhe," 77.

19. *Jiaoyubu qing cankao shishi banli Shanghai yixueyuan Nanjing jinda jiaoshou Yan Fuqing, Chen Rong deng beisu wenhua hanjian an wendian* (Telegram from the

Ministry of Education regarding the cases of Yan Fuqing and Chen Rong), SHA (7)-8953, October 12, 1945.

20. *Zhongyang daxue ruxue xuzhi* (Instructions for newly enrolled students at the Central University), SHA (2078)-0117, March 1941

21. *Nanjing gaodeng fayuan xiang sifa xingzhengbu chengsong wei jiaoyubu ji fushu jiguan xuexiao zhuyao renyuan mingdan.*

22. *Jiaoyubu qing cankao shishi banli Shanghai yixueyuan Nanjing jinda jiaoshou Yan Fuqing, Chen Rong deng beisu wenhua hanjian an wendian.*

23. *Kangzhan qijian liuri xuesheng zhenshen banfa* (Resolutions for Investigating Students who Studied in Japan during the War), ibid., 17, SHA (7)-8953. *Guofu yijiao* (Teachings of the Founding Father) was a pamphlet issued by the Nationalist government that compiled the most important writings by Sun Yat-sen.

24. *Shanghai jiaoyu ju chengsong funi jiaozhiyuan mingdan jiyu jiaoyubu wanglai tongxin* (Lists of faculty and staff who attached themselves to the enemy, provided by the Shanghai Bureau of Education), in *Jiaoyubu yu ge jiaoyuju wanglai hanjian ji jiaoshi xunling yiyi* (Correspondence of the Ministry of Education and the Ministry's clarification of various ordinances), 11, SMA (Q257)-1-49.

25. Ibid., 12–13.

26. *Beiping shi jiaoyuju chengqing jieshi banli zhongxuesheng zhenshen shiyi yiyi* (Responses to the inquiry of the Beijing Education Bureau regarding the examination of high school students), in *Jiaoyubu yu ge jiaoyuju wanglai hanjian ji jiaoshi xunling yiyi*, 15.

27. Zi Gui, "Guanyu Zhou Zuoren" (About Zhou Zuoren), SMA (D2)-0-980-12.

28. "Yancheng wenhua jiaoyu *hanjian*" (Severely punish cultural *hanjian* from the educational circles), *Zhongyang ribao*, August 21, 1945.

29. "Yancheng chuban *hanjian*" (*Hanjian* in the publishing industry should be severely punished), *Zhongyang ribao*, August 21, 1945.

30. "Jianju juyingjie funi *hanjian*: Shanghai yulunjie qiwang shenyin" (Public opinion in Shanghai had high hopes of the Cinema and Play Association for exposing *hanjian*), *Yindu*, November 23, 1946.

31. For instance, Mao Dun, Ding Ling, Feng Xuefeng, Xia Yan, Tian Han, Feng Naichao, and Yu Dafu were members of both associations. Zhou Enlai, one of the earliest CCP members and later premier of the People's Republic of China, was an honorary council member. See Xu Zhifu, "Zhonghua quanguo wenyijie kangdi xiehui," 710.

32. Zheng Zhenduo, "Xi Zhou Zuoren" (The regrettable choice of Zhou Zuoren), *Mengya*, 3 (1946): 18.

33. Qian Liqun, *Zhou Zuoren zhuan*, 356–65. To this day, the attempted assassination in 1939 remains a subject of debate and speculation. Zhou insisted that the Japanese planned it to force him to cooperate, but the Japanese maintained that Chiang Kai-shek's agents did it. Some think that Zhou's own nephew did it to forestall his collaboration.

34. "Gei Zhou Zuoren de yifeng gongkaixin" (An open letter to Zhou Zuoren), *Kangzhao wenyi*, May 4, 1938, SMA (D2)-0-2623-25.

35. Zheng, "Xi Zhou Zuoren."

36. "Guanyu diaocha funi wenhuaren de jueyi" (The decision on investigating intellectuals who attached themselves to the enemy), *Kangzhan wenyi* 5 (1946): 6. The eighteen members were Lao She, Sun Fuyuan, Ba Jin, Yao Pengzi, Xia Yan, Yu Ling, Cao Jinghua, Jin Yi, Mei Lin, Ye Yiqun, Zhang Junxiang, Xu Chi, Shao Quanlin, Huang Zhigang, Xu Weinan, Ma Yanxiang, Zhao Jiabi, and Shi Dongshan. See also Ma and Li, *Zhongguo wenxue dacidian*, 3475.

37. "Guanyu diaocha funi wenhuaren de jueyi."

38. Ibid.

39. "Xingzhengyuan chaosong quanguo wenhuajie kangdi xiehui dui chengzhi funi wenhuaren yijian" (The decision on punishing cultural *hanjian* reached by the National Resistance Association of Cultural Circles), November 3, 1945, SHA (7)-8933.

41. Sima, *Wenhua hanjian zui'eshi*, 2.

40. Scott, *Gender and the Politics of History*, 46–48.

41. "Heping nüshen yifei wanbi" (The body of the Goddess of Peace is no longer intact), *Shenbao*, March 19, 1947.

42. On Mei Lanfang's wartime experience and his photos during the war, see Wang Hui, *Mei Lanfang huazhuan*, chapter 20.

43. *Hanjian choushi*, issue 5, 10. Rong, *Shiji enyuan: Xu Beihong* yu *Liu Haisu*.

44. Liu cofounded the groundbreaking Shanghai Art Institute in 1912 with several other artists and introduced the use of mannequins for studio art in 1919. He, "Shidai de xianfeng, meiti de jiaodian," 40–45. Sullivan, *Art and Artists of Twentieth-Century China*, 30.

45. *Hanjian choushi*, issue 5, 10.

46. Ibid., 12.

47. Ibid.; Zhang and Deng, *Yitu chunqiu*, 49–53.

48. In the climate of social reform and progressive public discourse in early twentieth-century China, concubinage was associated with backwardness, patriarchy, and lack of women's rights. Lawmakers made continuous efforts to legislate monogamy and discourage concubinage. See Tran, *Concubines in Court*.

49. *Hanjian choushi*, issue 5, 8.

50. Ibid., issue 2, 8.

51. Shi, "Funü zai kangzhan zhong de renwu" (Women's missions in the War of Resistance), *Jiuwang ribao*, October 30, 1937.

52. See, for instance, "Guonan qijian suo xiwang yu funüzhe" (What is wanted from women during a time of national crisis), *Jiuwang ribao*, October 30, 1937.

53. Hershatter and Wang, "Chinese History: A Useful Category of Gender Analysis," 1404–21.

54. *Rikou juedi xia de jinan tongbao* (Our compatriots in south Hebei are suffering from floods unleashed by the Japanese), February 1940, (SHA) 7.34-594. This pamphlet reported that female *hanjian* purchased children of different ages at different prices, but the county government failed to catch them.

55. Musgrove, "Cheering the Traitor."

56. Masui, *Kankan saiban shi*, 210; Jin, *Wang Zhengquan de kaichang yu shouchang*, chapter 12.

57. As an insider, Jin Xiongbai revealed that Ye Jiqing had little involvement in the Wang Jingwei regime. Jin concluded that Ye and She were tried and punished primarily because of their *hanjian* husbands. Jin, *Wangzhengfu de kaichang yu shouchang*, chapter 141.

58. For instance, Mo Guokang, Chen Gongbo's secretary and mistress, was punished for her scandalous relationship with Chen. Masui, *Kankan saiban shi*, 213.

59. See, for instance, "Jiandie hanjian Chuandao fangzi Zigong (Confessions of the *hanjian* and spy Yoshiko Kawashima)," *Shenbao*, March 8, 1947.

60. Masui, *Kankan saiban shi*, 275–78. One widely circulated rumor was that a woman who was seriously ill in prison died in Kawashima's place in exchange for ten gold bars. In December 2009, this rumor was disproved by the release in Taiwan of documents on Kawashima's trials and execution. Li Gang, *Chuandao fangzi shenpan dang'an da jiemi*.

61. *Nü hanjian choushi*, 5, 7.

62. For a discussion of Li Xianglan's role in promoting pan-Asianist propaganda and the controversies she aroused, see Yiman Wang, "Between the National and the Transnational," 39.

63. Nicole Huang, "Fashioning Public Intellectuals: Women's Print Culture in Occupied Shanghai (1941–1945)," in *In the Shadow of the Rising Sun*, 325–45.

64. Yingjin Zhang, *Chinese National Cinema*, 88.

65. Su, *Jiehun shinian*; Zhang, "Fengsuo," in Qian Liqun, *Zhongguo lunxianqu wenxue daxi*, 165–66.

66. Huang, "Fashioning Public Intellectuals," 327.

67. Lee, *Revolution of the Heart*, 142. For a discussion of these issues in the Republican era, see Goodman, "Appealing to the Public," 32–69.

68. Huang, "Fashioning Public Intellectuals," 338.

69. Another renowned female writer targeted by the anti-*hanjian* campaigns was Guan Lu, a left-wing writer in the 1930s and an underground agent for the CCP during wartime, in which role she maintained a close relationship with Li Shiqun and his wife. Hao, *Zhongguo mimizhan*, 461.

70. Liu Xinhuang, *Kangzhan shiqi lunxianqu wenxueshi*, 131.

71. *Magazine*'s chief editor was Yuan Shu (1911–87), a left-wing writer in the 1930s and a CCP member. He was ordered by the CCP to infiltrate the Wang Jingwei government. To include left-wing writers' work in *Magazine*, Yuan solicited contributions from writers from all political camps. Yuan's secret identity and CCP membership were not revealed until later, and he himself was called a *hanjian* at the time. Gu, "Zhang Ailing bushi 'zhaimao' hanjian," 117–20; Chen Zishan, "1945–1949 nianjian de Zhang Ailing," 54.

72. Liu Weirong, "Zuojia Su Qing yu da hanjian Chen Gongbo de 'liqi' jiaowang," 27–29.

73. Tan, "Lun Su Qing yu Zhang Ailing," in Tan, *Dangdan nüzuojia xiaoshuoxuan*, 44.

74. Sima Wenzhen, *Wenhua hanjian zui'e shi*, 51.

75. Xi, "Luanshi cainü Su Qing," *Zuijia tiandi* 4 (2007): 62–67.

76. Yingjin Zhang, *The City in Modern Chinese Literature and Film*, 325 n. 73.

77. Huang, "Fashioning Public Intellectuals," 338.

78. Liu Weirong, "Zuojia Su Qing yu da hanjian Chen Gongbo de 'liqi' jiaowang," 28.
79. Ibid.
80. Han Chunxiu, "Su Qing yu *Tiandi*."
81. Sima Wenzhen, *Wenhua hanjian zui'e shi*, 51–53.
82. On Zhang Jingsheng and his reevaluation of free love in the 1920s, see Leary, "Sexual Modernism in China"; Goodman, "Appealing to the Public;" Lee, *Revolution of the Heart*, chapter 4.
83. Tang, ed. *Zhang Ailing juan*, 222.
84. Han, "Su Qing yu *Tiandi*," 4.
85. *Nü hanjian choushi*, 9.
86. Sima Wenzhen, *Wenhua hanjian zui'e shi*, 51.
87. *Wenhui bao* (Wenhui daily), September 6, 1945, quoted in Su, *Xu jiehun shinian*, introduction.
88. Ibid. Su gave several examples of how tabloids fabricated details of her clothes at various events and her living habits.
89. Su, *Xu jiehun shinian*, 2, 6.
90. Ibid., 3, 7.
91. Wang Xiaofang, "Kangzhan niandai de nüxing shuxie."
92. In 1951, Su stopped writing fiction and applied to join the opera playwriting workshop organized by the Shanghai Bureau of Culture. She was almost rejected because she failed the examination on current politics. Fortunately, Xia Yan, a well-respected Communist playwright, recommended her, and Su Qing started work as a full-time playwright. Ibid., 3.
93. Zhong, "Youguan Su Qing Shanghai fangwenji," 24. Qu Yuan was a widely celebrated poet loyal to the state of Chu (476–221 BCE). In this play, Su Qing emphasized Qu Yuan's integrity and compassion for his compatriots.
94. The CCP launched the anti-rightist movement in late 1950s to punish the perceived "rightists" within and outside the party. For Hu Feng and the "Hu Feng Clique," see Denton, *The Problematic of Self in Modern Chinese Literature*.
95. Zhong, "Youguan Su Qing Shanghai fangwenji," 25.
96. Even today, some historians in the People's Republic of China and Taiwan still consider Zhang a female *hanjian*. For instance, see Chen Liao, "Zhang Ailing re yao jiangwen"; Liu Xinhuang, *Kangzhan shiqi lunxianqu wenxueshi*.
97. *Nü hanjian choushi*, 10. Zhang and Hu were legally married in 1944, after Hu's second wife divorced him (his first wife had passed away). There is no proof that Zhang wrote such a letter. Hu Lancheng, *Jinsheng jinshi*, 164–200.
98. Tran, *Concubines in Court*, chapter 7. According to Tran, the Nationalist laws from 1935 onward, which emphasized a proper ceremony as the sole proof of a valid marriage, inadvertently gave certain concubines the status of legal wife.
99. *Nü hanjian choushi*, 10.
100. Sima Wenzhen, *Wenhua hanjian zui'eshi*, 49.
101. *Haipai* (Shanghai School), March 30, 1946, quoted in Chen, "1945–1949 nianjian de Zhang Ailing," 52–53. "Jeep Girl" was an epithet applied to Chinese women who prostituted themselves to Allied soldiers and traveled around the city in their military jeeps.

102. Zhang Ailing, *Xiao tuanyuan*, 246–47.
103. Both plays, *Endless Love* and *Darling, Stay at Home*, were developed into successful movies by the director Sang Hu. Chen, "1945–1949 nianjian de Zhang Ailing," 54–55.
104. Zhang Ailing, *Se, jie* (Lust, caution); *Lust, Caution*, directed by Ang Lee (Universal Studios, 2007).
105. Zhang Ailing, "You jijuhua tong duzhe shuo," in *Chuanqi*. Zhang had no affection for the Japanese and saw no possibility that their rule in China would last. She once noted that popular songs in Japan sounded sad, suggesting that the Japanese empire would soon meet its demise. Hu Lancheng, *Jinsheng jinshi*, 178.
106. Lao She, "Lüetan kangzhan wenyi" (Some words on the wartime production of literature and arts), in *Lao She wenji* (A complete collection of works by Lao She), 15: 522–26.
107. Su, *Xu jiehun shinian*, 3.
108. Lee, *Revolution of the Heart*, 137. Some other female artists were also attacked.
109. Virgili, *Shorn Women*.

Chapter 5: Punishing *Hanjian* beyond Chinese Borders

1. See, for instance, Chiang and Heinrich, *Queer Sinophone Cultures;* Ho and Kuehn, *China Abroad;* Shih, *Visuality and Identity.*
2. Wang, "A Single Chinese Diaspora?" 7; Shih, "Against Diaspora."
3. Vasantkumar, "What Is This 'Chinese' in Overseas Chinese?," 427.
4. Chen Liwen et al., *Taiwan guangfu yanjiu*, 124.
5. Liang, "Riju shidai taimin fuhua zhi lüquan zhidu," in Liang, *Taiwan zongdufu de "dui'an" zhengce yanjiu*, 141–82.
6. Chen Liwen et al., *Taiwan guangfu yanjiu*, 124.
7. Ibid., 126–32.
8. For the set of principles, see Chen Liwen et al., *Taiwan guangfu yanjiu*, 125–26.
9. "Taiwan de jianglai" (The future of Taiwan), *Dagong bao*, February 17, 1946.
10. Ibid.
11. "Taiwan xing: Buzhi youqin, geng buzhi you han, taibaohai ba women dangzuo qingguoren," *Wenhui bao*, February 9, 1946. A more literal translation of the title is "Experiencing Taiwan: They know not the Qin or Han and imagine mainlanders still subjects of the Qing."
12. Qin and Zhang, *Kangzhan shiqi shoufu Taiwan zhi zhongyao yanlun*, 287–88.
13. Xie Shao, "Taiwan renmin zhi zhongxin xinyang yu diyu guannian"(The core values and regionalist views upheld by people in Taiwan), *Taiwan minsheng bao*, August 1, 1945.
14. Chen Xiaochong, "Taiwan geming tongmenghui kangri aiguo douzheng shulun," *Taiwan yanjiu* 5 (2012): 60.
15. Chiang's resolve on this issue can be seen from his diary entry of November 18, 1943. On the preparations that the Nationalist leadership made during and after the conference for the recovery of Taiwan, see Chen Liwen et al., *Taiwan guangfu yanjiu*, 163–94.

16. *Xinhua ribao*, April 17, 1943; cited in Chen Xiaochong, "Taiwan geming tongmenghui shulun," 84

17. The investigation committee compiled comprehensive reports on Taiwan's
economy, education, transportation, health, education, police force, and other
important sectors during colonial rule and in the current state. Chen et al.,
Taiwan guangfu yanjiu, chapter 2.

18. Chu, "Qiu Niantai yu Er'erba shibian," 52.

19. "Taiwan de gerang he bumie de minzu jingshen" (The cession of Taiwan and the
immortal national spirit), in Qin and Zhang, *Kangzhan shiqi shoufu Taiwan zhi
zhongyao yanlun*, 188.

20. The TPAEO was founded on August 29, 1945, with the mission of preparing for
Taiwan's full integration into the Nationalist administration. Taiwan Investigation Committee, "Taiwan jieguan jihua gangyao cao'an" (A draft plan for taking
over Taiwan), 1944, cited in Chen Liwen et al., *Taiwan guangfu yanjiu*, 181.

21. Zeng Jianmin, *1945: Poxiao shike de Taiwan*, 175.

22. The first five *hanjian* had all worked at the Wang Jingwei government's consulate
in Taiwan. "Taiwan gaodeng fayuan jianchachu chuli hanjian anjian diaocha-
biao" (Statistics on the *hanjian* cases received by the Office of Procurators of the
Taiwan Advanced Court), Academia Historica, Taipei, 151–1704.

23. Ibid., 175.

24. "Taiwan sheng tingzhi gongquan ren dengji guize" (Restrictions on the Political
Rights of Taiwanese under Suspicion), in Hou, *Guoshiguan cang Er'erba dang'an
shiliao*, 33–35.

25. "Sifa xingzhengbu wei taisheng 'Tingzhi gongquanren dengji guize' buhe fadu
cheng Xingzheng Yuan" (Ministry of Justice's official letter to the Executive
Yuan regarding the Restrictions on the Political Rights of Taiwanese under
Suspicion), in Hou, *Guoshiguan cang Er'erba dang'an shiliao*, 23.

26. "Qiu Niantai zhi lifayuan han" (Qiu Niantai's Petition to the Legislative Yuan),
ibid., 14–15.

27. Hou, preface to *Guoshiguan cang Er'erba dang'an shiliao*, 42.

28. "Qiu Niantai chengbao tesheng shiji weiji qing teshe Er'erba shibian renfan ji taiji
hanjian zhanfan" (A petition by Qiu Niantai regarding the special amnesty for
prisoners of the February 28 unrest, *hanjian*, and war criminals), January 11,
1948. Academia Historica, Taipei, 105-0-0000-03.

29. "Yu Youren zhi Xingzhengyuan han" (Yu Youren's letter to the Executive Yuan),
in Hou, *Guoshiguan cang Er'erba dang'an shiliao*, 1:18.

30. Hou, preface to *Guoshiguan cang Er'erba dang'an shiliao*, 7.

31. Qiu, *Linghai weibiao*, 242.

32. See Disan Zhanqu Jinxia Hanjian Anjian Chuli Weiyuhui, *Mintai hanjian zuixing shilu*.

33. "Zhongguo lujunbu banbu 'Chuli taiwanren banfa'" (The Chinese Ministry of
Army issued Resolutions on Dealing with Taiwanese Persons in the Mainland),
Jiang sheng bao, January 21, 1946.

34. Hong, *Taiwan guangfu qianhou*, 110; "Benshi 8000 yu taibao you banshu shenqing
huiji" (Half of the eight thousand Taiwanese compatriots applied to return to
Taiwan), *Jiang sheng bao*, February 10, 1946.

35. Lai Guomin, preface to Disan Zhanqu Jinxia Hanjian Anjian Chuli Weiyuanhui, *Mintai hanjian zuixing shilu*.

36. Ibid., 13.

37. Judicial Explanation of the Supreme Court, No. 3078, cited in Disan Zhanqu Jinxia Hanjian Anjian Chuli Weiyuanhui, *Mintai hanjian zuixing shilu*, 6.

38. Disan Zhanqu Jinxia Hanjian Anjian Chuli Weiyuanhui, *Mintai hanjian zuixing shilu*, 121.

39. "Jinxia sujianhui fabiao jingban hanjian anjian qingxing" (Updates on *hanjian* cases handled by the Jinmen-Xiamen *hanjian* processing committee), ibid., 113.

40. Disan Zhanqu Jinxia Hanjian Anjian Chuli Weiyuanhui, *Mintai hanjian zuixing shilu*, 5-7.

41. Ibid., 9.

42. Ibid., 10.

43. "Jinxia sujianhui fabiao jingban hanjian anjian qingxing," 113-15.

44. "Sifa jiguan panjian jingguo" (How the judiciary handled *hanjian* cases), in Disan Zhanqu Jinxia Hanjian Anjian Chuli Weiyuanhui, *Mintai hanjian zuixing shilu*, 116. This piece was originally published in *Jiang sheng bao*, a major local newspaper in Xiamen.

45. "Guomin dahui Taiwansheng daibiao Dong Guoshu deng qingyuanshu" (A petition from Dong Guoshu and other representatives of Taiwan at the National Assembly), SMA (Q187) 1-352, 22,

46. See, for instance, Hou, *Guoshiguan cang Er'erba dang'an shiliao*, 1997; Huang Zhangjian, *Er'erba shijian zhenxiang kaozheng gao*; Chen Cuilian, *Taiwanren de dikang yu rentong*, chapter 8; For a recent publication that overturns the mainstream narrative and evaluation of the incident in Taiwan, see Xi Xiande, *Jingcha yu Er'erba shijian*.

47. "Qiu Niantai chengbao taisheng shiji weiji qing teshe Er'erba shibian renfan ji taiji hanjian zhanfan."

48. "Guomin dahui Taiwansheng daibiao Dong Guoshu deng qingyuanshu," 20-25.

49. Zhou Wanyao, *Taiji Ribenbing zuotanhui jilu bing xiangguan ziliao*, 46.

50. Ibid., 51.

51. Ching, *Becoming Japanese*, 37, 29.

52. Some modern Vietnamese scholars consider this period as one of Chinese colonization, marked by political domination, Chinese settlement in Vietnam, intermarriage, and cultural assimilation. See Khanh, "Ethnic Chinese in Vietnam and Their Identity," 268.

53. Ibid., 269-70.

54. Li Qingxin, "Cantonese in Vietnam from the Fifteenth Century to the Seventeenth Century," 13.

55. Khanh, *The Ethnic Chinese and Economic Development in Vietnam*, 15.

56. Chiuang, "Identity and Indigenization," 95; Khanh, *The Ethnic Chinese and Economic Development in Vietnam*, 15.

57. Chiung, "Yuenan de mingxiang ren yu huaren yimin de zuqun rentong yu bentuhua chayi," 96.

58. Khanh, *The Ethnic Chinese and Economic Development in Vietnam*, 272.

59. Li Qingxin, "Cantonese in Vietnam from the Fifteenth Century to the Seventeenth Century," 11–13.

60. According to an official French source, in Cochin China in 1921 there were about 46,500 Minh Huong, who formed 42 percent of the total Chinese population in that area. In 1950 there were 75,000 Minh Huong, who accounted for 10 percent of the total Chinese population. Khanh, *The Ethnic Chinese and Economic Development in Vietnam*, 21–28.

61. The construction of racial hierarchy and racism was complex, with whites at the top and various nonwhite groups being associated with distinct stereotypes and holding different judicial status. See Vann, "The Good, the Bad, and the Ugly," 187–205.

62. In March 1930, China and France signed the Nanjing Agreement, granting Chinese in Vietnam a range of privileges in trade and industrial investment never previously extended to foreigners in Indochina. Khanh, "Ethnic Chinese in Vietnam and their Identity," 274.

63. Shiu, "Yuenan huaren gongmin diwei de bianqian," 148; Ko, *Nationality and International Law in Asian Perspective*, 35.

64. "Materials and Discussion on the Issue of Minh Huong," Academica Historica, Taipei, 020-011007-0018-0142.

65. Zhang Yu, "Yuenan huaqiao kangri jiuwang yundong jilüe," 55; *Hua Qiao Zhi*, 202.

66. *Hua Qiao Zhi*, 201.

67. With a daily circulation of more than five thousand copies, *Quanmin ribao* was the most influential newspaper in Indochina before it was shut down by the French colonial government. Xu Anru, "Yuenan huaqiao aiguo baozhi *Quanmin ribao*," 26.

68. "Declaration of the National Salvation Committee in South Vietnam," Academia Historica, Taipei, 020-019908-0017, 55.

69. Mitter, *Forgotten Ally*, 206–9.

70. Guo, *Zhonghua minguo shishi rizhi*, 4:2888.

71. "Declaration of the National Salvation Committee in South Vietnam," Academia Historica, Taipei, 020-019908-0017, 56.

72. Ibid., 39.

73. Ibid., 105, 39.

74. Guo, *Zhonghuaminguo shishi rizhi*, 4:136–42, 4:172–73.

75. *Hua Qiao Zhi*, 203.

76. Zhang Yu, *Yuenan, Laowo, Jianpuzhai huaqiao huaren manji*, 47.

77. On Japan's economic policies in Vietnam and a list of collaborationist organizations and figures, see Shiu, "Yuenan huaren zai zhanzheng qijian de sunshi," 3–26.

78. Ibid., 14.

79. Marr, *Vietnam*, introduction.

80. In July 1941, an agreement between the Japanese and the Vichy government in France allowed the French regime to continue in Japanese-controlled Indochina, with much-curtailed powers. In March 1945, the Japanese overturned the French administration in Vietnam. Ibid., 4.

81. In addition, the Nationalist government argued that since China had fought the Japanese for the longest and suffered the greatest losses, it should have the right to pick first. Qin, *Zhonghua minguo zhongyao shiliao chubian*, 7:68–76.

82. Marr, *Vietnam*, 277.

83. Yang, "Postwar Sino-French Negotiations about Vietnam, 1945–1946," 218.

84. Marr, *Vietnam*, 274.

85. "Telegraph from the Chinese Consulate in Saigon, no. 20," in "The Ming Huong problem in Vietnam and citizenship status of overseas Chinese." Academia Historica, Taipei, 172-1-0554-1.

86. "Zhongguo Guomindang zhu Henei zhishu zhibu zhi Waijiaobu han" (Telegraph from the Nationalist Party's Hanoi Branch to the Ministry of Foreign Affairs," in "*Hanjian* Cases in North Vietnam, 1945–1951," Academia Historica, Taipei, 020-011007-0073, 15.

87. Khanh, *The Ethnic Chinese and Economic Development in Vietnam*, 59.

88. Ibid., 46.

89. Marr, *Vietnam*, 279.

90. "Zhongguo Guomindang zhu Henei zhishu zhibu zhi Waijiaobu han," 15.

91. Ibid., 45.

92. "Zhongguo Guomindang zhu Henei zhishu zhibu zhi Waijiaobu han," 48.

93. "Letter from the Wife of Huang Jiu, Huang Li Huanyu," Academia Historica, Taipei, 020-011007, 1.

94. *Zhufa dashi Qian Tai yu sifa xingzheng buzhang guanyu faguo qing jiang fajihanjian yu zaiyue hanjian jiaohuan yindu yijian laiwang han* (Correspondence between the Chinese ambassador in France and the minister of justice regarding exchanging *hanjian*), September 3–October 30, 1947, SHA 7 (2)-119. One of the convicted, Raymund Bossuet, was half French and half Japanese.

95. *Faguo dashi genju huhui jiaohuan fajian hanjian yuanze yaoqiu teshe zhuri weihai zhongguofan Aiminuofu* (Reports on the French ambassador's request for the pardon of Emelionoff), SHA 7 (2)-120. October 1946.

96. *Zhufa dashi Qian Tai yu sifaxingzheng buzhang guanyu faguo qingjiang faji hanjian yu zaiyue hanjian jianhuan yidu yijian laiwanghan*, September 1946.

97. Ibid., October 30, 1946.

98. This comparison was not an original argument by Guo but one that the Nationalist government had meticulously formulated and articulated in the mass media and through the judicial process. Zanasi, "Globalizing *hanjian*: The Suzhou Trials and the Post–World War II Discourse on Collaboration."

99. *Zhufa dashi Qian Tai yu sifaxingzheng buzhang guanyu faguo qingjiang faji hanjian yu zaiyue hanjian jianhuan yidu yijian laiwanghan*, October 30, 1946.

Epilogue

1. The saying was a juxtaposition of two otherwise unrelated idioms: "There is order and logic" and "There is no law and no heavenly rules" (*youtiao youli; wufa wutian*). In this saying, the two idioms were interpreted to be shortened forms for

you jintiao cai you daoli, wu fabi jiuwu qingtian, as translated in the text. Zhang Qizhi, *Wanqing minguo shi*, 555.

2. Mühlhahn, *Criminal Justice in China*, 167.
3. *Jinchaji bianqu hunyin tiaoli cao'an* (A draft of the marriage law of the Jin-Cha-Ji Border Region), July 7, 1941, in Hebeisheng shehui kexueyuan lishiyanjiusuo, *Jinchaji kangri genjudi shiliao xuanbian*, 119.
4. Wang Xiaohua, *Hanjian da shenpan*, 130.
5. "Guanyu ruogan teshu tudi de chuli wenti" (On the handling of special types of land), *Jiefang ribao*, February 6, 1942.
6. Xu Shilie, *Xiangfan laoqu jiaoyu jianshi*, 69.
7. Masui, *Kankan saibanshi*, 291. The local currency was called "border area currency" (*bianqu quan*).
8. Masui, *Kankan saiban shi*, 290–92.
9. Meng and Cheng, "Chengzhi hanjian gongzuo gaishu," 108; Wang Xiaohua, *Hanjian dashenpan*, 134–47.
10. Interviews conducted by the author with several individuals from Henan. Interviewees preferred to remain anonymous. "Death by a thousand cuts" (*lingchi*) was the most painful form of capital punishment in the traditional legal system and was usually reserved for those convicted of the most heinous crimes. Brook, Bourgon, and Blue, *Death by a Thousand Cuts*.
11. Wang Daoping, *Zhongguo kangri zhanzheng shi*, 2:625. The estimate is based on the exchange rate of 1937.
12. Meng and Cheng, "Chengzhi hanjian gongzuo gaishu," 111.
13. Yuan Ling, "Shanghai dang'an lide fangeming," 17.
14. Zeng, *Wode fuqin Yuan Shu*, 331–33. The complicated wartime activities of the three and the reasons for their persecution in the 1950s remain subjects of debate and speculation.
15. "The Traitor Act," *China Critic*, September 1945, 64.
16. Feng Xiaocai, "Zhengzhi yundong de jiceng luoji ji richanghua," 39–48.
17. Zhang Jinfan, *Zhongguo fazhi liushinian*, 107–8.
18. Ibid., 99. "Zhonghua Renmin Gongheguo chengzhi fangeming tiaoli" (The statute on punishing counterrevolutionaries of the PRC), *Renmin ribao*, February 22, 1951.
19. See, for instance, Strauss, "Morality, Coercion and State Building by Campaign in the Early PRC," 891–912; Yang Kuisong, "Reconsidering the Campaign to Suppress Counterrevolutionaries," 102–21.
20. *Zhonghua Suweiai Gongheguo chengzhi fangeming tiaoli* (The statute on punishing counterrevolutionaries in the Chinese Soviet Republic).
21. Shen and Zhao, "Zhengzhi shuyu de fazhihua shijian," 147.
22. Zhang Jinfan, *Zhongguo fazhi liushinian*, 93–98.
23. Chiang, *Weihe hanjian biwang qinlüe bibai*.
24. Ibid., 3–15.
25. *Tiantang chunmeng* (A heavenly dream), directed by Tang Xiaodan (Shanghai: Zhongyang dianying qiye gufen youxian gongsi, 1947).
26. *Se, Jie* (Lust, caution), directed by Ang Lee (Taipei: Haishang Films, 2007).

27. *Di Dao Zhan* (Tunnel warfare), directed by Ren Xudong (Beijing: Zhongguo sanhuan yinxiang she, 2004 [1965]); *Ip Man*, DVD, directed by Wilson Yip (Hong Kong: Dongfang dianying, Ltd., 2008); *Jinling shisan chai* (Flowers of War), directed by Zhang Yimou (Beijing: New Picture Film Co., 2011).

28. Lin Nansen, "Guomindang henpi qian zongtong Lee Teng-hui" (The Nationalist Party renounces the former president Lee Teng-hui), www.bbc.com/zhongwen /simp/china/2015/08/150821_kmt_leetenghui, accessed September 2, 2015.

29. "Za pingguo shi aiguo? Chi KFC shi hanjian?" (Is smashing iPhones an act of patriotism? Does eating KFC make one *hanjian?*) *Sina Domestic News*, http://news .sina.com.cn/c/2016-07-21/doc-ifxuhuma7460817.shtml, July 26, 2016.

30. Zhi Ling, "Lifa jinjue 'hanjian yanlun' shanghai xueshu ziyou" (Outlawing "*hanjian* speech" is a violation of academic freedom), *Zhongguo qingnianbao*, March 5, 2007.

31. The full text of the Austrian law can be accessed at the Bundeskanzleramt Rechtsinformationssystem website, www.ris.bka.gv.at/GeltendeFassung.wxe ?Abfrage=Bundesnormen&Gesetzesnummer=10000207.

32. "Jingti riben jiandie he hanjian de pohuai huodong" (Beware of the sabotage of Japanese spies and *hanjian*), http://blog.sina.com.cn/s/blog_ae1a2cb001018evh .html, September 19, 2012.

33. "The South China Sea Case and China's New Nationalism," *Diplomat*, July 19, 2016.

GLOSSARY

Terms are Chinese unless marked otherwise: (J) Japanese

ba ling hou 八零後 those born after the 1980s
baobian 褒貶 praise-or-blame approach
baoquanzhe da, xishengzhe xiao 保全者大，犧牲者小 a minor sacrifice to preserve
   something more important
baozhang 保長 head of mutual surveillance unit

Chengzhi Hanjian Tiaoli 懲治漢奸條例 Regulations on Punishing *Hanjian*
Chengzhi Hanjian Yanlun Fa'an 懲治漢奸言論法案 Resolutions on Punishing
   Hanjian Speech or Opinion
chujian 鋤奸 eradicating *hanjian*
chunqiu zebei xianzhe 春秋責備賢者 noble men always take the blame in history

Dadongya Zhanzheng 大東亞戰爭 the Great East Asian War
dagoutuan 打狗團 the dog-killer squad
Dai Li Xingdongdui 戴笠行動隊 Dai Li's Action Team
dajie 大節 political integrity
dang buke fen, guo bi tongyi 黨不可分，國必統一 the party cannot be divided, and
   the nation must be unified
danggun 黨棍 Nationalist Party stick
Dashe 大赦 Great Amnesty
dayi mieqin 大義滅親 to place righteousness above family loyalty
Daying yebao 大英夜報 *Daying Evening Paper*
Diwei Chanye Chuli Weiyuanhui 敵偽產業處理委員會 Enemy and Puppet Property
   Processing Committee

Erchenzhuan 貳臣傳 *Biographies of Twice-Serving Ministers*

faji hanjian 法籍漢奸 French nationals who betrayed the Han
fangeming 反革命 counterrevolutionary
fatuan 法團 legal organization
funi lüshi 附逆律師 collaborating lawyers

Geming Qingniantuan 革命青年團 Revolutionary Youth Group
gongzei hanjian 工賊漢奸 traitors to the nation and the working class
gongzhi 公職 public positions
Guofang Zuigao Weiyuanhui 國防最高委員會 Supreme Council of National Defense
guohuo 國貨 national goods
guxuan haiwai 孤懸海外 isolated from the homeland and left floating on the sea

Hanguo Jiuguotuan 韓國救國團 Korean Salvation Group

hanjian 漢奸 traitors to the Han Chinese

Hanjian choushi 漢奸醜史 *Hideous Histories of* Hanjian

hanjian meiti 漢奸媒體 *hanjian* media

hanjian wenren 漢奸文人 *hanjian* literati

hanren 漢人 people of Han ethnicity

hanzhong 漢忠 loyalty to the Han

hezuo 合作 cooperation

huajian 華奸 traitors to the greater Chinese nation

huanbingzhiji 緩兵之計 delay policy

Huangmin Fenggonghui 皇民奉公會 Associations for the Devoted Subjects of the Japanese Emperor

huaqiao 華僑 overseas Chinese

huayuan yangfang 花園洋房 grand mansion with garden

Huazhong Hongjishantang 華中宏濟善堂 Central China Grand Charity Hall

huoguo yangmin 禍國殃民 to wreck the country and ruin the people

jianshang 奸商 treacherous merchants

jianshu 奸屬 family members of *hanjian,* or those of the *hanjian* type

Jidong Zhengfu 冀東政府 Eastern Hebei Government

jimo chaojia 籍沒抄家 a house search and confiscation of all possessions

Jinyan Zongju 禁菸總局 General Bureau for the Opium Embargo

jinzhong 盡忠 to fulfill one's obligation of loyalty

Juntong 軍統 a Nationalist intelligence office; short for Junshi Weiyuanhui Tiaocha Tongjiju 軍事委員會調查統計局 Bureau of Investigation and Statistics under the Military Affairs Commission

juyao 劇妖 theatrical evil

Kangri Jiuguojun 抗日救國軍 Anti-Japanese National Salvation Army

Kangri Zhanzheng 抗日戰爭 War of Resistance against Japan

kangzhan jianguo 抗戰建國 resistance against the Japanese and rebuilding the nation

kangzhanfenzi 抗戰份子 contributors to the War of Resistance

kyōryoku 協力 (J) collaborationist

lianzuo 連坐 guilt by association

lingchi 凌遲 death by a thousand cuts

lishi wenti 歷史問題 problematic past

liumang xiaoshuo 流氓小說 pornographic novel

maiguozei 賣國賊 sellout

mingzhi 明志 to demonstrate one's virtue

Minh Huong 明香/ 明鄉 those carrying the Ming incense

minzuzhuyi 民族主義 nationalism

mu siling 母司令 the female commander

neiluan 內亂 internal rebellion
Nühanjian choushi 女漢奸醜史 *Hideous Histories of Female* Hanjian

pantu 叛徒 traitor

Qianxian ribao 前線日報 *Warfront Daily*
qie 妾 concubine
Qingxiang yundong 清鄉運動 Clearing the Villages movement

ren zei zuofu 認賊作父 to take foes for parents
renxinxiangbei 人心向背 the question of retaining popular support
Rexue Chubanshe 熱血出版社 Hot-Blooded Press
Riben diguozhuyi hanjian 日本帝國主義漢奸 *hanjian* deputies of Japanese imperialism
Riben hanjian zougou 日本漢奸走狗 traitors and running dogs for the Japanese
rimei 日煤 Japanese coal

Sanqingtuan 三青團 The Three Principles of the People Youth League; short for Sanminzhuyi Qingniantuan 三民主義青年團
Shanghai Lüshi Sujiantuan 上海律師蕭奸團 Shanghai Lawyers' *Hanjian*-Elimination Team
Shangtonghui 商統會 Commodity Control Commission
shangwei faxian you funi xianyi 尚未發現有附逆嫌疑 those who had probably collaborated but were yet to be exposed
Shenbao 申報 *Shanghai Daily*
sifajie 司法界 legal circles
Songhu Jingbei Silingbu 淞滬警備司令部 Songjiang-Shanghai Garrison Headquarters
suanzhang 算帳 to settle accounts
sujian 蕭奸 cleansing of *hanjian*
Suzhewan Diwei Chanye Qinglichu 蘇浙皖敵偽產業清理處 Jiangsu-Zhejiang-Anhui Enemy and Puppet Property Liquidation Committee

taiji hanjian 台籍 Taiwanese *hanjian*
Taiwan xing: Buzhiyouqin, gengbuzhi you han, taibaohaiba women dangzuoqing-guoren 台灣行: 不知有秦, 更不知有漢, 台胞還把我們當做清國人 Experiencing Taiwan: They know not the Qin or Han and imagine mainlanders still subjects of the Qing
Taiwan Xingzheng Zhangguan Gongshu 台灣行政長官公署 Taiwan Provincial Administrative Executive Office
Taose xinwen 桃色新聞 sex scandals
tongbao 同胞 compatriots, literally "those born of the same womb"
tongmoudiguo 通謀敵國 collaborating with the enemy nation
tongzhi jingji 統制經濟 control economy
tudi 徒弟 discipline

waihuan 外患 external aggression
weijun 偽軍 puppet militia
weiyuan 偽員 puppet staff
wenyao 文妖 literary devils
wugao 誣告 false accusations
wushang bujian 無商不奸 there is no merchant who is not treacherous
Wuyouzhixiang 烏有之鄉 Utopia (website)

xiaoyi 小義 personal duty/attachment
xincun hanshi 心存漢室 to remain loyal to the Han and their destiny
xuyu fuyan 虛與敷衍 to cope with courteously yet perfunctorily

yihuazhihua 以華制華 using the Chinese to rule the Chinese
yizhi 遺志 unfulfilled will
youtiao youli, wufa wutian 有條有理, 無法無天 with gold bricks comes innocence;
    being penniless means no access to justice
yuyong shishen 御用士紳 scholar gentry in the service of the (Japanese) emperor

zhanfan 戰犯 war criminals
zhengtong 正統 the orthodoxy
zhengzhi touji 政治投機 political speculation
zhengzhifan 政治犯 political criminals
Zhongchenlu 忠臣錄 *Biographies of Ming Loyalists*
Zhongtong 中統 Nationalist intelligence organization, short for 中國國民黨中央執行
    委員會調查統計局 Bureau of Investigation and Statistics of the Party Central Office
zhongyang zhengfu 中央政府 central government
zhongyao hanjian 重要漢奸 major *hanjian*
Zhongyi Jiuguojun 忠義救國軍 Loyal and Righteous National Salvation Army

BIBLIOGRAPHY

Archives

Academia Historica, Taipei
Chiang Kai-shek Diaries, Hoover Institution, Stanford, CA
Henan Provincial Archives, Zhengzhou
Second Historical Archives of China, Nanjing (SHA)
Shanghai Municipal Archives, Shanghai (SMA)
Zhejiang Provincial Archives, Hangzhou
Zhejiang University Archives, Hangzhou

Periodicals

Jiangsheng bao (Jiangsheng daily), Xiamen, 1927–1950
Jiefang ribao (Liberation daily), Yan'an, 1941–49
Jiuwang ribao (National salvation daily), Shanghai, 1937–41
Kangzhan ribao (Resistance daily), Changsha, 1938–39
Kangzhan sanrikan (Resistance biweekly), Shanghai, 1937–38
Renmin ribao (People's daily), Beijing, 1949–present
Shenbao (Shanghai daily), Shanghai, 1872–1949
Taiwan minshengbao (Voices from Taiwan), Chongqing, April–October 1945
Wenhui bao (Wenhui daily), Shanghai, 1938–47
Xinhua ribao (New China daily), Wuhan 1938–47

Published Sources

Alford, William. "Of Arsenic and Old Laws: Looking Anew at Criminal Justice in Late
    Imperial China," *California Law Review* 6 (1984): 1180–256.
Ban Gu. *Han shu* (The book of the Han). Beijing: Zhonghua Shuju, 1962.
Barrett, David P., and Larry N. Shyu, eds. *Chinese Collaboration with Japan, 1932–1945:
    The Limits of Accommodation.* Stanford, CA: Stanford University Press, 2001.
Beijing Municipal Archive, ed. *Riwei Beijing Xinminhui* (The puppet New Citizens
    Association of Beijing). Beijing: Guangming Ribao Chubanshe, 1989.
Bing Ying. *Hanjian xianxingji* (Exposure and elimination of *hanjian*). N.p.: Wartime
    Press, 1938.
Boyle, John Hunter. *China and Japan at War, 1937–1945: The Politics of Collaboration.*
    Stanford, CA: Stanford University Press, 1972.

Brook, Timothy. *Collaboration: Japanese Agents and Local Elites in Wartime China.* Cambridge, MA: Harvard University Press, 2005.

———. "Hesitating Before the Judgement of History." *Journal of Asian Studies* 1 (2012): 103–14.

———. "The Shanghai Trials, 1946: Conjuring Postwar Justice." In *Zhanhou bianju yu zhanzheng jiyi* (Postwar changes and war memories), ed. Lü Fangshang, 127–55. Taipei: Academia Historica, 2015.

Brook, Timothy, Jérômy Bourgon, and Gregory Blue. *Death by a Thousand Cuts.* Cambridge, MA: Harvard University Press, 2008.

Brunero, Donna. *Britain's Imperial Cornerstone in China: The Chinese Maritime Customs Service, 1854–1949.* Oxford: Routledge, 2006.

Cai Dejin. "Guanyu kangzhan shiqi Wang Jingwei yu Wangwei zhengquan de jige wenti zhi wojian" (Several issues concerning Wang Jingwei and his puppet regime during the War of Resistance). *Kangri zhanzheng yanjiu* 1 (1999): 4–12.

Cai Dengshan. "Buxue youshu de Chen Binhe" (Chen Binhe: A poorly educated yet resourceful individual). *Shucheng* 8 (2009): 70–77.

Cao Dachen, "Riben qinhua jigou: Huazhong Hongjishantung" (Central China Grand Charity Hall: An institution founded by the Japanese to poison the Chinese people). *Kangri zhanzheng yanjiu* 1 (2004): 113–37.

Cassel, Pär. "Excavating Extraterritoriality: The 'Judicial Sub-prefect' as a Prototype for the Mixed Court in Shanghai." *Late Imperial China* 2 (2003): 156–82.

Cavanaugh, Jerome. *Who's Who in China: 1918–1950.* Hong Kong: Chinese Materials Center, 1982.

Chai Degeng, ed. *Zhongguo jindaishi ziliao congkan: Xinhai geming* (A collection of primary sources on modern Chinese history: the 1911 Revolution). Shanghai: Shanghai Renmin Chubanshe, 1957.

Chan Wing-ming. "Official Historiography and Ideological Indoctrination in High Qing: Emperor Qianlong's Compilation of the *Erchen Zhuan* and *Nichen Zhuan*." *Oriens Extremus* 44 (2003.4): 253–74.

Chang, Chihyun. *Government, Imperialism and Nationalism in China: The Maritime Customs Service and Its Chinese Staff.* Oxford: Routledge, 2013.

———. "Zhongguo haiguan de guanyuan shencha he zhanhou fuyuan (1943–1945)" (Investigation of collaborators within the Chinese Maritime Customs Service and its postwar restoration, 1943–1945). In Zhou Huimin, *Guoji zhixu yu zhongguo waijiao de xingsu*, 189–219. Taipei: Chengchi University Press, 2014.

Chang Kai, ed. *Zhongguo gongyunshi cidian* (A dictionary of China's labor movements). Beijing: Laodong Renshi Chubanshe, 1990.

Chen, Joseph Kai Huan. "Chinese Law in Transition: The Late Qing Law Reform, 1901–1911." PhD diss., Brown University, 1976.

Chen Cuilian, *Taiwanren de dikang yu rentong* (The resistance and identities of the Taiwanese people). Taipei: Yuanliu Publishing, 2009.

Chen Gan, ed. *Chen Gongbo shiji* (Collected poetry of Chen Gongbo). Hong Kong: Haiyang Yinwu Youxian Gongsi, 2015.

Chen Gongshu, *Yingxiong wu ming* (The unknown heroes). Taipei: Zhuanji Wenxue Chubanshe, 1981.

Chen Liao, "Zhang Ailing re yao jiangwen" (The Zhang Ailing fever needs to cool down). *Wenyi bao* (Literary Post), May 3, 1996.

Chen Liwen, Zhong Shumin, Ou Suying, and Lin Zhenghui. *Taiwan guangfu yanjiu* (A study of the liberation of Taiwan). Nanjing: Nanjing University Press, 2015.

Chen Tong. "Zai falü yu shehui zhijian: Minguo shiqi Shanghai bentu lüshi de diwei he zuoyong" (Between law and society: Status and function of locally trained lawyers in Republican Shanghai). *Shilin* 1 (2006): 55–69.

Chen Xiaochong. "Taiwan Geming Tongmenghui kangri aiguo douzheng shulun" (The resistance efforts of the Taiwan Revolutionary Alliance), *Taiwan yanjiu* 5 (2012): 60–64.

Chen Zishan. *Shuobujin de Zhang Ailing* (An unceasing discussion of Zhang Ailing). Beijing: Sanlian Shudian Chubanshe, 2004.

———. "1945–1949 nianjian de Zhang Ailing" (Zhang Ailing between 1945 and 1949). *Nantong daxue xuebao* 3 (2007): 51–55.

Chiang, Howard, and Ari Larissa Heinrich, eds. *Queer Sinophone Cultures*. New York: Routledge, 2014.

Chinese Ministry of Information. *China Handbook, 1937–1945*. Revised and enlarged edition. New York: Macmillan, 1947.

Ching, Leo T. S. *Becoming Japanese: Colonial Taiwan and the Politics of Identity Formation*. Berkeley: University of California Press, 2001.

Chiung, Wi-vun Taiffalo. "Yuenan de mingxiang ren yu huaren yimin de zuqun rentong yubentuhua chayi" (Identity and Indigenization: Minh Huong People versus Ethnic Chinese in Vietnam). *Taiwan International Studies Quarterly* 4 (2013): 87–114.

Chu Jingtao. "Qiu Niantai yu 228 shibian" (Qiu Niantai and the February 28 incident). *Mintai wenhua jiaoliu* 1 (2008): 51–58.

Ch'ü T'ung-tsu. *Law and Society in Traditional China*. Paris: Mouton, 1961.

Cihai bianji weiyuanhui. *Cihai* (Comprehensive dictionary of the Chinese language). Shanghai: Shanghai Cishu, 1979.

Coble, Parks. *Facing Japan: Chinese Politics and Japanese Imperialism, 1931–1937*. Cambridge, MA: Harvard University Press, 1991.

———. *Chinese Capitalists in Japan's New Order: The Occupied Lower Yangzi, 1937–1945*. Berkeley: University of California Press, 2003.

Cochran, Sherman and Andrew Hsieh, *The Lius of Shanghai*. Cambridge, MA: Harvard University Press, 2013.

Crossley, Pamela Kyle. *The Wobbling Pivot: China since 1800*. Malden, MA: Wiley-Blackwell, 2010.

Cui Meiming. "Dajieshou yu Shanghai minying gongye" (The catastrophic takeover and Shanghai's private industry). *Dang'an yu shixue* 3 (1998): 43–55.

Deák, István. *Europe on Trial: The Story of Collaboration, Resistance and Retribution during World War II*. Boulder, CO: Westview Press, 2015.

De Ceuster, Koen. "The Nation Exorcised: The Historiography of Collaboration in South Korea." *Korean Studies* 2 (2001): 207–42.

Denton, Kirk. *The Problematic of Self in Modern Chinese Literature: Hu Feng and Lu Ling*. Stanford, CA: Stanford University Press, 1998.

Ding, Wei. "Kangzhan shiqi Juntong Shanghaiqu de chujian xingdong" (Juntong's *hanjian*-elimination operations in wartime Shanghai). *Wenshi tiandi* 10 (2012): 56–59.

Disan Zhanqu Jinxia Hanjian Anjian Chuli Weiyuanhui, ed. *Mintai hanjian zuixing shilu* (A faithful account of criminal deeds by *hanjian* in Fujian and Taiwan). Xiamen: Jiangsheng Wenhua Chubanshe, 1947.

Duan Ruicong. "Jiang Jieshi yu kangzhan shiqi zongdongyuan tizhi zhi goujian" (Chiang Kai-shek and the wartime total mobilization). *Kangri zhanzheng yanjiu* 1 (2014): 34–53.

Eichensehr, Kristen E. "Treason in the Age of Terrorism: An Explanation and Evaluation of Treason's Return in Democratic States." *Vanderbilt Journal of Transnational Law* (November 2009): 1443–1507.

Esherick, Joseph, and Matthew T. Combs, eds. *1943: China at the Crossroads.* Ithaca, NY: Cornell University Press, 2015.

Fang Xuanling, *Jin shu* (The book of the Jin dynasty). Beijing: Zhonghua Shuju, 1974.

Fang Zhanhong. "Da Hanjian Yuan Lüdeng shoushenji" (A record of the trial of Yuan Lüdeng, a major traitor). *Wenshi tiandi* 1 (2010): 31–33.

Fay, Peter Ward, *Opium War, 1840–1842.* Chapel Hill: University of North Carolina Press, 1997.

Feng, Chongyi, and David S. G. Goodman, eds. *North China at War: The Social Ecology of Revolution, 1937–1945.* Lanham, MD: Rowman & Littlefield, 2000.

Feng Bing. "Kangzhan shenglihou Guomin zhengfu chengjian zhong de caichanxing yunyong" (The application of penalties for the *hanjian* crime in the postwar period). *Jinan xuebao* 6 (2014): 137–45.

Feng Chongyi. *Kunan, zai guohun zhong zhengzha: Kangzhan shiqi de zhongguo wenhua* (Chinese cultural trends during the War of Resistance). Guilin: Guangxi Shifan Daxue Chubanshe, 1995.

Feng Xiaocai, "Zhengzhi yundong de jiceng luoji yu richanghua: Yige 'hanjian' de faxian yu shencha" (The fundamental logic and routinization of political movements: The discovery and investigation of a *hanjian*). *Ershiyi shiji* 12 (2012): 39–48.

Field, Andrew. *Mu Shiying: China's Last Modernist.* Hong Kong: Hong Kong University Press, 2014.

Fitzgerald, John. *Awakening China: Politics, Culture, and Class in the Nationalist Revolution.* Stanford, CA: Stanford University Press, 1998.

Fogel, Joshua, ed. *The Nanjing Massacre in History and Historiography.* Berkeley: University of California Press, 2000.

Fu, Poshek. *Passivity, Resistance, and Collaboration: Intellectual Choices in Occupied Shanghai, 1937–1945.* Stanford, CA: Stanford University Press, 1993.

Gangcun ningci huiyilu (A memoir of Okamura Yasuji). Translated by Tianjinshi Zhengxie bianyi weiyuanhui. Edited by Inaba Masao. Beijing: Zhonghua Shuju, 1981.

Gerth, Karl. *China Made: Consumer Culture and the Creation of the Nation.* Cambridge, MA: Harvard University Asia Center, 2004.

Goodman, Bryna. *Native Place, City and Nation: Regional Networks and Identities in Shanghai, 1853–1937.* Berkeley: University of California Press, 1995.

———. "Appealing to the Public: Newspaper Presentation and Adjudication of Emotion." *Twentieth Century China* 2 (April 2006): 32–69.

The Great Qing Code. Translated by William C. Jones. New York: Oxford University Press, 1994.

Gu Yuanqing. "Zhang Ailing bushi 'zhaimao hanjian'" (Zhang Ailing was never a *hanjian* to begin with). *Xueshujie* 6 (2008): 117–20.

Guo Tingyi. *Zhonghua minguo shishi rizhi* (Chronicles of the Republic of China). Vol. 1. Taipei: Academia Sinica, 1985.

Guofangbu Qingbaoju, ed. *Zhongyi Jiuguojun zhi* (A history of the Loyal and Righteous National Salvation Army). Taipei: Guofangbu Qingbaoju, 1970.

Guominzhengfu Junshiweiyuanhui, ed. *Mingmo hanjian liezhuan* (Biographies of *hanjian* in the fall of the Ming). n.p., 1936. Shanghai Municipal Archives (SMA) (K827)-117872.

Han Chunxiu, "Su Qing yu *Tiandi*" (Su Qing and her *Heaven and Earth*). MA thesis, Shandong University, 2008.

Hanjian choushi (Hideous histories of *hanjian*). Shanghai: Datong Chubanshe, 1945.

Hao Zaijin. *Zhongguo mimizhan: Zhonggong qingbao baowei gongzuo jishi* (A faithful account of the intelligence and security work of the Chinese Communist Party). Beijing: Zuojia Chubanshe, 2005.

Harrison, Henrietta. *The Making of the Republican Citizen: Political Ceremonies and Symbols in China, 1911–1929.* Oxford: Oxford University Press, 2000.

He Deting. "Kangri genjudi sujian yanjiu" (A study of anti-*hanjian* campaigns in the Chinese Communist Party base areas). PhD diss., Central China Normal University, 2009.

He Dong, Yang Xiancai, and Wang Shunsheng, eds. *Zhongguo gemingshi renwu cidian* (A dictionary of important figures in the history of Chinese revolution). Beijing: Beijing Chubanshe, 1991.

He Haifeng, "Shidai de xianfeng, meiti de jiaodian: Liu Haisu jiqi Shanghai Tuhua Meishu Xuexiao" (Pioneer in art and focus of the media: Liu Haisu and his Shanghai Art Institute), *Meiyuan* 6 (2009): 40–45.

He Shengsui and Chen Maiqing. *Hanjian choushi* (Hideous history of collaborators). Shanghai: Fudan Daxue Chubanshe, 1999.

Hebeisheng Shehui Kexueyuan Lishiyanjiusuo, ed. *Jinchaji kangri genjudi shiliao xuanbian* (A selection of historical materials on the Shanxi-Chaha'er-Hebei base area). Shijiazhuang: Hebei Renmin Chubanshe, 1983.

Hershatter, Gail, and Wang Zheng. "Chinese History: A Useful Category of Gender Analysis." *American Historical Review* 5 (2008): 1404–21.

Hevia, James. *Cherishing Men from Afar: Qing Guest Ritual and the Macartney Embassy of 1793.* Durham, NC: Duke University Press, 1995.

———. *English Lessons: The Pedagogy of Imperialism in Nineteenth-Century China.* Durham, NC: Duke University Press, 2003.

Ho, Elaine Yee Lin, and Julie Kuehn. *China Abroad: Travels, Subjects, Spaces.* Hong Kong: Hong Kong University Press, 2009.

Hong Buren, *Taiwan guangfu qianhou: 1943–1946* (Key moments of the liberation of Taiwan: 1943–1946). Xiamen: Xiamen University Press, 2010.

Hou Hongkun, ed. *Guoshiguan cang Er'erba dang'an shiliao* (Archival materials on the February 28 Incident held by the Academia Historica). Taipei: Academia Historica, 1997.

Hsiung, James, and Steven Levine. *China's Bitter Victory: The War with Japan, 1937–1945.* New York: M. E. Sharpe, 1997.

Hu Jubin. *Projecting a Nation: Chinese National Cinema before 1949*. Hong Kong: Hong Kong University Press, 2003.

Hu Lancheng. *Jinsheng jinshi* (This life, this world). Taipei: Yuanxing Chubanshe, 1976.

Hua Qiao Zhi (Chronicle of overseas Chinese). Taipei: Huaqiaozhi Bianzuan Weiyuanhui, 1958.

Hua Yougen. "Dong Kong yu jindai Zhongguo lifa" (Dong Kang and modern Chinese law). *Nanjing daxue falü pinglun* 2010 (2): 73–87.

Huang, Nicole. *Women, War, Domesticity: Shanghai Literature and Popular Culture of the 1940s*. Leiden: Brill, 2005.

Huang, Philip C. C. *Code, Customs and Legal Practice in China: The Qing and the Republic Compared*. Stanford, CA: Stanford University Press, 2001.

Huang Huiying. "Wen Lanting de shoushen he gaipan" (The trial and retrial of Wen Lanting). *Minguo chunqiu* 2 (1996): 61–62.

Huang Zhangjian, *Er'erba shijian zhenxiang kaozheng gao* (The truths about the February 28 Incident). Taipei: Lianjing Publishing, 2007.

Hung, William S. H. *Outlines of Modern Chinese Law*. Arlington, MA: University Publications of America, 1976.

Hwang, Dongyoun. *Some Reflections on Wartime Collaboration in China: Wang Jingwei and His Group in Hanoi*. Durham, NC: Asian/Pacific Studies Institute, Duke University, 1998.

——. "Wartime Collaboration in Question: An Examination of the Postwar Trials of the Chinese Collaborators." *Inter-Asia Cultural Studies* 1 (2005): 75–97.

Jacobs, Justin. "Preparing the People for Mass Clemency: the 1956 trials of Japanese War Criminals in Shenyang and Taiyuan." *China Quarterly* 1 (2011): 152–72.

Jiang Zhaoxin, *Zhongguo falü kanbujian zhongguo: Ju Zheng sifa shiqi yanjiu (1932–1948)* (The lack of Chinese elements in Chinese law: A study of the Chinese legal system under Ju Zheng, 1932–1948). Beijing: Qinghua Daxue Chubanshe, 2010.

Jin Xiongbai. *Wang zhengfu de kaichang yu shouchang* (The beginning and ending of the Wang Jingwei regime). Taipei: Li Ao Chubanshe, 1988.

Ju Zheng. "Zhongguo faxi zhi chongxin jianli" (On reestablishing a Chinese legal system). *Zhongguo faxue zazhi* 1(1944): 124.

——. *Weishenme yao chongjian falü tixi* (On the necessity of rebuilding the legal system). Shanghai: Dadong Shuju, 1946.

Kataoka, Tetsuya. *Resistance and Revolution in China: The Communists and the Second United Front*. Berkeley: University of California Press, 1974.

Kawanabe, Ryusaku. *Hiroku Kawashima Yoshiko: Sono shogai no shinso to nazo* (The truths and myths about Kawashima Yoshiko). Tokyo: Bancho Shobo, 1972.

Khanh, Tran. *The Ethnic Chinese and Economic Development in Vietnam*. Hanoi: Institute of Southeast Asian Studies, 1993.

——. "Ethnic Chinese in Vietnam and Their Identity." In *Ethnic Chinese as Southeast Asians*, edited by Leo Suryadinata, 267–92. Singapore: Institute of Southeast Asian Studies, 1997.

Ko, Swan Sik, ed. *Nationality and International Law in Asian Perspective*. Dordrecht, Boston and London: Martinus Nijhoff Publishers, 1990.

Kushner, Barak. *The Thought War: Japanese Imperial Propaganda*. Annotated ed. Honolulu: University of Hawaii Press, 2007.

———. *Men to Devils, Devils to Men: Japanese War Crimes and Chinese Justice*. Cambridge, MA: Harvard University Press, 2014.

Lao She. *Lao She wenji* (Complete works of Lao She). Beijing: Renmin Wenxue Chubanshe, 1980–91.

Larson, Carlton. "The Forgotten Constitutional Law of Treason and the Enemy Combatant Problem." *University of Pennsylvania Law Review* 863 (2006): 863–926.

Larson, Wendy. *Literary Authority and the Modern Chinese Writer: Ambivalence and Autobiography*. Durham, NC: Duke University Press, 1991.

Lawson, Konrad. "Wartime Atrocities and the Policies of Treason in the Ruins of the Japanese Empire, 1937–1953." PhD diss., Harvard University, 2012.

Leary, Charles. "Sexual Modernism in China: Zhang Jingsheng and 1920s Urban Culture." PhD diss., Cornell University, 1994.

Lee, Haiyan. *Revolution of the Heart: A Genealogy of Love in China, 1900–1950*. Stanford, CA: Stanford University Press, 2007.

Li Chengji. "Ruotao sixiong reshang guansi" (My cousin Li Ze was involved in a lawsuit). *Zhongshan wenshi* 59 (2006): 92–97.

Li Gang. *Chuandao Fangzi shenpan dang'an dajiemi* (Unveil the trial records of Kawashima Yoshiko). Hong Kong: Wanguo Xueshu Chuban Gongsi, 2012.

Li Gang and He Jingfang. *Chuandao fangzi shengsi zhi mi jiemi* (The mystery of Kawashima Yoshiko's death unveiled). Changchun: Jilin Wenshi Chubanshe, 2010.

Li Man. "Rumour, *hanjian* 漢奸, and identity: Who led the 'barbarians' to burn the Yuanming Yuan?" *Crossroads* 4 (2011): 169–241.

Li Qingxin. "Cantonese in Vietnam from the Fifteenth century to the Seventeenth Century." Paper presented at the Second International Overseas Chinese Studies Conference, Hong Kong Chinese University, March 2003.

Li Xiangshu. "Du Ju Zheng yuanzhang *Weishenme yao chongjian falü tixi*" (A review of *Weishenme yao chongjian falü tixi*). *Falü pinglun* 729 (1947): 20–22.

Li Zonghuang. *Xianxing baojia zhidu* (The mutual surveillance system in its current state). Beijing: Zhonghua Shuju, 1945.

Li Zuyin. "Chengzhi 'wugao' de fashiguan" (A legal history of "malicious accusation" and its punishment), *Falü pinglun* 730 (July 1947): 4–5.

Liang Huahuang. *Taiwan zongdufu de "dui'an" zhengce yanjiu* (A study of the colonial government's policies toward mainland China). Taipei: Daoxiang Chubanshe, 2001.

Liang Jingchun. *The Sinister Face of the Mukden Incident*. New York: St. John's University Press, 1969.

Lin Zexu, "Mina hanjian zhagao" (A proposal on secretly arresting *hanjian*). In *Lin Zexu ji* (A collection of works by Lin Zexu). Beijing: Zhonghua Shuju, 1963.

Linz, J. "Legitimacy of Democracy and the Socioeconomic System." In *Comparing Pluralist Democracies: Strains on Legitimacy*, edited by M. Dogan, 65–113. Boulder, CO: Westview Press, 1988.

Liu, Jixing. "Kangzhan chuqi bei Chusi de Hanjian Dacaizi" (A gifted scholar turning into *hanjian*: Executed at the beginning of the War of Resistance). Sina blog, July 26, 2011. http://blog.people.com.cn/article/1315296711200.html.

Liu Danian, ed. *Zhongguo fuxing shuniu: Kangri Zhanzheng de banian* (The turning point for China's rejuvenation: The eight years' War of Resistance). Beijing: Beijing Chubanshe, 1997.

Liu Shanshu. "Wenguan kaoshi zhidu jianjie" (A brief introduction to the Nationalist Government's civil service examination). In *Wenshi ziliao cungao xuanbian—zhengdang, zhengfu,* edited by Xu Chaojian. Beijing: Zhongguo Wenshi Chubanshe, 1982.

Liu Tong. "Guomin zhengfu shenpan Riben zhanfan gaishu: 1945–1949" (A brief overview of the Nationalist trials of Japanese war criminals, 1945–1949). *Minguo dang'an* 1 (2014): 72–84.

Liu Weirong. "Zuojia Su Qing yu da hanjian Chen Gongbo de 'liqi' jiaowang" (The curious relations between Su Qing, the writer, and Chen Gongbo, a major *hanjian*). *Dang'an tiandi* 3 (2006): 27–29.

Liu Xiaoyuan. *Frontier Passages: Ethnopolitics and the Rise of Chinese Communism, 1921–1945.* Washington, DC: Woodrow Wilson Center Press, 2004.

Liu Xinhuang. *Kangzhan shiqi lunxianqu wenxueshi* (A history of literature in occupied regions during the war). Taipei: Chengwen Chubanshe, 1980.

Lo Jiu-jung. "Juntong tegong zuzhi yu zhanhou hanjian shenpan"(Juntong and the postwar trial of *hanjian*). *Zhongyangyanjiuyuan Jindaishi Yanjiusuo jikan* 6 (1994): 267–91.

——. "Lishi qingjing yu kangzhan shiqi 'hanjian' de xingcheng: yi 1941 nian Zheng-zhou Weichihui wei zhuyao anli de tantao" (The historical circumstances and the emergence of *hanjian*: A case study of the Zhengzhou Local Maintenance Council, formed in 1941). *Zhongyangyanjiuyuan Jindaishi Yanjiusuo jikan* 24 (1995): 818–41.

Long Xiangzhen. "Liu Haisu chongdang hanjian shifei bian" (A defense for Liu Haisu against the accusation of collaboration). *Dawutai* 5 (2009): 102–3.

Lottman, Herbert. *The People's Anger: Justice and Revenge in Post-liberation France.* London: Hutchinson, 1986.

Lu Jianxin, ed. *Ershi shiji Shanghai ziliao wenku* (Collections of twentieth-century Shanghai archives). Shanghai: Shanghai Shudian, 1999.

Luo Guanzhong, *Sanguo yanyi* (Romance of the Three Kingdoms). Beijing: Renmin Wenxue Chubanshe, 1998.

Ma Liangchun and Li Futian, eds. *Zhongguo wenxue dacidian* (Dictionary of Chinese literature and literary figures). Tianjin: Tianjin Renmin Chubanshe, 1991.

MacMinnon, Stephen, and Diana Lary, eds. *China at War: Regions of China, 1937–1945.* Stanford, CA: Stanford University Press, 2007.

Marr, David. *Vietnam: State, War, Revolution, 1945–1946.* Berkeley: University of California Press, 2013.

Martin, Brian. The *Shanghai Green Gang: Politics and Organized Crime, 1919–1937.* Berkeley: University of California Press, 1996.

Masui, Koichi. *Kankan saiban shi: 1946–1948* (A history of trials of *hanjian*, 1946–1948). Tokyo: Misuzu Shobo, 1977.

Meng Guoxiang and Cheng Tangfa. "Chengzhi hanjian gongzuo gaishu" (A brief account of the punishment of *hanjian*). *Minguo dang'an* 2 (1994): 105–12.

Meyer, Kathryn, and Terry Parssinen. *Webs of Smoke: Smugglers, Warlords, Spies, and the History of the International Drug Trade.* New York: Rowman and Littlefield, 2002.

Mitter, Rana. *Forgotten Ally: China's World War II, 1937–1945*. Boston: Houghton Mifflin Harcourt, 2013.

Mo Han. "Guanyu Shen Jianshi zai kangzhan qijian ruogan wenti zhi kaobian" (On several issues regarding Shen Jianshi's activities during the War of Resistance). *Dang'an tiandi* 12 (2013): 35–37.

Mote, Frederic. *Imperial China, 900–1800*. Cambridge, MA: Harvard University Press, 2003.

Mühlhahn, Klaus. *Criminal Justice in China: A History*. Cambridge, MA: Harvard University Press, 2009.

Mullaney, Thomas, James Leibold, Stéphane Gros, and Eric Vanden Bussche, eds. *Critical Han Studies: The History, Representation, and Identity of China's Majority*. Berkeley: University of California Press, 2012.

Musgrove, Charles D. "Cheering the Traitor: The Post-war Trial of Chen Bijun, April 1946." *Twentieth-Century China* 30 (2005): 3–27.

Nora, Pierre. "Between Memory and History: Les Lieux de Mémoire," *Representations* 26 (Spring 1989): 7–24.

Nühanjian choushi (Hideous histories of female *hanjian*). Shanghai: Shanghai Dashid-aishe, 1945.

Nühanjian lianpu (Who's who of female *hanjian*). Shanghai: Shanghai Dashidaishe, 1945.

Ouyang Hua, *Kangzhan shiqi Shaan-Gan-Ning bianqu chujian fante fazhi yanjiu* (A study of the laws against *hanjian* and spies in the Shaanxi-Gansu-Ningxia base area). Beijing: Zhonghua Zhengfa Daxue Chubanshe, 2013.

Paine, S. C. M. *The Sino-Japanese War of 1894–1895: Perceptions, Power and Primacy*. Cambridge: Cambridge University Press, 2005.

———. *The Wars for Asia, 1911–1949*. New York: Cambridge University Press, 2012.

Peng Ming, ed. *Zhongguo xiandai shi ziliao xuanji* (A selection of important documents in modern Chinese history). Beijing: Renmin Daxue Chubanshe, 1993.

Peng Weicheng, "Zhanhou Guomin Zhengfu chengzhi *hanjian* yanjiu: Yi meiti baodao wei zhongxin de kaocha" (A study of the postwar trials of *hanjian* based on reports from the media). MA thesis, University of Shanghai, 2009.

Qian Liqun. *Zhou Zuoren zhuan* (A biography of Zhou Zuoren). Beijng: Shiyue Wenyi Chubanshe, 1990.

———, ed. *Zhongguo lunxianqu wenxue daxi* (A comprehensive collection of Chinese literature in occupied regions). Nanjing: Guangxi Jiaoyu Chubanshe, 1998.

Qian Qinglian. *Chengzhi hanjian fa* (Laws on punishing *hanjian*). Zhengzhong Shuju, 1941.

Qin Xiaoyi, ed. *Zhonghua Minguo zhongyao shiliao chubian: Duiri kangzhan shiqi* (A collection of important historical materials on the Republic of China: The War of Resistance). Taipei: Zhongyang Wenwu Gongyingshe, 1981.

Qin Xiaoyi and Zhang Ruicheng, eds. *Kangzhan shiqi shoufu Taiwan zhi zhongyao yanlun* (Important speeches and opinions regarding the liberation of Taiwan during the War of Resistance). Taipei: Jindai Zhongguo Chubanshe.

Qing shilu (A faithful record of the Qing dynasty). Beijing: Zhonghua Shuju, 2008.

Qiu Niantai, *Linghai weibiao* (An autobiography of Qiu Niantai). Taipei: Haixia Xueshu Chubanshe, 2002.

Rong Hongjun. *Shiji enyuan: Xu Beihong yu Liu Haisu* (Decades-long enmity between Xu Beihong and Liu Haisu). Beijing: Tongxin Chubanshe, 2009.

Rousso, Henry. *The Vichy Syndrome: History and Memory in France since 1944.* Translated by Arthur Goldhammer. Cambridge, MA: Harvard University Press, 1991.

Sartre, Jean-Paul. "What Is a Collaborator?" In *The Aftermath of War,* translated by Chris Turner, 41–64. New York: Seagull Books, 2008.

Schoppa, Keith. *In a Sea of Bitterness: Refugees during the Sino-Japanese War.* Cambridge, MA: Harvard University Press, 2011.

Scott, Joan Wallach. *Gender and the Politics of History.* New York: Columbia University Press, 1999.

Second Historical Archive, ed. *Zhonghua minguoshi dang'an ziliao huibian* (A collection of archival materials on the Republic of China), Vol. 5. Nanjing: Jiangsu Guji Chubanshe, 1994.

———. *Riwang de Qingxiang* (The Clearing the Villages movement of the Japanese and the Wang Jingwei government). Beijing: Zhonghua Shuju, 1995.

Shanghai Huobaoshe. *Bujian lumi* (Secret accounts of arresting *hanjian*). Shanghai: Qingnian Wenhua Fuwushe, 1948.

Shanghai Municipal Archives, ed. *Riben diguo zhuyi qinlüe Shanghai zuixing ziliao huibian* (A selection of materials on the crimes committed by the Japanese imperialists in Shanghai). Shanghai: Shanghai Renmin Chubanshe, 1997.

Sheldon, Mark. *China in Revolution: The Yenan Way Revisited.* London: M. E. Sharpe, 1995.

Shen Weiwei and Zhao Xiaogeng. "Zhengzhi shuyu de fazhihua shijian: Lun 1951 nian qianhou de fangeming zui" (Legalizing political terms in practice: An analysis of the counterrevolutionary crime around 1951). *Zhongguo Renmin Gong'an Daxue xuebao* 6 (2010): 147–53.

Shi Bifan, "Guomindang tongzhi shiqi ziyou zhuyi renquan yuandong pingxi" (An evaluation of the human rights movement during Nationalist rule). *Anhui shixue* 6 (2008): 78–84.

Shi Bolin. "Lun kangzhan shiqi Guomin Zhengfu de zhanshi zhengzhi tizhi" (An analysis of the Nationalist government's wartime political system). *Kangri zhanzheng yanjiu* 1 (1994): 25–41.

Shi Jiashun. *Liangguang shibian zhi yanjiu* (A study of the 1936 Guangdong-Guangxi Incident). Gaoxiong: Fuwen Tushu Chubanshe, 1992.

Shi Liang, "Funü zai kangzhan zhong de renwu" (Women's roles in the War of Resistance). *Jiuwang ribao,* October 30, 1937.

Shih Shu-mei. *Visuality and Identity: Sinophone Articulations across the Pacific.* Berkeley: University of California Press, 2007.

———. "Against Diaspora: The Sinophone as Places of Cultural Production." In *Global Chinese Literature: Critical Essays,* edited by David Der-wei Wang and Jing Tsu, 29–48. Leiden: Brill, 2010.

Shiu Wen-tang. "Yuenan huaren zai zhanzheng qijian de sunshi" (Inquiry into the material losses of Chinese in Vietnam during wartime, 1941–1947). *Taiwan dongnanye xuekan* 8 (2011): 3–26.

———. "Yuenan huaren gongmin diwei de bianqian" (An evolution of the citizenship status of Chinese in Vietnam). In *Haiwai huaren zhi gongmin diwei yu renquan* (On the citizenship, social status, and human rights of overseas Chinese), edited by Chen Hongyu, 147–72. Taipei: Huaqiaoxiehui Zonghui, 2014.

Sima Changfeng. *Zhongguo xin wenxue shi* (The history of modern Chinese literature). Hong Kong: Zhaoming Chubanshe, 1978.

Sima Wenzhen, *Wenhua hanjian zui'e shi* (Criminal histories of cultural *hanjian*). Shanghai: Shanghai Shuguang Chubanshe, 1945.

Snow, Philip. *The Fall of Hong Kong: Britain, China and the Japanese Occupation*. New Haven, CT: Yale University Press, 2003.

Song Lian. *Yuanshi* (The history of the Yuan dynasty). Beijing: Zhonghua Shuju, 1976.

Strauss, Julia. "Morality, Coercion and State Building by Campaign in the Early PRC: Regime Consolidation and After, 1949–1956." *China Quarterly* (December 2006): 891–912.

Sun Kekuan. "Lun dui fei junren de junfa shenpan" (On military tribunals for civilian cases). *Falü pinglun* 742 (October 1947): 1–2.

Su Qing. *Xu jiehun shinian* (A sequel to *Ten Years of Married Life*). Shanghai: Lili chubanshe, 1947.

———. *Jiehun shinian* (Ten years of married life). Nanjing: Jiangsu Wenyi Chubanshe, 2009.

Sullivan, Michael. *Art and Artists of Twentieth-Century China*. Berkeley: University of California Press, 1996.

Tan Zhengbi. "Lun Su Qing yu Zhang Ailing" (On Su Qing and Zhang Ailing). In Tan Zhengbi, ed., *Dangdan nüzuojia xiaoshuoxuan* (Selected works by contemporary female writers). Shanghai: Taipingyang Shuju, 1944.

Tang Wenbiao, ed. *Zhang Ailing juan* (A collection of works by Zhang Ailing). Taipei: Yuanjing Chubanshe, 1982.

Taylor, George. *The Struggle for North China*. New York: Institute of Pacific Relations, 1940.

Tran, Lisa. *Concubines in Court: Marriage and Monogamy in Twentieth-Century China*. London: Rowman & Littlefield, 2015.

Treat, John. "Choosing to Collaborate: Yi Kwang-su and the Moral Subject in Colonial Korea." *Journal of Asian Studies* 1 (2012): 81–102.

van de Ven, Hans, Diana Lary, and Stephen R. Mackinnon. *Negotiating China's Destiny in World War II*. Stanford, CA: Stanford University Press, 2014.

Van Schaack, Beth, and Ronald Slye. *International Criminal Law and Its Enforcement*. St. Paul, MN: Foundation Press, 2010.

Vann, Michael. "The Good, the Bad, and the Ugly: Variation and Difference in French Racism in Colonial Indochine." In *The Color of Liberty: Histories of Race*, edited by Sue Peabody and Tyler Stovall, 187–205. Durham, NC: Duke University Press, 2003.

Vasantkumar, Chris. "What Is This 'Chinese' in Overseas Chinese? Sojourn Work and the Place of China's Minority Nationalities in Extraterritorial Chinese-ness." *Journal of Asian Studies* 2 (2012): 423–46.

Virgili, Fabrice. *Shorn Women: Gender and Punishment in Liberation France.* Oxford: Bloomsbury Academic, 2002.

Wakeman, Frederic, Jr. *The Shanghai Badlands: Wartime Terrorism and Urban Crime, 1937–1941.* New York: Cambridge University Press, 1996.

———. "*Hanjian* (Traitor)! Collaboration and Retribution in Wartime Shanghai." In *Becoming Chinese: Passages to Modernity and Beyond,* edited by Wen-hsin Yeh, 298–341. Berkeley: University of California Press, 2000.

———. *Spymaster: Dai Li and the Chinese Secret Service.* Berkeley: University of California Press, 2003.

Wang, Gungwu. "A Single Chinese Diaspora? Some Historical Reflections." In *Imagining the Chinese Diaspora,* edited by Annette Shun Wah and Gungwu Wang, 1–17. Canberra: Australian National University, 1999.

Wang, Yiman. "Between the National and the Transnational: Li Xianglan/Yamaguchi Yoshiko and Pan-Asianism." *IIAS Newsletter,* September 2005, 39.

Wang Chunying. "Zhanhou jingji hanjian shenpan: Yi Xinxin gongsi Li Ze an weili" (Trials of economic *hanjian* after the war: A discussion of the case of Li Ze, manager of the Xinxin Company). *Lishi yanjiu* 2 (2008): 132–46.

Wang Daoping, ed. *Zhongguo Kangri Zhanzheng shi* (A history of the War of Resistance against Japan). Beijing: Jiefangjun Chubanshe, 2005.

Wang Hui. *Mei Lanfang huazhuan* (An illustrated biography of Mei Lanfang). Beijing: Zuojia Chubanshe, 2004.

Wang Junxi, ed. *Zhang Shizhao quanji* (A complete collection of the writings of Zhang Shizhao). Vol. 1. Beijing: Wenhui Chubanshe, 2000.

Wang Ke. "'Hanjian': xiangxiang zhong de danyi minzu guojia huayu" (*Hanjian:* An expression resulting from the imagined nation-state). *Twenty-First Century* 3(2004): 63–73.

Wang Tongqi. "Kangri Zhanzheng shiqi de wenhua sichao" (Cultural trends during the War of Resistance). PhD diss., Nankai University, 2000.

Wang Xiaofang. "Kangzhan niandai de nüxing shuxie: Lun Su Qing sanshishi niandai de wenxue chuangzuo" (Literature production by female writers during the war: Su Qing and her writings during the 1930s and 1940s). MA thesis, Shanghai Normal University, 2005.

Wang Xiaohua. *Guogong kangzhan dasujian* (The grand anti-*hanjian* campaigns by the Nationalist government and the Chinese Communist Party during the War of Resistance). Beijing: Zhongguo Dang'an Chubanshe, 1996.

———. *Hanjian da shenpan* (The momentous trials of *hanjian*). Nanjing: Nanjing Chubanshe, 2015.

War Measures Act Conference. *The Japanese Canadian Experience: The October Crisis.* London: Peter Anas, 1978.

Wasserstein, Bernard. "Ambiguities of Occupation: Foreign Resisters and Collaborators in Wartime Shanghai." In *Wartime Shanghai.* Edited by Wen-hsin Yeh. London: Routledge, 1998, 24–41.

Weng Youwei. "Kangri genjudi minzhu zhengquan chengzhi hanjian de lifa he zhengce yanjiu" (A study of anti-*hanjian* laws and policies in the Communist base areas). *Zhonggong dangshi yanjiu* 2 (2006): 56–65.

Wenshi Ziliao Wenyuanhui. *Wenshi ziliao cungao xuanbian: Kangri zhanzheng* (A selected collection of literary and historical archives: The Anti-Japanese War period). Beijing: Zhongguo Wenshi Chubanshe, 2002.

———, ed. *Wenshi ziliao xuanji* (Selections of literary and historical materials). Beijing: Zhongguo Wenshi Chubanshe, 1996.

Wesley, Fishel. *The End of Extraterritoriality in China.* Berkeley: University of California Press, 1952.

White, Theodore H., and Annalee Jacoby, *Thunder out of China.* New York: William Sloane Associates, 1946.

Wills, John E. *Past and Present in China's Foreign Policy: From "Tribute System" to "Peaceful Rise."* Honolulu: University of Hawaii Press, 2011.

Woodside, Alexander. *Vietnam and the Chinese Model: A Comparative Study of Vietnamese and Chinese Government in the First Half of the Nineteenth Century.* Cambridge, MA: Harvard University Asia Center, 1971.

Wright, Tim. *Coal Mining in China's Economy and Society, 1895–1937.* Cambridge: Cambridge University Press, 2009.

Wu Chucai, ed. *Guwen guanzhi* (A collection of the best classical Chinese essays). Beijing: Zhonghua Shuju, 2001.

Wu Mi. "Qingdai guanshu dang'an suojian 'hanjian' yici zhicheng jiqi bianhua" (The evolution of the word *hanjian* as seen in Qing documents). *Lishi dang'an* 1 (2010): 56–67.

Xi Chi. "Luanshi cainü Su Qing" (The talented female writer Su Qing in turbulent times). *Zuojia tiandi* 4 (2007): 62–67.

Xiao Yiping, ed. *Zhongguo Gongchandang Kangri Zhanzheng shiqi dashiji* (Significant events of the Chinese Communist Party during the War of Resistance) Beijing: Renmin Chubanshe, 1988.

Xie Guansheng, ed. *Zhanshi sifa jiyao* (A brief record of laws and judicial activities during the war). Taipei: Sifayuan Xingzhengbu, 1971.

Xu Anru. "Yuenan huaqiao aiguo baozhi *Quanmin ribao*" (*National People's Daily*: The patriotic newspaper of overseas Chinese in Vietnam). *Indochina Studies* 3 (1982): 26.

Xu Chaojian, ed. *Wenshi ziliao cungao xuanbian: zhengdang, zhengfu* (A selection of historical accounts: The volume on political parties and governments). Beijing: Zhongguo Wenshi Chubanshe, 1982.

Xu Hongxin. "Zhenshi de Zheng Pingru" (The true story of Zheng Pingru) (article in three parts). *Dang'an chunqiu* 4 (2008): 36–40; 5 (2008): 39–45; 6 (2008): 32–37.

Xu Jin. "Chen Fan yu Subao an"(Chen Fan and the case of *Subao*). *Jindaishi ziliao* 3 (1983): 65–71.

Xu Shilie, ed. *Xiangfan laoqu jiaoyu jianshi* (A brief history of the education system in Communist areas in Hubei). Wuhan: Xiangfan Laoqu Jiaoyu Yanjiuhui, 1998.

Xu Xiaoqun. "The Fate of Judicial Independence in Republican China, 1912–1937." *China Quarterly* 147 (1997): 1–28.

———. *Chinese Professionals and the Republican State: The Rise of Professional Associations in Shanghai, 1912–1937.* Cambridge: Cambridge University Press, 2001.

———. *Trial of Modernity: Judicial Reform in Early Twentieth-Century China, 1901–1937.* Stanford, CA: Stanford University Press, 2008.

Xu Zhifu. "Zhonghua Quanguo Wenyijie Kangdi Xiehui" (The National Resistance Association of Cultural Circles). *Wenshi zazhi* 5 (2005): 7–10.

Xuanzong Chenghuangdi shilu (A faithful record of the Daoguang reign). Taipei: Huawen Shuju, 1964.

Yamamuro, Shinichi. *Manchuria under Japanese Domination*. Philadelphia: University of Pennsylvania Press, 2005.

Yang Ji'an. "Minguo shiqi xianggan bianjie baojia zhidu de shishi jiqi xiaoneng: Yi Jiangxi Waizan xian wei ge'an" (A case study of the Baojia system in Wanzai, Jiangxi, during the Republican era). *Jinggangshan Daxue xuabao* 9 (2012): 11–15.

Yang Kuisong. "Reconsidering the Campaign to Suppress Counterrevolutionaries." *China Quarterly* 193 (2008): 102–21.

Yang Sichang. "Zhaocai shuixi shanhou shu" (Memorial on the southwest rebellion and its solutions). In *Xuxiu siku quanshu*, edited by Gu Tinglong, 181. Shanghai: Shanghai Guji Chubanshe, 2002.

Yang Tianyu, ed. *Liji yizhu* (Annotated book of rites). Shanghai: Shanghai Guji Chubanshe, 2007.

Yeh, Wen-hsin. *Shanghai Splendor: Economic Sentiments and the Making of Modern China, 1843–1949*. Berkeley: University of California Press, 2007.

———, ed. *Wartime Shanghai*. New York: Routledge, 1998.

Yeh, Wen-hsin, and Christian Henriot, eds. *In the Shadow of the Rising Sun: Shanghai under Japanese Occupation*. Cambridge: Cambridge University Press, 2004.

Young, Louise. *Japan's Total Empire: Manchuria and The Culture of Wartime Imperialism*. Berkeley: University of California Press, 1999.

Yu Qichang. "Chengzhi hanjian tiaoli zhi Zhengdang shiyong" (On the proper application of the Regulations on Punishing *Hanjian*). *Falü pinglun* 779 (August 1948): 1.

Yu Renlin. *Gujin hanjian maiguo shilu* (A faithful record of *hanjian* sellouts in the past and present). Guangzhou: Kangri Jiuguojun Zhengzhibu/Political Division of the Japanese-Resisting National Salvation Army, 1936.

Yuan Ling. "Shanghai dang'an lide fangeming." (Counterrevolutionaries in Shanghai Archives). *Yanhuang chunqiu* 4 (2015): 17.

Yuan Lüdeng. "Yuan Lüdeng huiyilu"(A memoir of Yuan Lüdeng). *Dang'an yu shixue* 10 (1995): 28–33, 71.

———. "Yuan Lüdeng zibai shu" (A confession by Yuan Lüdeng). *Dang'an yu shixue* 4 (2000): 19–21.

Yuenan huaqiao guoji wenti yanjiu (A study of the issue of citizenship of Chinese in Vietnam). Taipei: Haiwai Chubanshe, 1957.

Zanasi, Margherita. "Globalizing *Hanjian*: The Suzhou Trials and the Post–World War II Discourse on Collaboration." *American Historical Review* 3 (2008): 731–51.

Zarrow, Peter. *China in War and Revolution, 1895–1949*. Oxford: Routledge, 2005.

Zeng Jianmin. *1945: Poxiao shike de Taiwan* (1945: Daybreak in Taiwan). Taipei: Taihai Chubanshe, 2007.

Zeng Long, *Wode fuqin Yuan Shu* (My father Yuan Shu). Taipei: Duli Zuojia, 2016.

Zhang, Yingjin. *The City in Modern Chinese Literature and Film: Configurations of Space, Time and Gender*. Stanford, CA: Stanford University, 1996.

———. *Chinese National Cinema*. New York: Routledge, 2004.

Zhang Ailing. *Chuanqi* (Legend). 2nd enlarged ed. Shanghai: Shanhe Tushugongsi, 1946.

———. *Se, jie* (Lust, caution). Taipei: Huangguan Chubanshe, 2007.

———. *Xiao tuan yuan* (Little reunion). Taipei: Huangguan Wenhua Chuban Youxiangongsi, 2009.

Zhang Dainian and Deng Jiuping. *Yitu chunqiu* (Vicissitudes in the lives of artists). Beijing: Beijing Shifandaxue Chubanshe, 1997.

Zhang Jinfan. *Zhongguo fazhi liushinian* (Sixty years of Chinese legal history). Xi'an: Shaanxi Renmin Chubanshe, 2009.

Zhang Pengyuan and Shen Huaiyu, eds. *Guomin zhengfu zhiguan nianbiao* (Annual reports on the Nationalist Bureaucracy). Taipei: Zhongyang Yanjiuyuan Jindaishi Yanjiusuo, 1987.

Zhang Qizhi, ed. *Wanqing minguo shi* (A history of the late Qing and Republican period). Taipei: Wunan Tushu Chubangongsi, 2002.

Zhang Rujie and Yang Junming, eds. *Qingdai yeshi* (The unofficial histories of the Qing). Chengdu: Bashu Shushe, 1987.

Zhang Shizhao. "Hanjian bian" (A debate on the usage of *hanjian*). In *Zhang Shizhao quanji* (Complete writings of Zhang Shizhao), vol. 1, ed. Zhang Hanzhi. Shanghai: Wenhui Chubanshe, 2000.

Zhang Xibo and Han Yanlong. *Zhongguo geming fazhishi* (A history of revolutionary lawmaking in China). Beijing: Zhongguo Shehui Kexue Chubanshe, 2007.

Zhang Yu. "Yuenan huaqiao kangri jiuwang yundong jilüe" (A brief history of the national salvation movements among Chinese in Vietnam). *Bagui qiaoshi* 3 (1991): 53–58.

———. *Yuenan, Laowo, Jianpuzhai huaqiao huaren manji* (Casual notes on the overseas Chinese in Vietnam, Laos, and Cambodia). Hong Kong: Shehuikexue Chuban Youxiangongsi, 2002.

Zhang Yuanjie. *Chuli hanjian anjian tiaoli qianshi* (An interpretation of the Regulations on Punishing *Hanjian* and related laws). Yuyao: Zhengze Chubanshe, 1945.

Zhang Yushu. *Kangxi zidian* (Kangxi dictionary). Reprint. Beijing: Zhonghua Shuju, 1958.

Zhao Erxun. *Qingshigao* (A draft of the history of the Qing). Beijing: Zhonghua Shuju, 1976.

Zhong Ya. "Youguan Su Qing Shanghai fangwenji" (Interviews conducted in Shanghai on the life of Su Qing). *Shucheng* 11 (2000): 25.

Zhongguo Guomindang dangshi bianzuan weiyuanhui, ed. *Geming wenxian* (Primary documents on Chinese revolutionaries). Taipei: Zhengzhong Shuju, 1979.

Zhongguo Renmin Jiefangjun Junshi Kexueyuan Junshi Lishi Yanjiubu. *Zhongguo Kangri Zhanzheng shi* (A history of the War of Resistance against Japan). Beijing: Jiefangjun Chubanshe, 2005.

"Zhonghua Suweiai Gongheguo chengzhi fangeming tiaoli" (The statute on punishing counterrevolutionaries in the Chinese Soviet Republic). Reprinted in *Jiangxi shehui kexue,* S1 (1981): 134–36.

Zhou Shuzhen. *Sanqingtuan shimo* (The history of the Three People's Principles Youth League). Nanchang: Jiangxi Renmin Chubanshe, 1996.

Zhou Wanyao, ed. *Taiji Ribenbing zuotanhui jilu bing xiangguan ziliao* (Minutes of the meeting with Taiwanese veterans from the Japanese Imperial Army and related materials). Taipei: Academia Sinica, 1997).

Zou Bei and Li Zhen, eds. *Zhongguo gongren yundong shihua* (A history of China's labor movements). Beijing: Zhongguo Gongren Chubanshe, 1993.

Zou Rong. *Gemingjun* (Revolutionary Army). Reprint. Beijing: Zhonghua Shuju, 1958.

INDEX

Wu Bin, 39, 203n105
Wu Jie, *hanjian* case of, 68–69
Wu Kunsheng, 96
Wu Mingfang, 76, 131, 210n103
Wu Tiecheng, 106
Wu Zhaozhang, 93–94

X

Xi Rungeng, *hanjian* case of, 209n79
Xia Qin, 87–88
Xia Wenyun, secret identity of, 73
Xia Yan, 222n92
Xiamen (Fujian): *hanjian* of, 150–51; Japanese occupation of, 53; Taiwanese in, 143, 144
Xiang Kangyuan, 109–10
Xiang Yingquan, 75–76
Xiao Baicai, 108, 217n114
Xingtai (Hebei), mass *hanjian* trial at, 176
Xinsheng bao (newspaper), anti-*hanjian* campaign of, 148
Xinxin Company: CCP at, 103; on Li Ze, 103, 104, 105, 107, 108, 109; Li Ze's management of, 101–3
Xu Caicheng, 92, 213n47
Xu Guangping, 123
Xu Xilin, assassination of Enming, 205n11
Xu Xing, 100
Xuan Tiewu, 33, 104, 105; Chiang's support for, 105

Y

Yan Bingzhen, 131
Yan Fuqing, *hanjian* charges against, 119
Yan Lunkui, 38
Yang Naiwu, 108, 217n114
Yang Xingzhi, 218n8
Yang Xiulun, 169
Yang Yushen, 178
Ye Changyi, 40
Ye Jiqing: imprisonment of, 130; trial of, 221n57
yi (foreign peoples): division from Han, 17; *hanjian* and, 15
Yi Kwang-su, trial of, 60
Yi Zicai, *hanjian* conduct of, 163–64
Yin Rugeng, 43; execution of, 44
Yin Zhanqin, assassination of, 54

Yu Qichang, 42
Yu Youren, 87
Yuan dynasty, use of *hanjian* terminology, 15
Yuan Lüdeng, 43, 68, 204n124; charges against, 95; death of, 177; media coverage of, 213n46; on National Commodity Control Commission, 97, 98; Nationalist Party contacts, 97; public speeches of, 98; on Rice and Grain Control Commission, 214n71; trade activities of, 92; trial of, 94, 97–98; war relief work of, 95
Yuan Shu, 178, 221n71
Yuci (Shanxi), puppet officials of, 50

Z

Zhan Fangzi, 131
Zhang Ailing, 124; audience of, 112; celebrity of, 132, 137; *hanjian* charges against, 132–33, 140, 222n96; on Japanese empire, 223n105; marriage to Hu Lancheng, 137, 138, 139, 222n97; popularity of, 138; public degradation of, 138. Works: "Blockade," 132; *Darling, Stay at Home*, 138, 223n103; *Endless Love*, 223n103; "Little Reunion" (Xiao tuanyuan), 138; *Lust, Caution*, 139
Zhang Bin, 18, 199n22
Zhang Fakui, General, 63
Zhang Jingsheng, 222n82
Zhang Naiqi, 106, 218n8
Zhang Shenwei, corruption of, 155
Zhang Shizhao, 3; defense of Li Ze, 43, 106; on Han heroes, 18, 199n20; on *hanjian* trials, 62–63; on Han victimization, 19; on malicious accusations, 65; reinterpretation of *hanjian*, 18, 181
Zhang Ziping, 124
Zhao Chen, 75
Zhao Xiaokun, 125, 128
Zheng Zhenduo, 93, 122, 123
zhongchuquan: exchange for *fabi*, 214n77; Wang Jingwei administration's use of, 211n18

www.ingramcontent.com/pod-product-compliance
Lightning Source LLC
Chambersburg PA
CBHW031415270326
41929CB00010BA/1462